Irigaray and Kierkegaard

Irigaray and Kierkegaard

On the Construction of the Self

Helene Tallon Russell

MERCER UNIVERSITY PRESS
MACON

MUP/P394

© 2009 Mercer University Press
1400 Coleman Avenue
Macon, Georgia 31207
All rights reserved

First Edition.

Books published by Mercer University Press are printed on acid free paper that meets the requirements of American National Standard for Information Sciences—Permanence of Paper for Printed Library Materials.

Mercer University Press is a member of Green Press initiative (greenpressinitiative.org), a nonprofit organization working to help publishers and printers increase their use of recycled paper and decrease their use of fiber derived from endangered forests. This book is printed on recycled paper.

ISBN: 978-0-88146-166-4

Library of Congress Cataloging-in-Publication Data

Contents

Dedication / vii
Preface / ix
Introduction / 1
1. Augustine's Theological Anthropology:
Unity versus Division / 19
2. Søren Kierkegaard: Multi-Spheres of Living / 57
3. Kierkegaard's Pseudonymity: Multiple Voices of a Genius / 94
4. Luce Irigaray: Critique of the Economy of the Same / 136
5. Irigaray's Embodied Feminine Subject / 177
6. Both at Once: A Multivalent and
Dialectically Relational Self / 219
Bibliography / 257
Index / 263

This book is dedicated to
The Rev. Jacquelyn Tallon Russell, my mother.

She raised me with love, careful thought, and eccentric grace, teaching me:

To study with my heart,

To understand with my spirit,

To act with integrity.

I wish she were still with me to see it in published form.

Preface

This book is a creative construction of selfhood based upon the insights of nineteenth century religious philosopher Søren Kierkegaard and French feminist psychoanalytic theorist Luce Irigaray. It brings together two thinkers from distinct schools of thought in a dialectical approach to offer a new way of thinking about the importance of multiplicity and relationality within the self. In this process it hopes to accomplish three particularly important tasks. First in arguing for a critical awareness of the embedded assumption of singularity and oneness in our current dominant discourse concerning selfhood, I suggest that the apparent unity of the self is a problematic and fictitious conception. This construct is a prodigious illusion that has not only outworn its usefulness, but has become detrimental to more inclusive concepts of the self, in which diversity and relationality are encouraged.

Second, this book offers an alternative conceptualization of human selfhood as multiple. There are many parts within a person, many dimensions and that self consists in these parts and in the network of relations between these parts. I construct a dialectical method that mirrors the dialectical structure of the notion of the self that I propose.

Thirdly, I utilize an integrative approach by bringing together a 19th century thinker with a postmodern feminist theorist. Søren Kierkegaard and Luce Irigaray both offer critical alternatives to such a unitary conception of selfhood. Kierkegaard views the self as complex, relational, and processive. The self consists of three pairs of polar elements, such as temporal and eternal, within three spheres of existence. The spheres and the elements are dialectically inter-related to each other. Irigaray criticizes the cultural and philosophical norms of Western discourse as phallocentric and monistic. This "economy of the same"—a system in which only one universal norm of behavior is accepted and valued is built upon the repression of the feminine. She looks to women's embodied experience to uncover the feminine. Her (psycho-) analysis highlights that which has been repressed, such as multiformity and fluidity, to be excellent candidates for the lost feminine. It is my contention that a dialogue between these two diverse thinkers provides a fruitful groundwork for re-envisioning and building-up the concept of a self as multiple, embodied, and relational.

This work could not have been brought to fruition without the gracious help of many sister and fellow travelers along the way. My dearly departed parents set the stage for this work in nurturing in me a critical approach to ideas combined with a hospitable approach to diversity and difference.

I am grateful to my thesis adviser, Dr. Marjorie Suchocki, who treated me like a colleague from the first time we met. Her insightful wisdom, critical questions and the affectionate "Marjorie's plan for my life," gave me great guidance and inspiration. She continues to inspire and challenge me as a beloved friend and colleague. I would also like to thank Dr. Jack Verheyden, whose clear and insightful understanding of Kierkegaard, especially his nineteenth-century framework, kept my sometimes unorthodox interpretation of Kierkegaard grounded in the text and its context. He responded to my choice of French Feminist Luce Irigaray as a dialogue partner with Kierkegaard by saying "that's…creative." And he meant it. He encouraged my creative approach both in understanding Kierkegaard in an unusual way as well as in my bringing together these two thinkers.

I thank my editor at Mercer University Press, Marc Jolley for his patience and kind guidance throughout the process of moving this work from manuscript to published book.

I would like to thank my colleagues at Christian Theological Seminary, whose up-building presence sustained me in the long process of writing and rewriting this manuscript. I am particularly grateful to Dr. Rufus Burrow whose frequent inquiries about the progress of the writing kept my nose to the grindstone. Special thanks go to Dr. K. Brynolf Lyon and to the students in our team-taught class on Christian Theological Anthropology, who read and offered critical responses to my final chapter. Thank you for both your clarifying questions and for raising the most profound issues of relationality. Further, I want to extend my appreciation to the administration of CTS and the faculty development fund for its generous support to make this publication possible.

Last, but not least, I want to thank Jeremy Fackenthal, whose unending devotion to this project is manifest both in his patient listening and insightful responses to my revisions upon revisions and in his painstaking work in editing this project with me. I am deeply grateful.

Introduction

Multiplicity Within: Introducing the Issues

We are one, But we are not the same—Bono, of U2.

This book is about selfhood, difference, and diversity. Diversity is a buzzword these days in a variety of contexts from the corporate work place to the classroom, in political arenas and in the entertainment industry, in religious discussions and in everyday personal conversation. We ask questions such as "Do we have enough diversity on the faculty? Does our standpoint represent a variety of perspectives? How can we get more diversity? In what ways and places do we need to improve our diversity?" Academically and in seminaries these issues approach the deep questions of truth and justice as well as legal responsibilities and practical pedagogies. A greater diversity of perspectives and experiences not only exposes the student to more options and contexts, it broadens their experiences and resources. The more viewpoints engaging in a solution to a problem, the greater the depth of understanding and breadth there are for possible solutions. Encouraging multiple experiences exposes students to the actualities in the world and gives them a more realistic education. Including more voices, promoting those who have previously been marginalized is a justice issue as well.

Alternative approaches that have focused on the inclusion of other voices and persons have made significant strides. Yet even when these struggles are successful, the result has tended to continue to reduce difference. The actual different-ness of those who have been marginalized is often absorbed into a so-called universality, so that the result is merely more of the same. One of the unexamined issues in previous approaches to promoting diversity and difference is the presence of an embedded assumption that exalts oneness and sameness. This book examines this assumption and critiques these claims about singularity and sameness as they relate specifically to common theories about selfhood.

Allow me to clarify the difference between the mere fact of multiplicity and relational multiplicity. The difference lies in the positive value ascribed to the multiplicity and the intentional relating of the different parts. This distinction is in a vein similar to that made between the fact that there are many religions in the world on the one hand, and the positive engagement of these religious viewpoints, on the other. The first is called *plurality*, the other characterized by the term *pluralism* or diversity. The fact is that there are many religions. No one can dispute that. What is in dispute is the value of this fact and the issue of how these religions should relate to each other and how each is related to that which is divine. We can use the same logical distinction in denotation for discussing the difference between the "plurality" of multiple parts within a self on the one hand and the pluralism of these parts and their relations to each other, on the other.

The dominant Western view of the self is characterized by singularity, sameness, and homogeneity. This conceptualization of apparent unity of the self is a construct that has been imposed upon the popular understandings of the human self. It has outworn its usefulness and has become a hindrance to a more full expression of selfhood. This work in feminist anthropology evaluates the supreme value ascribed to the quality of oneness in the Western tradition's view of religious selfhood and works toward developing a constructive theory of selfhood that corrects the problems in the traditional theological and contemporary conceptualizations of self by developing theories that acknowledge the fundamental multiplicity and inner relatedness of the self.

This constructive project builds upon the insights of two apparently dissimilar authors—nineteenth century philosopher Søren Kierkegaard and twentieth century feminist Luce Irigaray—to challenge the centuries-old understanding of the self as One, and to construct a relational understanding of a healthy self as inherently multiple.

The importance of this endeavor is highlighted by the increasing necessity in twenty-first century society to deal constructively with diversity. The notion of the "One" and the "Same" wreaks havoc with social relations in a world where cultures are continuously intermingling. Persons who deviate from the normative construct of what it means to be a subject are ignored, repressed, and mistreated, even to the extent of genocide. Women bear the brunt of this hegemony. The incapacity to deal with diversity at the social level reflects the deeper problem of dealing with diversity at the inner personal level. Addressing the diversity within the self in a healthy and creative way opens the possibility of respecting and appreciating the plethora of difference in the world. Furthermore, the implications for identity and selfhood developed from analysis and experiential resources of persons of color and women and others who have been repressed and oppressed are consistent with this constructive view of multiplicity of selfhood.

The emphasis on oneness of self is problematic in three especially significant ways. First, such oneness is a construct and not an *a priori* truth, as is often assumed. It does not fit with or take into account the experience of many persons, especially women and other marginalized groups. Second, the exclusive emphasis on oneness of self inhibits a conceptualization of the self as relational, both within itself and externally with others. When the self is viewed as one, the meaning of unity is distorted into the reduction of all else to the same. "Unity" comes to connote conformity to the least common denominator, and "oneness" comes to connote sameness. When oneness becomes the norm, the particularizations of parts of the self become absorbed into the hegemony of the dominant group/self. With a proclivity toward this type of uniform unity, the internal relationality of the self is inhibited and even prohibited.

This hegemony in turn has negative effects upon social relationality and society in general, which leads us to the third problematic implication/impact of oneness of self. The diversity external to the self is repressed and ignored, or even demonized and devalued. When one can't accept the multiplicity within one's self, the diversity outside of oneself is also difficult to appreciate and can even become a scapegoat and screen for the rejection/projection of the unrealized and unrecognized difference and otherness within one's self. The more we can and do recognize the multiplicity within, the easier it becomes to be open and appreciative of the diversity and pluralism outside of oneself.

The over-valuation of oneness thus inhibits a conceptualization of the self as constituted by intimate relatedness. This proclivity toward uniformity reduces all differences and otherness to conformity with the normative model of selfhood. This reduction to the same occurs in society, in personal social relationship and for individuals. It also occurs discursively and theoretically. The differences in society between people are thus judged according to a singular standard of right/good behavior and being. Cornel West writes that a "hegemonic culture subtly and effectively encourages people to identify themselves with the habits, sensibilities, and worldviews supportive of the status quo and the class interests that dominate it."[1] This "normative gaze"[2] is singular in its form, and this singularity is its power to oppress. Because it excludes both the characteristics that are not part of the norm and those persons who have these

---

[1] Cornel West, *Prophesy Deliverance!* (Philadelphia PA: Westminster Press, 1982) 119.

[2] Ibid., 34. This is a term used by West in *Prophesy Deliverance!* In it he argues that the American society has accepted and perpetuated a visual standard by which everything is noticed and judged.

characteristics, it proves to be absolute and hegemonic. Those characteristics associated with this one model of true and good selfhood are valued, while other charac-teristics are either ignored or demonized as the reverse image of the positive characteristics associated with the one. Likewise, the different characteristics and aspects within a single individual are reduced to conformity with those characteristics most like the dominant norms of society.

The effects of this discourse of singularity rub both ways, inside out and outside in, creating a downward spiral of reduction to the same. In other words, the reduction of the complexity within the self influences the way that difference is addressed externally, and the way that diversity is repressed in society shapes the way that internal multiplicity is viewed. A constructive view of the self as multiple subverts both the internal and external normative gaze and leads to freer self-expression and better societal relations. By accepting internal multiplicity and thus sabotaging the normative gaze, individuals and society become free to express the full complexity and diversity within and among themselves.

Living as a self is not a uniform experience, nor an experience of uniformity. Concrete living does not necessarily yield a uniform self. Feminist author Kathleen Sands, in her work, *Escape From Paradise* agrees, claiming that life is "genuinely plural and conflicted."[3] A way of theorizing about human selfhood that takes into account this plurality and conflict is needed. Addressing the pluralism at the macrocosmic level is ineffective without also addressing the pluralism at the microcosmic level, that is, within each individual self. The multicultural movement is insufficient because it treats the symptoms of bigotry and small-mindedness while ignoring the systemic disease of hegemony. To adequately address the crisis in the world marked by the disregard for difference between individuals, groups, and nations,

---

[3] Kathleen Sands, *Escape From Paradise* (Minneapolis: Fortress Press, 1994) 28.

one must address the disregard for multiplicity and pluralism within the individual self.[4]

The interest in selfhood as constituted in and by relationality and multiplicity is developing in a variety of arenas, including critiques of the oneness of God, deconstruction's revaluation of difference, and process thought's claims of the primacy of relationship in the process of becoming for all entities.[5] This present work investigates the possibilities for models of multiplicity and relationality of selfhood. I utilize insights found in bringing together two unlikely bedfellows: Søren Kierkegaard and Luce Irigaray. Kierkegaard is a nineteenth century Danish religious writer concerned with how to become subjective. His insights give voice to the dialectical tensions within human becoming. On the other end of the spectrum, Luce Irigaray is a contemporary French feminist psychoanalyst concerned with the repression of the feminine in Western discourse. Her insights give voice to the multiplicity of the body and a critical analysis of the dominant Western discourse and its "economy of the Same." Each offers significant elements toward establishing a helpful groundwork to reconstruct theological anthropology in terms of manyness, difference and relationality. I use these two thinkers dialectically, mirroring in the format of this project the very dynamic of dialectical relationship that I suggest is at the heart of selfhood.

I begin examining this exaltation of oneness that has become so deeply ingrained in Western, and specifically, Christian, thought, with Augustine's formulation of sin. Augustine views evil as the

---

[4] In a sense, the multicultural movement has failed because it only treats the symptoms while ignoring the systemic disease. To adequately address the crisis in the world marked by disregard for pluralism between individuals and groups, the disregard for multiplicity and pluralism within the individuals must also be addressed.

[5] See Laurel Schneider, *Re-imaging the Divine* (Cleveland OH: Pilgrim Press, 2000) and *Beyond Monotheism: A Theology of Multiplicity*, (New York, New York: Routledge, 2007).

privation of good and I argue that he also views sin as the privation of oneness. He brings a Plotinian dualistic structure into a Hebraic-Christian value of the unity of the body and soul, resulting in a problematic conception of human selfhood. The body is reduced to a figment of the soul, while multiplicity is made a scapegoat as the form of sinfulness.

He synthesizes the Greek notion in which the self is naturally sinful or evil due to its connection to the manifold of the body into the Hebraic view of the natural and created good unity of the body and soul. The problem arises when the Hebraic notion of unity is identified with the Plotinian One. Sin then, is viewed as a movement against this oneness. In the original state of the soul, Augustine claims, the contemplative part of the mind rules the will and body absolutely. Sin is the rebellious movement of the body and will against the mind. This movement makes division and multiplicity in the self. Sin is the division of the will away from the soul and toward the body, moving toward the natural multiplicity associated with the body. This movement is a reversal of the proper hierarchy, and causes the person, like the Rome of his time, to divide against itself and fall. Thus, sin is the privation of oneness. Implicit in Augustine's system of value remains the Plotinian identification of the good with the One. Evil may be the privation of *good*, but sin is the privation of *oneness*.

Augustine changes the view of sin as a conflict between flesh and spirit in which the body is pitted against the soul to a conflict within the soul itself. Augustine's formulation of sin, while a move in a good direction (toward including the body as an important part of the whole person), has outworn its usefulness. Currently it and the views it has influenced reinforce the detrimental effects incurred by the dominant exaltation of oneness. Profound changes in the view of human selfhood are necessary.[6]

---

[6] Naturally, these changes also call for changes in the view of sin, but that is another project.

Søren Kierkegaard and Luce Irigaray each offer critiques of the unitary conceptualization of selfhood and suggest alternative views of human selfhood in which the self is viewed as more than one. I begin with the insights of Kierkegaard who offers an alternative to the dominant model of a singular self. While Luce Irigaray's view of selfhood arises from a feminist and psychoanalytic perspective, Kierkegaard's alternative view is from the perspective of religious insight. Although Kierkegaard is in the Western religious tradition, his theological anthropology strays from the tradition's dominant view. His analysis takes the form of an attack upon Christendom and upon what he perceives to be Hegel's abstract and finished system of existence. He writes against the common assumptions and norms of the crowd. I use Kierkegaard to construct a model of multiple selfhood based on three aspects of his thought: the dialectical binary structure of ontological elements; the three spheres of human existence, which are the aesthetic sphere, the ethical sphere, and the religious sphere; and a polynymity of authors. A genuine self is complex, multiple, and internally related to itself.

The three pairs of constitutive elements of existence—finitude and infinity, temporality and eternity, freedom and necessity—are not reducible to each other, nor reducible to a third term. Instead, the tensions between the contradictory elements of the finitude of human existence and the infinity of the human spirit remain within the person throughout life. Life is a dynamic struggle of these two poles, three spheres of living, and the dialectical movement back and forth between and among the spheres and elements. Human subjectivity is a both-at-once-ness in existence, a simultaneity of divergent elements and their relationships. The tension must remain "liminal" in the sense that presence of the self is found in presevering rather than resolving the tensions between the polar ontological elements.

My interpretation of Kierkegaard varies a bit from traditional and popular interpretations in that I use one particularly significant element of his work, the dialectic of faith, to facilitate and enlighten my understanding of other facets of his thought. Scholars of Kierkegaard disagree about how best to interpret many aspects of his thought. For instance, some argue that the spheres of existence are three different types of personality and a person should choose between them. This view is like Sartre's "you are alive, choose"...choose either the aesthetic, or the ethical, or the religious. Other scholars believe that these three spheres are stages of development that a person goes through as s/he matures into a religious Christian self, a knight of faith. Others argue that Kierkegaard's primary purpose is merely to clarify the distinctions between those who are Christians and those who are confused about whether or not they are Christian. These interpretations of Kierkegaard are inadequate because they do not address the dialectical character of his thought. The spheres of existence are part of the structure of his dialogue of the self. *Either/Or*, his first publicly published work under a pseudonym, is an illustration of the movement and relationality in his view of the self. *Either/Or* is not saying either be an aesthete absolutely, or be an ethical person absolutely. It is not a choice of one or the other. Nor is this book's main thesis merely an attempt by Kierkegaard to get aesthetically minded readers to realize that the aesthetic values are not so good and they should just live ethically.

Keeping in mind that Kierkegaard's style of communication is indirect, we can guess that perhaps he has entitled his work in this way with his tongue in cheek. *Either/Or* is partially a spoof on Hegel's dialectic. In Hegel's dialectic the first element, an idea, or shall we say, thesis,[7] meets its opposite, an antithesis. These two ideas are contradictory, an "either/or." Next in Hegel's thought these two conflicting ideas are synthesized into a third idea, a synthesis, which

---

[7] Please note that thesis, antithesis, synthesis is not Hegel's own terminology. But this language does correspond to Hegel's system.

collapses elements from each of the first two into a third harmonized entity—a one. Then the one, in turn, is the next thesis. This progression is the basic structure of Hegel's dialectic, his view of the movement of the Spirit, as expressed in the march of history, or at least is Kierkegaard's reading of Hegel.

Kierkegaard does not agree with this view of the movement of the spirit. He sees this synthetic unity as just that, *synthetic*—constructed, not real, and certainly not an expression of the Spirit. He believes that real persons do not live this way. Rather, in actual existence the two elements corresponding to Hegel's thesis and antithesis are not reduced or blended together to progress to another thesis, nor to be absorbed into the collective. Instead, they remain distinct from each other, an "either/or" within the individual. I interpret Kierkegaard's theory of spheres of existence through his dialectic of faith. I understand the elements of existence, represented by a polarity between the finite and the infinite, as the structure of human selfhood. These oppositional elements need to be held together, yet they cannot be collapsed into a singular synthetic one/whole. The ability to hold these elements together internally can only be found in the religious sphere, which provides the necessary balance to hold together the tension. Rather than a "one," these elements form an "either/or," which in the religious sphere, is more like a "both/and." The elements that appear to be in conflict with each other are brought together into a dialectical relationship, each retaining their integrity, while being in the midst of relating to each other. Further, with regard to the aesthetic sphere and the ethical sphere, a person's progression through the spheres in not a simple linear development from one to the next. In real selfhood these spheres, like the elements of existence, cannot be divided from each other. In a real, concrete life, one is not "either" aesthetic "or" ethical but rather, the authentic self in existence is *both* aesthetic *and* ethical, *and* thus in the religious sphere. The ethical sphere takes the aesthetic sphere into itself, yet the aesthetic sphere is not collapsed or reduced to the ethical sphere. And the religious sphere, which is the highest and most desired way of existence, brings together these two dimensions of living and holds them together in tension, through a dialectic movement of the self's center from immediate subjectivity to objectivity and back again to a transformed subjectivity.

These elements of existence come together, relate to each other and are held in tension together. The relating of this relation to itself is the form of the human self, the religious sphere. As Kierkegaard says in the prelude to *Sickness Unto Death*: "The self is a relation that relates itself to itself or is the relation's relating itself to itself in the relation; the self is not the relation but is the relation's relating itself to itself."[8] The self is always in the process of becoming itself through relating reflexively to itself; it is a dynamic relational matrix. I make use of this non-reductionistic dialectical relationship to form the structure of my construction of selfhood.

In the religious sphere the individual holds together the elements of existence and the other two spheres in tension before God. The operative and functional quality of religious selfhood is relationality. The subjectivity that Kierkegaard calls truth is possible only as the individual is internally related with itself. Further, this internal, constant relationality is possible only in relationship with the divine. Kierkegaard conceives of selfhood as non-uniform and inherently relational. Kierkegaard's employment of pseudonymous authors is also an aspect of the multiplicity of the self, in which the multitude of authors reveal the multiplicity of Kierkegaard's own subjectivity and his understanding of the multiple parts of human selfhood. I will analyze in greater depth these multiple elements of Kierkegaard's theological anthropology of multiplicity.

This work continues with a thorough feminist critique of embedded assumptions in Western discourse that exalt oneness and

---

[8] Søren Kierkegaard, *The Sickness Unto Death*, trans. Howard V. Hong and Edna H. Hong (Princeton NJ: Princeton University Press, 1980) 13. All following citations of SUD will be from this edition unless explicitly noted otherwise.

sameness. Among others I utilize Luce Irigaray's critical insights and methods. Chapter Four criticizes the cultural and philosophical norms of Western discourse. Irigaray argues that the tradition's emphasis upon oneness and uniformity leads to what she calls the "economy of the Same," a system that values a universal norm of behavior and existence, which is singular. She shows that this dominant discourse is constructed for and by particular experience, and not *the* discovered truth, as its masquerade indicates. It is constructed *from* exclusively male experience and meaning, *for* exclusively male need and desire, and *by* exclusively male voices and articulation. She argues that this "phallocentric" construction is built upon the repression of sexual difference. The feminine is oppressed, ignored, and repressed into the unconscious. This is problematic because it leaves women able to find themselves only in that which the culture denies and thus leaves women unable to find themselves at all. Women's subject/ivity is unconscious. There is no genuine sexual difference in this economy of the Same, says Irigaray. Her solution is to uncover that which has been buried by the discourse of universal sameness. Looking for possible candidates for this lost feminine, she highlights that which has been forced into the unconscious of individuals, culture and discourse and especially women's experience of themselves sexually.

Irigaray offers both a critical evaluation of the conceptualization of selfhood in Western discourse and constructive alternative views of the feminine self. She reinterprets the phallocentric definition of the feminine as "not one,"[9] to mean more than one. Employing the principles of psychoanalysis philosophically in her "analysis" of Western discourse, she demonstrates the ways in which the feminine is repressed in this economy of the Same. Female subjectivity, female sexuality and female discourse are subverted and submerged into unconsciousness. In focusing on Freud and Lacan as philosophy, her

---

[9] See Jacques Lacan, *Écritis, A Selection* (London: Tavistock, 1977).

psycho-analysis of Western discourse yields its recovery of what has been repressed by Western culture into the unconscious: the feminine. Her constructive work elicits candidates for the characteristics and forms of the feminine. In this way, she not only proposes likely candidates for the lost feminine, but also subverts patriarchy by highlighting what phallocentric culture denies, thus disrupting its balanced harmony.

In the fifth chapter, we see that Irigaray's techniques yield several candidates for feminine characteristics and form, such as multiplicity and multiformity of selfhood, fluidity, non-specular (such as tactile), and simultaneity (both at once). She explores these possibilities poetically and experimentally, looking to the female body and morphology, especially sexuality, to discover the origin of the feminine. Paralleling Freud and Lacan's theories of the transition of an individual through developmental stages toward individuation, her technique seeks to enable women to regress to the pre-Oedipal stage and then to transit through it again as genuine feminine subjects. She looks to women's sexuality for exploring new ways of experiencing the pleasure and *jouissance* of the feminine. These experiences in turn, she believes, can function as metaphors for the plurality of women's sexuality that might yield for discursive knowledge. Feminine sexuality includes both the morphology of female sex organs as well as feminine desire. Her goal is to create, tap into, and contribute to the feminine imaginary, a rich system of meaning and source of the feminine, which acts as a resource of feminine symbols, allusions, metaphors, metonyms, and values. Since she believes that there is a direct relationship between language and women's determination and actualization of herself as a subject, she seeks to elicit a feminine discourse, including grammar and syntax.

For the pairs of labia, Irigaray pens "both at once," because the labia are both one and two. She suggests "both at once" as a fundamental feminine metonymy to express a genuine reality corresponding to the not-one-ness of phallocentrism's projection onto the feminine. The two lips, even the two pairs of lips, represent the feminine. They are simultaneously both singular and double, both open and closed. This metonymy indicates that the feminine is simultaneously singular and double, open and closed. Irigaray says, "She is neither one nor two. Rigorously speaking, she cannot be identified either as one person, or as two."[10] The two labia are not reducible to ones. The feminine is "both at once;" two or more elements are simultaneously brought together and held apart.

These two views of subjectivity offered by Kierkegaard and Irigaray, while divergent in many ways are also similar in content and structure. The final chapter suggests an alternative theory of selfhood based on relationality and multiplicity. What does being a subject look like under the categories of multiplicity and relationality? This chapter first examines the ways that Irigaray's exploration of the feminine yields a model of subjecthood similar to Kierkegaard's dialectical "both/and," in which the religious self is comprised of multiple and relating parts. The religious sphere of existence is structured by a dialectical movement between the particularity of the finite individual and the universality of the infinite. The dialectical movement back and forth between this "either/or," together with the relationship to the absolute, gives the self in the religious sphere its unique and essential structure. The dialectic between these two irreconcilable factors of existence seems paradoxical—it is the paradox of faith, and it is possible only in relationship with the absolute, or as Kierkegaard says, in willing to become oneself before God.

The metaphor/metonymy of two lips for the feminine self as posited by Irigaray is an analogous metaphor for Kierkegaard's understanding of human subjectivity. The human is neither objective, nor subjective; s/he is neither merely aesthetic, nor ethical, but both

---

[10] Luce Irigaray, "This Sex Which is Not One," in *This Sex Which is Not One* (Ithaca NY: Cornell University Press, 1985) 26.

at once—neither fully finite, nor fully infinite, but both at once. Taken together, Irigaray's critical analysis and the constructive metonymy of fluidity, multiplicity, and openness, with Kierkegaard's theory of the self as dynamic dialectical and relational, provide the groundwork for a reconstructive model of selfhood that is both more genuine to human experience and more beneficial to diversity in the world. Irigaray's embodiment of selfhood yields multiplicity of parts of the self, while Kierkegaard provides the emphasis upon the conscious internal relationality of the different elements of the self.

The format of my work serves as a model/example for multiple selfhood. Each thinker provides one side of the conversation. The constructive work is not a mere comparison/contrast, nor even a synthesis of these two authors, but is a dynamic dialectic of the insights of these thinkers with my own voice providing the conduit of relation (like sound waves of a conversation) between them. Thus, the format of the work itself is an example of the "multiplicity within."

Thus, this book makes use of the insights of these disparate thinkers. There are parallels in their insights, but the differences between these thinkers will also be highlighted. As the content argues for conceptualizations of human selfhood of dialectical dynamism, so too, the format and methodology holds the ambiguity and tension between these different thinkers, drawing on each for a distinct element in this new construction of selfhood as dialectically dynamic.

Multiplicity of self is a productive and insightful way of viewing the self. It is consistent with experience, particularly the experience of women and others who have been marginalized by this dominant metaphysics of singularity and sameness. And it enables the self to be more aware of all the multiplicity and relationality within itself. Further, this constructive view opens persons to the significance and diversity of external relationships with others in one's personal social spheres as well as in society in general.

A model of selfhood as multiple coincides with recent discoveries in psychology that understand the human ability to maintain the multiplicity of the self as normal and healthy. This constructive model of theological selfhood based on multiplicity is not to be confused with the psychological disorder of Multiple Personality, nor other forms of psychosis or even neurosis.[11] Rather, I am speaking of healthy persons, with a healthy and beneficial awareness of many parts, many selves within their integrated whole person. The word "whole," suggests that parts are brought together into a whole. Yet they are not integrated into a singularity. The pathology in Multiple Personality Disorder, now named Dissociative Identity Disorder, is not about the making of multiple personalities, but is the dissociation of the parts from each other. The many parts are not aware of each other; they are not fully internally related. There is nothing pathological about the ability to make multiplicity within one's self, for it is a given feature of human personality. This ability is neutral in terms of health and well-being, and varies across culture and gender. Multiplicity is a result of a coping mechanism for stress usually involving some sort of invasion or interaction. This response could occur because the multiplicity of parts within the self is related to the multiple relations one has with others, who interpenetrate our subjectivity. The more deeply one is related with others, the more one is affected internally by these different persons. This in turn leads to the development of more complexity within the self. In healthy situations, this complexity within the self can lead to acceptance of complexity and difference outside of the self and a healthy tolerance of ambiguity.

---

[11] While I want to distinguish between the healthy and nonfunctional forms of multiplicity, I also want to affirm that the difference is not a difference between multiplicity and oneness. The exact reason for the difference is not part of my discussion. Rather this discussion puts forth the assertion that being multiple is a given human ability, as is integration.

I argue that there is more than one singular and authentic element within the human individual. These many parts within each person are internally related to each other in harmonious, analogous, complementary, and/or conflicting ways, which are not reducible to each other. The multiplicity within the human self can be understood as positive. It can be viewed as the largeness of a person's self, meaning the ability to encompass many competing worldviews and paradigms. Such a new model of selfhood that includes and encourages multiplicity and relationality is needed in our ever-increasingly diverse world.

The format of my work serves as a model/example for multiple selfhood. Each of the subject thinkers provides one side of the conversation. The constructive work is not a mere comparison/contrast, nor even a synthesis of these two authors, but is a dynamic dialectic of the insights of these thinkers, with my own voice providing the conduit of relation (like the sound waves in a conversation) between them. Thus, the format of the work itself is an example of "the multiplicity within."

It is the dissimilarities between Søren Kierkegaard and Luce Irigaray that structure this book and mimic the constructive structure of selfhood that is suggested in this book. There are parallels in their insights, but the differences between these thinkers will be highlighted. As the content of this book argues for a new concept of a human selfhood based on dialectical dynamism, the format and methodology reinforces this idea by highlighting the ambiguity and tension between Kierkegaard and Irigaray. Thus both the content and format communicate my point—that the coherence and integrity of selfhood is not dependent upon a singularity or conformity to the form of oneness. But rather, meaningful selfhood can, and should, encompass internal multiplicity within a complex web of internal and external relationality. From each author I draw a distinct element in this new construction of selfhood as dialectically dynamic.

Multiplicity of self is a productive and insightful model of the self. It is consistent with experience, particularly the experience of women and other groups marginalized by the dominant metaphysics of singularity and sameness. For example, womanist theologian Jacquelyn Grant develops W.E.B. Du Bois' historic concept of the two-ness of the self-consciousness of African American into a concept of triple consciousness of African-American Women.[12] The view I suggest here promotes awareness and acceptance of multiplicity, ambiguity, and relationality within a self. Further, this constructive view opens one to the significance and diversity of external relationships, both in one's personal social spheres and in society generally as a whole.

---

[12] Jacquelyn Grant, "The Sin of Servanthood," in *A Troubling in My Soul*, ed., Emile M. Townes (Maryknoll, New York: Orbis, 1993).

1

Augustine's Theological Anthropology: Unity versus Division

> "...in goodness there was unity, but in evil disunion of some kind. It seemed to me that this unity was the seat of the rational mind and was the natural state of truth and perfect goodness; whereas the disunion consisted of irrational life...."[1]
> --St. Augustine's *Confessions*

The exaggerated value ascribed to oneness pervades the dominant Western Christian theological and philosophical conceptualizations of human selfhood. The exaltation of uniformity and oneness in theological anthropology explicitly devalues multiplicity while, at the same time, implicitly devalues pluralism. One area in which this exaltation is particularly visible is Western theological anthropology. Here there is an unquestioned assumption that singularity is exclusively the only healthy and only holy form of selfhood. While the privileging of unity and the One in philosophical and theological conceptualizations predates and reaches beyond Saint Augustine (354-430 CE), his conceptualizations of human personhood and sin illustrate it paradigmatically. As one of the must influential writers in the Western Christian theological and philosophical traditions, his conceptualization of human nature provides the foundation upon which the dominant Western Christian understandings of theological

---

[1] Saint Augustine, *Confessions*, trans. R. S. Pine-Coffin (London: Penguin Books, 1961) 86.

and spiritual anthropology are constructed. This chapter explicates the prevalence of the assumptions of singularity and the exaltation of the quality of oneness and unity in Augustine's doctrine of human nature. Augustine's theological anthropology assumes a metaphysical and moral dualism of form in which unity and oneness are exalted while multiplicity and division are denigrated. These assumptions are particularly evident in his claims that multiplicity of self is an indication of sin and sickness.

Augustine's view of the relationship of the body and soul and his portrayal of the division of the human will against itself as the paradigm of sin both demonstrate the exaltation of oneness in his thought. His fear of multiplicity and ambiguity also contributes to his perception that particularity is one of the detrimental consequences of sin.

Augustine's formulation of human nature is influenced by three major factors: the Neoplatonic exaltation of oneness directly through Plotinus's doctrines concerning the form and telos of human nature; the Manichaean mythology in which a person consists of two souls, one good and one evil; and Christianity's concept of the relationship of the body and soul, especially in terms of sin as an ontological state characterized by division and multiplicity within the body and soul.

Augustine and his contemporary Christians view personhood in relation to God. In the beginning, God created humans in the image of God, and thus, ideally, human nature is a reflection of the form of God (which in Neoplatonism is identified with absolute oneness). This original harmony is lost when Adam's original sin corrupts the very structure of human nature. In its fallen form human nature is characterized by division and rebellion against God. The act of dividing itself and the multiplicity that results from this division is the form of sin, and thus multiformity is contrary to God's plan. Augustine's structural view of sin gives sin a formal criterion: uniformity versus multiformity. This "formal" criterion, the form of a person's soul, is established by the object of his/her will. In other words, desire is at the core of a person's self. The soul becomes accustomed to the object of its desire. The object of desire can be either the multiplicity of the creature, or the unity of God. Concupiscence, his core metaphor for sin, scatters a person's self across the chaotic discontinuities of creation, leaving the human's will mortally weakened by a division against itself. Originally, with God's absolute singularity of unity as the object of a person's desire, his/her will would have been unified and thus his/her whole self would work together in a divinely ordained order and systematic unity.[2] Under original sin, the human self is scattered and divided against itself, not able to find its integrity or its peace until the soul is reunited with God. "You made us for yourself and our hearts find no peace until they rest in you."[3] This rest, this peace, which is the opposite of sin and the strife of sinful living, is identified exclusively with internal unity of the self.

Augustine strives to limit his own life to that which is singular and unified. This is illustrated in his recollection of his personal life as told in his *Confessions*. Here he reinterprets the variant events and ideas of his life in two ways: either as divine heuristic devices which functioned to return him to his religious path, or as discontinuous with the rest of his unified existence, so that these events and thoughts must be eradicated.[4]

Augustine's personal concern for unity is also illustrated in the structure and normative flow of his *Confessions*, in which he characterizes his sinful life as dissipated and distracted in a myriad of desires and directions. First he tries to find himself in the camaraderie of stealing pears with his friends, then in the philosophy of the good

---

[2] However, as the later Augustine believes, original sin has so radically damaged a person's will, that a major portion of it always remains uncontrollable and even unconscious.

[3] Augustine, *Confessions*, 21

[4] This tendency is also illustrated in his *Retractions*, where he reviews his past works and "corrects" any contradictions.

life, then in the strict asceticism of the Manichean cult, then in the Neoplatonic philosophy of Plotinus, and finally he finds unity in a simple conversion to Christianity.

Augustine's view of sin as the division against one's self is the most obvious nexus of his overvaluation of the quality and form of oneness within the self. His doctrine of sin shifts the emphasis from the evilness of the body, which is prevalent in both Plotinian and Manichean conceptualizations of sin, inwardly to human subjectivity and human activity. In doing this, he clearly releases God and anything God created from any culpability for sin and evil, but in order to accomplish this he scapegoats human movement toward multiplicity.

Influences Upon Augustine's Theological Anthropology[5]

His doctrine of theological anthropology, which sets the context for his view of sin, is formulated in the context of three primary influences: 1) his early adherence to the Manichean cult and its mythology of two souls, one evil and one good; 2) Plotinus's Neoplatonic metaphysical dualism of body and soul, also one good and one evil; and 3) Christianity and its sense of wholeness from Hebraic heritage, in collaboration with Paul's spirit/flesh dualism. He reformulates what he believes to be the true Christian doctrine of sin in an attempt to integrate Christianity with the intellectual and spiritual theories and questions of his age. After I delineate these significant influences upon Augustine's view of human nature, I will

---

[5] Michael Hanby in his book *Augustine and Modernity* (New York: Routledge, 2003) has recently argued that Augustine's view of the problematic nature of multiplicity within the self is due to the fact of conflict and not the fact of multiplicity. He focuses upon Augustine's work *On the Trinity* and his notion that the human self is a reflection of the Divine Trinity. My response to his argument is that while it is quite intriguing, and it may more accurately reflect Augustine's mature positions about multiplicity of self, I am addressing the Augustinian tradition and his legacy.

offer an analysis of the place that unity, division and multiplicity hold in his anthropology.

Augustine's view of the relationship of the body and soul hinges upon his emphasis on the faculty of the will. In accord with many schools of thought at his time, Augustine believes that there is an intense conflict within the human person. He experiences this struggle personally, which he reveals so dramatically in his *Confessions*.

In both the Manichean cult and Neoplatonic thought the body and soul are viewed as antithetical to each other. The Manicheans view the relationship between body and soul as oppositional: the body is opaquely dark and evil, while the soul is light and good. The human subject is the battleground of these two forces, and thus existence is a function of never-ending internal conflict. The Manichean understanding of human nature is based on a model of warfare. This metaphor carries over in Augustine's assumptions against ambiguity and multiplicity.

The Manichean cult to which Augustine belonged for ten years of his youth interpreted the experience of inner conflict as a personification of a mythological war between two kingdoms, one dark and the other light. The dark kingdom was evil and the Prince of Darkness created the world for the purpose of inflicting suffering. His army had invaded the Realm of Light, which is good, and had taken prisoners. These prisoners are sparks of light trapped by the Prince of Darkness through encapsulating the light with the dark opaque heavy bodies of matter. Thus, humans are the mixture of soul and body, of the spark of light and the body of darkness. Augustine sometimes refers to these two elements of the human subject as the two souls. Mani saw the god of creation as evil and the god of redemption as good. The Manichean cult encouraged various ascetic practices, such as refraining from eating meat and from sexual intercourse, to aid the soul of light in escaping the evil soul of darkness. Augustine retains this intense sense of being captive or bound in the midst of this cosmic conflict playing itself out within his own person. Augustine's personal internal struggle against a part of himself that is distracted from God remains just as intense and as potentially destructive. Augustine also retains the distrust of the body's needs, desires, and functions. In addition, he brings to his Christian doctrine the Manichean sense of internality, its sense of being bound, the struggle of good versus evil, and the ascetic practices they ingrained into all inductees.

Yet he also discards much that is characteristically Manichean, especially that which is incompatible with Neoplatonism and with Christianity. Furthermore, Augustine's understanding of sin and theological anthropology is influenced by both his retention of Manichean elements and his reaction against the Manichaean doctrines of two souls and two gods. The Hebraic unity of body and soul embedded in Christianity contradicts Mani's view that the body is separate from the soul; that the body is evil, while the soul is good; and that there are two divine realities, an evil one who created the body out of war and a good god who seeks to redeem the soul of light from the prison of the body. Augustine's belief that the one good God creates human nature as a whole and that everything God creates is good maintains continuity with Christianity. Both the body and soul are, therefore, good. Everything that has being is created by God and is good. Evil can only exist by feeding off of that which is good; it must be a deprivation of what is good. Thus he argues that evil is being less good than one could be, and he arrives at his famous definition of evil as the privation of good. Augustine refutes the Manichean doctrine of two souls by emphasizing the singularity of God: "whatever is, ... has its existence from the one God,"[6] and in quoting St. Paul, "'One God of whom are all things, and one Lord Jesus Christ...'"[7] Augustine thus argues against the Manichean notion

---

[6] Augustine, "Concerning Two Souls, Against the Manicheans," trans. Richard Stothert, in *The Nicene and Post Nicene Fathers of the Christian Church*, 14 vols., ed. Philip Schaff. (Grand Rapids MI: Wm. B. Eerdmans, 1956) 4:99.

[7] Ibid.

that sin is a result of the evil nature of the body, the dark soul, created by the Prince of Darkness. Rather, sin is an activity of the human will. Sin is not the result of an evil *nature*, but the effects of human *movement* and choices away from God. In the following quotation, Augustine is speaking of angels, but his argument concerning human nature is the same in this respect:

> There is no reason to doubt that the contrary dispositions which have developed among these good and bad angels are due, not to different *natures* and origins, for God the Author and Creator of all substances has created them both, but to the dissimilar *choices and desires* of these angels themselves.[8]

While Augustine agrees with Mani that human existence is a moral struggle of good versus evil taking place violently within one's very soul, he does not agree that this struggle is a cosmic re-enactment of creation and redemption. Rather, in Augustine's schema the internal division is the result of original sin. In Adam's fall the structure of human will was damaged such that human ability to act to do the good, even when one knows what the good demands, is radically compromised. Further, although the struggle against sin is a moral dichotomy of evil versus good, it is not a struggle of two materials, one evil and one good, occurring inside of the mind and body as the Manichean myth supposes. Rather, within Augustine's system, all substance is good: the mind, the soul, and the body, and even the will. All elements of human nature are created good. God's creation of human nature is thus not culpable for sin. God looked at creation and said, "It is good." Sin and evil have no substance, but feed off the power and being of good. Mani views good and evil as a moral dichotomy, but not an ontological one. Soul and body are of the same substance: matter. Augustine concurs with the moral dichotomy, but not with the ontological monism. His thinking about

---

[8] Augustine, *City of God*, trans. Marcus Dods (New York: The Modern Library, 1950) 244. Emphases mine.

human nature changes fundamentally when he leaves the Manicheans and discovers in Plotinus the metaphysical tools for understanding spiritual reality as substantially distinct from material reality.

Neoplatonist Plotinus (205-270 CE) is the second profound influence upon Augustine's conceptualization of human nature. Plotinus's thought was published by his disciple, Porphyry, in the fourth century in six books called the *Enneads*. Augustine credits Neoplatonism for saving him from the materialism of the Manicheans by providing him with the intellectual means to think clearly about God as spiritual and non-material.[9] Instead of a moral dichotomy within an ontological monism, Plotinus offers an ontological dualism that corresponds to this moral binary. Plotinus's view of the human person is characterized by a metaphysical dualism of body and mind. Rather than the metaphorical myths of ethical morals of the Manicheans, the Neoplatonists make metaphysical statements about what is actually ontologically real. In their way of thinking, reality is actually dualistic. The structure of reality is a hierarchical ontological dualism in which spiritual reality is immaterial, such as the One and the Intellect, and is higher than the material reality of physical bodies. Humans are both material via bodies, and spiritual via intellect or mind. Here is a definite metaphysical dualism, not simply a metaphorical opposition taken literally as in the Manichean system. Yet like the Manichean view, two substances, which constitute the human, are at odds with each other.

Along with this discovery of metaphysical immutability, Augustine is also taken with Plotinus's absolute emphasis upon oneness. For Plotinus, the ultimate principle of the truth of all reality is the One, which is unity-itself: a "self-sufficing principle will be

---

[9] Augustine writes addressing Plato in his imagination, "You have persuaded me that the truth is seen not with the bodily eyes but by the pure mind and that any soul that cleaves to truth is thereby made happy and perfect." "Of True Religion," trans. John H. S. Burleigh in *Augustine: Earlier Writings* (Philadelphia: Westminster Press, 1953) 226.

Unity-Absolute, for only in this unity is there a nature above all need whether within itself or in regard to the rest of things...."[10] Plotinus believes that the ontological structure of all reality is grounded in and empowered by the One. Out of the One everything proceeds and back into the One everything recedes. In *The Enneads*, he writes, "Seeking nothing, possessing nothing, lacking nothing, the One is perfect and, in our metaphor, has overflowed, and in its exuberance has produced the new...."[11] Plotinus overvalues oneness in general, as well as overvaluing it in the relationship of the body and soul. The human soul is born from and must return to the "transcendent and unknowable One." The One is the source of all reality, it is "God," it is the Good, it is beyond plurality and unity, it is homogenous. Returning to the One cannot be accomplished solely through knowledge, or reason, but only by desire. While the One is the source of all reality here on earth and otherwise, the One is not a personal being reaching out to humans, rather it is an unchanging/unchangeable, self-sufficient absolute singularity that can have no real concern for the position or reality of anything other than itself. Further, in Plotinus's anthropology the body is not considered an essential or good aspect of the person. He writes of his own experience:

Many times it has happened: lifted out of the body into myself; becoming external to all other things and self-encentered; beholding a marvelous beauty; then, more than ever, assured of community with the loftiest order; enacting the noblest life, acquiring identity with the divine... [12]

Plotinus believes that matter itself is evil, for it is "That Kind whose place is below all the patterns, forms, shapes, measurements, and limits...a mere image as regards Absolute Being but the

---

[10] Plotinus, *The Enneads,* trans. Stephen MacKenna (New York: Pantheon Books, 1957) 620.
[11] Ibid., 380.
[12] Ibid., 357.

Authentic Essence of Evil—in so far as Evil can have Authentic Being."[13] Augustine's general evaluation of human nature is affected by this overvaluation of singularity.

This hierarchical dualism entails various levels of being, which are structured like a ladder of being, with the absolute immaterial reality of the One at the top and the absolute material, inert matter at the bottom. The human person is constituted by both the physical extension of the body and the spiritual reality of the mind. Properly, the mind ought to govern the organized functions of the body, like the governor of the "city-state." Like Plato, Plotinus also uses the metaphor of "chariot driver" to express the relationship between mind and body. The mind as the driver must control the passions of the horse/body, in order to steer the whole person. In this view, the problems of evil and suffering arise because the "energies of the mind and those of the body and the emotions are opposed."[14] Persons are motivated toward the multiplicity of the body and the world, and abandon the spiritual drive toward rejoining the blessed unity of the One. Thus, the existing human being is understood in contrast with the One. As Marjorie Hewitt Suchocki's analysis of Plotinus reveals:

> Insofar as the being is directed toward multiplicity, then the Threeness of the One will be hard to discern. But if, in the reflection of the One which is present even in the discrete units of multiplicity, the being is recalled to the source of all being, then the being turns from multiplicity toward the One....[15]

The parallels to Augustine's mature thought are obvious.

---

[13] Ibid., 68.

[14] Karen Jo Torjesen, "The Body" (unpublished paper, Claremont Graduate University, 1993).

[15] Marjorie Suchocki, "The Correlation between God and Evil," (PhD diss., Claremont Graduate University, 1974) 12.

Plotinus views human beings as a mixture of multiplicity with a hint of the remnant of the quality of oneness.[16] Multiplicity for Plotinus is not only the movement away from the One, but it is also the conflict between these two different substances that constitute the human person, body and mind. The conflict between body and mind is drastic and is apparent in three areas. First, the mind is ontologically distinct from the body. The mind is viewed as real and consists of the same substance as the One, while the body is viewed as not really real, for it consists of the same substance as inert mass. Second, the mind is perfect, while the body is an imperfect imitation. And third, the mind is morally good, while the body is morally evil and responsible for sin. The mind is stronger than the body and can dominate it by mental power, spiritual desire, moral virtue, and ascetic practice. In the next section, we will see how Augustine's mature viewpoint follows Plotinus's evaluation of multiplicity and the problematic role it plays for spiritual concerns, and yet it diverts from Plotinus's location of sin in the nature of the human body.

While it is clear that Augustine's thought is deeply influenced by the schools of thought derived from Mani and Plotinus, there are, however, two significant differences between Augustine's view and these systems. First, he believes that the conflict within the person is not original, nor inherent in human nature. Rather, this division within the human occurs in time and by human agency as a

---

[16] See Suchocki's dissertation, which shows the connection between these qualities of absolute singularity, immutability, and self-sufficiency, on the one hand, and unrelatedness, on the other hand. She has offered a critique of the notion of love, which supposedly flows out of the One. This love is without concern for the dependent beings it supposedly loves, and without relationality with anything. I seek to demonstrate that the problem is not simply in the implications of this quality of oneness, but lies with the quality of oneness itself. Her critique of Augustine's exaltation of the quality of oneness centers on his doctrine of God. I seek to offer a corollary critique of the implications of this quality of oneness centering on theological anthropology.

consequence of sin. It is not a necessary conflict, nor one created by God. Secondly, Augustine does not name this conflict as an original conflict between body and soul. Rather, Augustine argues for the original wholeness and eschatological unity of the human body and soul. The war is internal, and it is between sin and faith. The body and soul sin together and together find faith through the grace of God.

The third and strongest influence on Augustine's view of the divided soul is Christianity and its Hebraic heritage. The Hebraic view of human beings is characterized by an unbreakable wholeness of body and soul. God created both body and soul and created them to be united as a whole. There is no dichotomy of matter and spirit, nor are the values of good and evil determined by a cosmic battle of light and dark. God creates both light and dark, body and soul and they are all good. Given this sensibility Augustine rejects Plotinus' ontological division within the person in favor of an ethical or religious division between sin and grace. Sin and grace is a theme developed in the New Testament, especially in those books attributed to Paul.

Augustine reads Paul's writings in the complex context of these differing schools of thought and belief. Paul conceives of the body and soul relationship as a function of an antithesis between the *flesh* and the *spirit*. Paul writes in a way that pits *flesh* against *spirit*, such as in Romans 8:6, "To set the mind on the *flesh* is death, but to set the mind on the *Spirit* is life and peace." Augustine's mature thought interprets this distinction not as the inevitable fight of the body and the soul as interpreted in the Greek and Manichaean thought, but as a struggle within a single soul between *sin* and *grace*.[17] In his early study of Paul, he concludes that free will enables the sinner to turn

---

[17] James Patout Burns, "Grace: the Augustinian Foundation," in *Christian Spirituality: Origins to the Twelfth Century*, vol. 16 of *World Spirituality: an Encyclopedic History of the Religious Quest*, ed. Bernard McGinn and John Meyerdorff (New York: Crossroad, 1985) 337.

from his sin and helplessness to Christ and beg divine aid in dying to sin completely, in a way similar to Plotinus's view that the mind is stronger and can control the flesh through religious practice. In this scenario the body and soul are separated. However, as Augustine's thought matures, he begins to interpret the "flesh" of Paul's dichotomy between flesh and spirit not as the body and its natural needs, but rather as the unnatural, sinful, disobedient turning *away* from God and God's eternal glory, toward the finite, empty human and its puny power and carnal desires. Note then that the flesh has no ontological reality, nor does the sprit. Both are qualities, movements and forms of the soul and the body.

Each of these schools of thought see particular oppositions within the human person, such as the body versus the mind, the light versus the dark, the good versus the evil, etcetera. Augustine struggles through these various significations, retaining particular notions from each influence with the process culminating in his understanding of the flesh and the spirit as an antithesis between sin and grace. Augustine's mature thought still sees a difference between flesh and spirit but he interprets this difference not as body versus soul, but in terms of sin versus grace, not in terms of ontological reality, but in terms of qualities of that ontological reality.

Augustine's Own Synthesis

Augustine's own synthesis is deeply influenced by Christianity and its Hebraic tradition. He believes he must conform his ways of thinking to Christianity's created wholeness of body and soul or reinterpret Christianity to be consistent with his beliefs. In formulating his own doctrine of theological anthropology, he retains the primacy of conflict and discord within his concept of human nature that is present in previous viewpoints. Yet he does abandon the Manichean belief in a mythological cosmic war waged between two opposed material souls within a single person. Utilizing Neoplatonism's ontological dualism of the substance of spirit (soul) and that of matter (body), he critiques Mani's ontological monism of materiality. He then transforms this Greek metaphysical dichotomy of body and mind, which corresponds to the Manichean ethical dichotomy between good and evil, into a more subtle, but not less intense, struggle *within* the human mind. The early Christian Augustine moves away from these classical dualisms in which the "true self, the soul, was drawn to reason, virtue, and higher spiritual realities, while the demeaning urges of...the body distracted the soul through its senses."[18] He adapts St. Paul's antithesis of spirit and flesh to articulate the essential unity of body and soul, reinterpreting this Pauline metaphor, not as a dualism of mind versus body, or of a good soul versus a bad soul, but as a struggle between sin and grace within a single soul. The primary battle of being human is not between two different substances, such as body and soul, but between two different forms and two different stances.

In *On the Trinity,* Augustine proposes a tripartite structure of the human mind in correlation with the Trinitarian structure of the *Imago Dei,* which is the doctrine that humankind is made in the image of God and therefore reflects the divine image. The human soul is comprised of three functions: contemplative mind, practical mind, and will. In Book IX he argues that the image of God is presented in humanity's mental nature. The mind is structured triadically into memory, understanding, and will. The parallel structure between human nature and God's nature is no coincidence, for it is an ontological correspondence. In fact the direction of correspondence flows both ways. We learn about the Trinitarian structure of God from knowing the inner structure of the human soul.

There is a hierarchical structure to the relationship of the parts of the human mind. The first and highest element of the human soul,

---

[18] Paula Fredriksen, "Beyond the Body/Soul Dichotomy: Augustine's Answer to Mani, Plotinus, and Julian," in *Paul and the Legacies of Paul,* ed. William S. Babcock (Dallas: Southern Methodist University Press, 1990) 244.

the contemplative mind, functions to contemplate God. Next, the practical mind functions to discern practical living in the world in order that the higher mind can peacefully contemplate God. While Augustine does "distinguish practical knowledge from contemplative wisdom," he also emphasizes the underlying unity in these distinctions: "the higher reason which belongs to contemplation, and the lower which belongs to action, (but) are in one mind."[19] The third part, the will, executes the desires of the contemplative and practical parts of the mind. The will is the part of the human soul that is in charge of the body. The body is not part of the soul, and is thus excluded from the *Imago Dei*.

The influences of both Mani and Plotinus are apparent in his thinking about the relationship of these divinely created parts or functions of the human mind with each other. Plotinus's influence is evident in Augustine's view of the Trinitarian structure of human nature. Although Augustine clearly proclaims the undivided unity and equality of substance within the Holy Trinity, he unwittingly infects the Christian doctrine of theological anthropology with Neoplatonic philosophy and its hierarchical and dualistic thinking.[20] It is more apt to describe Augustine's view of the Trinitarian structure within the human person as following Plotinus's hierarchical view of the One and its emanations rather than the Christian Holy Trinity's unity and equality. The contemplative mind parallels Plotinus's view of absolute divine reality as the One. Practical knowledge parallels the first emanation of the One, and the faculty of will corresponds with the second emanation into the multiplicity of the world.

Augustine's early influence from Manichaean mythology leads him to employ a model of warfare and military command in his

---

[19] Augustine, *On the Trinity*, trans. Stephen McKenna (New York: Cambridge University Press, 2002) 182. See also *On the Trinity*, Book XII, ch. 3. Note that he explains that "contemplative knowledge, which as I have argued, is properly called wisdom...the active which is properly called knowledge." *On the Trinity*, 208.

[20] See Augustine, *On the Trinity*, Books II and VIII.

understanding of the relationship of the parts of the human mind. The contemplative mind rightly rules the practical mind. The mind as a whole commands the will to carry out its desires, and the will rightly controls the body. The orders ought to be carried out unambiguously, for when the will hesitates just for a moment and wavers as to which voice to heed, the mind's voice or the body's voice, and then the whole person falls sinfully.

The Manichean view of two equally strong souls intensely struggling within the single person, evil versus good, and Plotinus's assertion of the hierarchical value of the mind over the body are combined with the Christian-Hebraic doctrine that the body and soul are created together as a whole. According to the Greeks, the mind thinks, contemplating God/Ideas, while the body acts in the world, taking care of practical concerns. Augustine retains this Greek hierarchy of mind over body in his complex order of the contemplative mind over practical mind, over will, over passions, over bodily needs.[21] Yet inheriting the Hebraic-Christian traditions, Augustine struggles to articulate a metaphysical, substantial unity or at least continuity/unity of body and soul.[22] The soul is the form of the body. It acts as the animator and director of the body's less than soul-like existence. Even within his understanding of the unity of body and soul, he continues the Plotinian notion of giving priority to the mind: "Man [sic] is a rational substance consisting of mind and body."[23] The mind properly rules over the body. Even though he asserts the eschatological unity of the body and soul, this unity is had at the expense of the self-sufficiency of the body. The so-called unity

---

[21] Plato then genderizes these aspects of the human, the mind is male and the body is female. Augustine accepts this genderization and further associates' gender with the internal hierarchies of the parts of the human as well.

[22] In some works, Augustine cannot fully accept a full metaphysical unity of body and soul.

[23] Augustine, *On the Trinity*, 201.

is in fact more precisely expressed as the proper order to the divinely created distinctions within the human person.

Although Augustine does not see the body as inherently evil, as do the dualists above, he does believe the body to be lower on the ontological hierarchy scale and less good than the soul. Yet, he carefully distinguished between *caro* (the body itself) and *qualitas carnalis* (the soul's carnal quality). Augustine interprets what Paul calls the flesh, as indicating *qualitas carnali*, but not *caro*.[24] *Caro* is the neutral material substance of the body, while *qualitas carnali* is that which results from the first sin. Sin lies not in the body itself, nor even its desires and needs; rather, it lies in the soul's turning toward the flesh. In sin this carnal quality of the soul is controlled by the desires of the flesh.[25] This state of affairs reverses the created order of the soul, which consists of three aspects hierarchically ordered according to their value: the contemplative mind, the practical mind, and the will.

Original Will versus Original Sin

Augustine's view of human personhood as a whole is shaped by his conceptualization of sin. Both doctrines combine elements from the three major influences in his thought: the Manichean model of warfare, the Plotinian metaphors of government and chariot riders, and the Pauline dichotomy between spirit and flesh, alongside the Hebraic/Christian respect for the original wholeness of the human, body and soul. This perspective distinguishes Augustine from the classical thinkers' views that either sin is a practical moral error in

---

[24] Fredriksen, "Beyond the Body," 230.

[25] In Augustine's early thought, then, Christ's unmerited grace enables the soul to completely resist the controlling distractions of the body and to become purely virtuous and free to contemplate God purely. Note that this scenario reflects the Plotinian optimism concerning the abilities of the soul.

thinking that can be corrected by thought or is the carnal needs and desires of the physical body.

Because selfhood is understood in relation to God, sin is understood in relation to selfhood. Sin lies in assuming a form of selfhood that is both multiple in form and tilted toward the creature in direction. Augustine integrates elements from each of these influences, offering a view of the self as a function of the self's form: either *unity* or *division*. He still views sin as a battle within the human self, not as one of the body against the soul, nor as dark against light, but rather as the moral struggle of the soul to *will* what it knows is right. He articulates this inner battle of sin in terms of division and insubordination. In the activity of insubordination, the will refuses to obey the commandments of the higher mind and faces away from God. In the activity of turning away from the mind, the will divides against itself and its form becomes *division itself*. Sin is the cause of the disruption of the original unity of the human self. It disrupts the connection of the body and soul by dividing the soul against itself. In the original unity of the soul with itself, the mind and the will are united, and the soul is united with the body. Sin creates a battle of the soul against itself, of the body against itself, and of the will against itself. It is not a battle of the body against the soul. Sin is not a conflict between parts already differentiated by God's creative hand; rather, sin is understood as a *new* division, a new occurrence in time. Thus, sin can be seen as contrary to God's created order, and in no way can God be responsible for sin.

In this formulation Augustine heeds Christianity's Hebrew heritage in affirming that everything God created is good. The world and all its creatures are a part of God's creation, embedded with God's purpose. Humans are made in the image of God. He differentiates his Christian viewpoint from Plotinus's assertion that the human soul consists of the same substance as God and that the body is an imperfect substance. Within the Christian tradition he finds a way of speaking about evil without giving it the material and ontological value that the Manicheans and the Greeks did. Evil is not a natural result of existence, but rather is a corruption of the good and the removal of the good. The paradigm of evil is the privation of good. Evil is not part of human nature; it is not what one is, but rather, it is the behavior of moving away from God. Evil is seen in the form of the human will, not as a part of human nature. He writes, "The will does not fall 'into sin'; it falls 'sinfully.'"[26]

Here Augustine revises the religious question of evil from a simple identification of mind/body with good/evil of the Greek and Manichean beliefs into a more complex concept of the wholeness of human nature and of the goodness therein. Human nature is good. The problem is in its weakened ability to execute its will. Thus, evil is not created by God, or a Prince of darkness, as the Manicheans believe, nor is it a natural occurrence of existence, as the Greeks believe. Rather, evil is the consequence of sins and their punishments. Sin is choosing that which is less good; it is moving toward the multiplicity of the world. In this movement, the will creates multiplicity and ambiguity within itself. The will's original role is to listen purely to the desires of the mind and execute these orders, which would move the whole person closer to God. However, in original sin, the will hears the mind's orders *and* it is distracted by the impulses of the body toward the various and particular pleasures of the world and the creature. Amongst all this ambiguity, the will divides against itself and part of it heeds the body. Thus, concupiscence is born and ever after, the will remains divided against itself. The will is weakened and no longer able to perform its duties effectively. As he writes of sinfulness as dividing:

The law in our members is opposed to the law of the mind, is not a mingling of two natures caused of contrary principles, but a division of one against itself caused through the desert of sin. We were not so in Adam, before that nature, having listened to and

---

[26] Augustine, *City of God*, 255.

followed its deceiver, had despised and offended its Creator; that is, not the former life of man created, but the latter punishment of man condemned.[27]

Early in his career, then, he sees sin as a free act of the mind/soul to disobey God, by loving its own goodness over God's goodness, creating disorder, and disrupting the natural order of creation and the divine purpose. Sin is the will's desire of finite, empty self-pleasure, over against the will's desire to fulfill the divine, eternal purpose.

Delineating the context of the original position of the faculty of the will and its functions and aspects in the human soul clarifies the complexity of original sin and its consequences. The major ingredient in Augustine's innovative interpretation of the division within the human is his emphasis on the faculty of *the will*. Augustine treats the will "not as the property of rational activity, but under the heading of a *libido dominandi* from which all action proceeds...."[28] In Latin, desire and will are closely related. To will and to want is *voluntas*, and desire is *appetitus*. The "will is defined as the appetitive faculty in man [sic]."[29] The intellect and the will are seen as related, as two functions of the human spirit. Latin distinguishes these functions as such: "intellect is that which knows objects, the will is that which has an appetite or desire for them."[30] Augustine believes that God created humankind with a chain of command built-in. Before original sin, the will acts as a bridge between the faculty of reason/knowledge and the body/physical needs. The will is what hears the wisdom of the contemplative mind and executes the proper activity for the body. It actualizes the mind's intention, when it works correctly.

---

[27] Augustine, "On Continence," trans. C. L. Cornish, in *The Nicene and Post-Nicene Fathers of the Christian Church*, 3:21.

[28] E.J. Hundert, "Augustine and the Sources of the Divided Self," *Political Theory* 20/1 (Feb 1992): 89.

[29] Robert Muller, *Dictionary of Latin and Greek Theological Terms* (Grand Rapids MI: Baker Book House, 1985) 330.

[30] Ibid.

However, something goes wrong in sin; the mechanism of execution becomes damaged. After original sin, this order becomes reversed, and the body's desires take over the attention and work of the will. The will still hears the wisdom of the mind, for it "knows the good"; however, it also hears the needs and pleasures of the body. It is unable to heed the mind exclusively and moves in two different directions, thus creating a rift in its integrity. He confirms will as the focal point of sin:

> Sinning therefore takes place only by exercise of will. But our will is neither well known to us . . . will is a movement of the mind, no one compelling, either for not losing nor for obtaining something…Sin…cannot exist apart from the will.[31]

Employing Augustine's military metaphors, the will rebels, or "defects," and heeds the impulses of the "foot soldiers," the body and all its multiplicity. As a consequence of this original breaking of the chain of command, the body will no longer obey the commands of the will, or of the soul in general (or the soul, the General). The problem in sin is depicted as a problem of dissension and ambiguity. In sin these hierarchically ordered parts begin to war with each other. The will's defection against itself creates a rift within human subjectivity itself.

Augustine also uses Mani's military metaphor to describe his experience of internal conflict as a war against sin. He writes of two different forces within the human self, speaking of the way of continence and the way of concupiscence as "the war in which we are engaged, and enkindles us to contend keenly."[32] Adopting Pauline terminology, he continues to utilize the metaphor of conflict as he refers to the force toward sin as *the flesh*, and one toward continence as *the spirit*. He writes that the "flesh is said to lust against the spirit,

---

[31] Augustine, "Concerning Two Souls, Against the Manichees," 102-4.
[32] Augustine, "On Continence," 9.

when the soul with fleshly lust wrestles against the spirit, this whole are we."[33]

Sin is not only division; it is the movement toward division, as Augustine writes: "progression towards inferior things is dangerous to that rational cognition that is conversant with things corporal and temporal."[34]

Augustine's emphasis upon the activity of the will in sin makes the desire of the soul the operative category. Sin is not an error in the mind. For the mind is associated with the form of unity that is evidenced by its ability to think a single thought with a single purpose, while the form of the will has been reformatted in the sinful division against itself. Rather, the soul in its entirety is the seat of sin, for it is the soul that does not will to do the good that the mind knows; instead, it desires its own glory. He writes:

> If one seeks the efficient cause of their evil, none is to be found…What made the bad will bad?…It (the will) becomes evil because the very turning itself and not the thing to which it turns is evil.[35]

Augustine sees the primary sinfulness of humans, not in our connection or bondage to the physical body, but in our pride in ourselves—in turning away from loving God's power and glory, toward loving our own puny existence. Augustine laments his own sin in the *Confessions* in these terms:

> But my sin was this, that I looked for pleasure, beauty, and truth not in Him [God] but in myself and his other creatures, and the search led me instead to pain, confusion, and error.[36]

---

[33] Ibid., 19.
[34] Augustine, *On the Trinity*, 159.
[35] Augustine, *City of God*, 251-2.
[36] Augustine, *Confessions*, 40-41.

The will turns away from what is most good, God, and turns toward itself. In so turning, the will creates a disorder of the internal elements that had constituted the essential unity of the human self. This disorder is the reversal of properly prioritized maxims for making decisions regarding one's activity in the world. The turning of the will has three dimensions: the will turns away from the absolute unity of God, it turns toward the multiplicity of the world and the creature, and the will turns against itself. Sin is the cause of the disruption of the original unity of the body and soul, and the original unity of the soul with itself: the mind and the will.

Early in his career, Augustine understands sin as a free act of the mind/soul to disobey God, by loving its own goodness over God's goodness. Sin creates disorder, disrupting the natural order of creation and the divine purpose. Sin desires finite empty pleasure, rather than the divine eternal purpose, seeking control over the material world. The results of sin are twofold: first, the mind loses control over the will; and second, the will loses control over the desires of the flesh. Note that the body is not the culprit. Health is lost to deterioration and death in the body and disharmony in the human spirit itself. Only the grace of God's act in Redemption converts the human mind back toward God. Sin creates unhappiness and conflicted divisions within these different functions of the person.[37]

Division and insubordination determine human existence under sin. Sin is the insubordination of one of these parts, the will. Augustine's interpretation of the events in the Garden of Eden found in his *The Literal Meaning of Genesis* illustrates the relationship of will and mind in the activity of original sin. Augustine allegorically interprets a confusing story in scripture as a truth about the internal

---

[37] His early view on sin and will has to do with his understanding of the origin of the soul. Earlier he believes with Origen that the soul is separate from the body. See Robert O'Connell's study of this development in Augustine's thought, *The Origin of the Soul in St. Augustine's Later Works* (New York: Fordham University Press, 1987).

parts of one person, one mind. Contemplative Wisdom, which he identifies with Adam, is primal, first. He happily goes about contemplating God and eternal truths, that is until Eve, Practical Will, arrives on the scene and is tempted by the serpent's promise of knowing both good and evil and being like God. The will takes the temptation and gives it to the mind, Adam, thereby making his power and control useless. Once the wisdom has listened to the will, he has lost his control over her. Augustine likens this story with these different characters to what occurred within the single mind in the original fall into sin. The will, like Eve, disobeys God's law. To the contrary, the contemplative mind, like Adam, knows this law and wishes to follow it. It is only after the will (Eve) disobeys, that the mind (Adam) is also lost.[38] This original disobedience supplies the condition by which the mind loses control of its will. The proper command order is disrupted and remains disrupted throughout life. Augustine characterizes sin in the *Confessions* as his inability to master himself, his body, his desire for sex and food. He quotes the Bible to illustrate his point: "No man (sic) can be master of himself, except for God's bounty."[39] Further, he writes, only with God's help of grace, is it "that my soul may follow me [meaning the contemplative mind] to you [God], freed from the concupiscence which binds it, and rebel no

---

[38] Note that Augustine's schema of sin is the disobedience of the will. The will disobeys the contemplative mind. Thus, this story does not actually fit the story of Adam and Eve in the garden. Remember from earlier, that Augustine uses that story as an allegory of the fall of humanity. Augustine sees Adam as the Contemplative Mind of humanity, and Eve is the Practical Will of humanity. In the biblical story, God commands both Adam and Eve not to taste the serpent's fruit, but in Augustine's story, the will disobeys its own contemplative mind. This is further evidenced in Augustine's statement that the punishment of sin is the internal conflict of the self against itself, to fit the crime of the will disobeying the mind. As I plug this schema back into the garden story, it is evident that sin would consist in Eve disobeying Adam. Thus, the very structure of original sin, as so forcefully articulated by Saint Augustine, is actually the structure of women not following the orders given by men.

[39] Augustine, *Confessions*, 235.

more against itself."[40] Here Augustine makes clear reference to the division within the self, the part that knows the good, wants to do the good, wants to resist temptation, and, on the other hand, the part that hampers the person's drive to do the good; yet both parts are within the same person. He refers to this second part as "my unhappy soul," which rejoices in the uncertainty about how much the body really needs to subsist, using this doubt "to vindicate and excuse itself. It is glad that the proper requirements of health are in doubt, so that under the pretense of caring for health it may disguise the pursuit of pleasure."[41] Sin, therefore, is a complex interaction of the soul and the body. Both can act for the purposes ordained by God and both can turn away from God's glory toward the finite.

Later in 396-398 CE, Augustine begins to reformulate his notion of free will, or more exactly, his notion of the ability of the soul to completely will the good. The soul, he decides (through his own experience and the experience of his congregation and through his identification with what he believes to be Paul's own biographical statements) is too weak to control its desires. All humanity is born and bound by Adam's sin into a collective sinful mass. The soul itself has been made defective in Adam, and the defect in the soul is inherited through the "*summa voluptus* [sexual passion] of orgasm necessary to achieve conception."[42] Earlier thinkers argued that the sin was passed on only through the flesh, the body. But in Augustine's eyes this dichotomy ignores the soul/body connection created by God. What is changed in the fall is "not man's great purpose, the begetting of children, but rather the psychological means by which this could be accomplished."[43] Sin is a radical rift in humanity's will

---

[40] Ibid., 234.

[41] Ibid., 235.

[42] Fredriksen, "Beyond the Body," 246. See also Augustine, "The Literal Meaning of Genesis," Book 3, chs. 21 and 33.

[43] Fredriksen, "Beyond the Body," 246. See also Augustine, "The Literal Meaning of Genesis," Books 9 through 11.

that changes the very structure of human subjectivity. It is by original sin that evil and further sins come into the world. All human beings after Adam and Eve are altered. It is as if the genetic codes have mutated. The ontological changes are passed down through the generations. This mutated subjectivity is characterized most fundamentally by division. The first sin is what disintegrates the original unity of the human body and soul, leaving the person divided against itself.

All evil is a result of sin and its consequences. The primary and lasting effect of the first sin is a perverted will in which Adam's sin lives on, disabling all of his descendants. Humans are no longer able to relate positively to God. Previously, Adam had direct and somewhat mutual interactions with God. But even more significant, Adam's will was fully intact, as was Eve's, according to Augustine. Being intact, they spoke with God. They were able to be one self, totally integrated and with one undivided and effective will.

The next major consequence of sin is the unhappy division within the soul between the *mind* and the *will* and the subsequent division between the weakened soul and the body. The loss of the ability to focus one's desire/will and the further loss of the ability to control one's body, particularly one's sexual "members" are also consequences of sin. The sinfulness of this division and distraction from the one goal of spiritual living then causes more sins.

The deterioration of the body's health is a third affect. Health is lost to the deterioration and death in the body caused by disharmony in the human spirit *itself*. When Adam and Eve sinned they incurred changes in their bodies and souls that remain effective for all humanity even to this day; they:

> lost their privileged state, their bodies became subject to disease and death, like the bodies of animals, and consequently subject to the same drive by which there is in animals a desire to copulate…Nevertheless, even in its punishment the rational soul gave evidence of its innate nobility when it blushed

because of the animal movement of the members of its body and...this movement of which it was ashamed came from the violation of the divine commandment.[44]

Disharmony is the paradigm for sin, death and evil.

Original sin has ontological consequences that cannot be fully rectified except by God at the resurrection. It is only by the grace of God that the soul and body are saved from the bondage to sin under which all humans now live. Only at the resurrection are the body and soul reunited into a whole as they were created to be, in one unconflicted nature. Because the body and soul are connected, they sin together and are redeemed together. Augustine's understanding of redemption[45] and the eschaton reveals the importance of the body and soul connection. He believes that the soul is only made wholly spiritual again at the resurrection when the soul and body are unified, together with one undivided will. Only then will the whole person be "*in pace*":

> Perfect your [God's] mercies in me until I reach the fullness of peace, which I shall enjoy with you in soul and body, *when death is swallowed up in victory*. [Augustine or the editor of the modern translation of Augustine uses the Italics to indicate that these words come from Corinthians.][46]

Augustine's words "in soul and body" indicate that at the resurrection, the body and soul will not only both be there, in such a way to indicate that the resurrection is also bodily as well as spiritual, but also to indicate that the body and soul will be together in harmony. The body will act solely on command of the soul, fulfilling

---

[44] Augustine, "The Literal Meaning of Genesis," in *Ancient Christian Writers*, 57 vols., trans. John Hammond Taylor (New York: The Newman Press, 1982) 42:165.

[45] Even once the person is "*sub graitia*" converted, s/he is still a sinner and sinners continue to sin.

[46] Augustine, *Confessions*, 234.

the purpose of God, known by the mind and now enacted by the body. Augustine contends that the internal unity of body and soul is correlated with salvation. Augustine believes that God's authority reformats the human self, providing the prerequisite unity that for Augustine is the necessary condition for the possibility of salvation.

Augustine's emphasis on oneness operates as a *formal* criterion for Christian selfhood/existence and salvation. He reveals the importance of "formal" criteria in sin in his understanding of how the soul must be restructured in its return from many-ness to its original oneness:

> It will be re-formed by the Wisdom which is not formed but has formed all things, and will enjoy God through the spirit, which is the gift of God. It becomes 'spiritual man, judging all things and judged of none...loving the Lord its God with all its heart and all its soul and all its mind, and loving its neighbor not carnally but as itself. He loves himself spiritually who loves God with all that lives within him.[47]

Augustine's doctrine of sin is a move toward acceptance of the body. He takes great effort to affirm the created goodness of the body and its genuine needs. Augustine's emphasis on the activity of the human will as the true culprit of evil influenced the theological understanding of sin and human agency in this evil for ages to come. His reformulation solves several theological quandaries. First, it interprets the problem of evil in a way that neither blames God for evil, nor sees human nature as evil. His thought allows God to be immaterial, without being responsible for evil. Further, it offers a view in which human nature remains good. Human *activity*, a radical occurrence in time, accounts for sin and evil. Evil is a result of sin and

---

[47] Augustine, "Of True Religion," 237. Note that Augustine speaks of the spiritual soul as "it" several times here. Also note his addition to Matthew's gospel, "loving its neighbor *'not carnally but'* as itself."

its consequences. Thus, Augustine shifts the focus of sin and evil from the locus of the body and its needs for external nourishment and stimulation to the internal realm of the mind and the will.[48] Sin begins its divisive effects in the will and spreads to all the functions and parts of being human.

Yet in order to accomplish these solutions, he denigrates multiplicity. He reveals his bias concerning many-ness and oneness as he writes about how if the soul overcomes its temptations, for its reward it "will return from the mutable *many* to the immutable *One*."[49] Augustine devalues multiplicity and division in his conceptualization of sin. Augustine shifts the location of evil away from the substance of the body to the form of the whole person. Sin is the formation of division itself, and the movement away from the unity that is oneness, toward the multiplicity, which constitutes the form of materiality. The paradigm of sin is then the form of multiplicity. Augustine's understanding of sin as the movement of the will against itself toward the multiplicity of the creature and its environs reveals his denigration of multiplicity. He associates sin with multiplicity, both in form and in content of sin's will/desire. The form of sin (which is also the form of concupiscence) is division, a division against the self.

Sin is the privation of the One

In this chapter, I have discussed Augustine's three primary influences on his doctrine of sin and theological anthropology. Both

---

[48] This shift begins theology's movement from concern for asceticism of the body to a concern for subjectivity. Subjectivity is about a person's stance and form. In shifting sin to its location in the mind, Augustine sets the stage for Luther's Reformation emphasis on faith as the opposite of sin and his view of sin as disbelief (the opposite of faith). Luther also views sin as a problem within human subjectivity; however, he expands on Augustine's formulation of sin as a defect in the will to include a defective mind as well as the defective will.

[49] Augustine, "Of True Religion," 236-7. Emphasis mine.

Mani and Plotinus describe sin as a conflict of universal elements actualized within each person, either between two material souls or between the mind and body. Augustine synthesizes these two notions and moves the struggle of sin further inward, into each individual soul as a conflict between a divided will. Augustine's insight is in retaining the power of the inner conflict from Mani and Plotinus while avoiding a straight identification between this conflict and the dualisms of each thinker.

Further, Augustine's analysis of sin removes the identification of sin with the body and identifies sin with the movement and structure of the will. Augustine internalizes and spiritualizes sin. Augustine's conceptualization of sin changes the very structure of how sin is viewed. Evaluation of sin no longer focuses on the body and its so-called evil needs. Rather, sin is named as a problem of the soul, of an activity of the will. Sin is an activity that occurs in the world's time, and is a rebellion against God and God's created order of nature. Next, I explored Augustine's understanding of the will and its position and activity before, after, and during original sin. The will's sinful activity has three turns. The will turns away from the unity of God, in its desire, toward the multiplicity of the world and the creature, and in so doing the will turns against itself and against the divinely created hierarchical order of control and command. Thereby the paradigm of sin is the creation of multiplicity and ambiguity within the human soul. And lastly, I have drawn out implications of Augustine's thought for the evaluation of multiplicity and division.

Next we move to an analysis of the function of multiplicity in Augustine's leading metaphor of sin: desire. Desire plays the primary role in Augustine's autobiographical analysis of sin, both in his experience and in his reflection on his experience, as we shall see in this current section that examines the *Confessions*. Desire is the primary term in Augustine's articulation and personal experience of sin. By moving sin's location from the body to the will, he detaches desire from the physical realm of the body itself. Desire is not seen as grounded in the body, but in the will. Augustine believes that people crave sex and food in a sinful way. However, sin is not due to the body's need or appetite or even the body's cycles of hormones, but rather sin is due to the sinful and defective will that is responsible for the desire and craving of any object other than the divine Himself.

Augustine's tendency is also found in his naming of sin in terms of desire in his conceptualization of concupiscence versus continence. Concupiscence is the desire for the creature. It is most often associated with sexual lust, as lust is Augustine's paradigmatic example of sin. Yet concupiscence can indicate desire for anything that is not the holy desire for union with God. There are two characteristics of concupiscence that are problematic for Augustine: the desire is characterized by *multiplicity* as opposed to *unification*, and this desire is a *variety,* rather than the *same.* This *form* of the desire consists in the *form* of the subject who has the desire and the *form* of the object desired.

Desire formats the human will. For Augustine one's desire constitutes oneself. The form of one's will conforms to the form of the object of one's will/desire. Here we can discern a double denigration of multiplicity in Augustine's conceptualizations. Not only is sin conceptualized in terms of a divided form of one's will, but also the object of this sinful will is multiple as well. All that is not God, not the One, is multiple and is creaturely. Desiring any object that is not God is *ipso facto,* desiring an object that is not an absolute unity. Such activity of the will has a catastrophic effect upon the ontological form of the will, causing the will to be divided. In sin, not only is the object of one's will a sinful object via its multiple form, but also the will that desires this sinful object is divided and thus sinful.

Desire is not just another example of Augustine's structure of sin as division within the will; it is the paradigm of Augustine's conceptualization of sin. It provides the very ontological structure of what occurs in human activity after original sin. Desire has ontological power to re-form the will.

Continence, on the other hand, is the restraint of one's desires and needs. Continence is associated with uniformity: "Truly it is by continence that we are made as one and regain that unity of self which we lost by falling apart in the search for a variety of pleasures."[50] More technically, continence is the control of one's bodily fluids. Augustine primarily thought of withholding the ejaculation in male sexual orgasm, but it includes the ability to withhold all of one's energy, power and fluids within the self. This is significant metaphorically. Spiritually Augustine believes that continence means withholding all of one's desire for God. Also in the literal sense, Augustine believes that his power and energy is lost, spent up and destroyed in the scattering of his seed. He sees himself and his soul likewise scattered and lost uselessly all over the world. "I was tossed and spilled, floundering in the broiling sea of my fornication...."[51] Until he finds rest in God, in whom his soul, his self, will be re-gathered from all the ends of the earth and the whole of his being will live to praise God's name.

Another illustration of the denigration of multiplicity in Augustine's thought is found in his fear of particularity and his exaltation of universality. This devaluation is prevalent in the praise-blame structure as demonstrated in Augustine's articulation and valuation of his own experience as revealed in *The Confessions*. Augustine blames his particular self while praising God who grants him access to a universal self. In his *Confessions*, the structure of Augustine's view of selfhood is shown first hand, as he offers an analysis of himself. He makes a strong contrast between his interpretation of himself as an unconverted sinner in the first part of the book, and his construction of the ideal converted selfhood of a

---

[50] Augustine, *Confessions*, 233.
[51] Augustine, *Confessions*, 43.

Christian, found in the second part of the work. The central focus and the turning point are found in the conversion in the scene in the garden.

Augustine describes himself before conversion as being a particular self with conflicts and contractions within his will and mind. At his conversion, he is faced with the fact of his existence as madness. To avert this fate, he believes that he must convert; he hears the book calling out, "read me, read me," like the Eucharist: "Take, Eat, Given for you." At this pivotal moment, his heart is converted. Afterward, he fits into the ideal of Christian selfhood. Differences between individuals because of any particularity, such as gender, race, or personal experiences are deemed unimportant for they are associated with the sinful unconverted state of being. He views the converted self as identical with the singular ideal of Christian selfhood. This dichotomy is the reason he highlights his own particular experience in the first nine chapters, which describe and interpret his pre-converted experiences as a confused and contradictory self, full of particularities and concupiscence expressed as desire for variety and multiplicity. These first three-fifths of his confessions emphasize his particularity and show that his life did not fit into the one singular ideal of Christian selfhood. Thus, he was to be blamed as sinful. He is not, as some have argued, aware of his own subjective perspective, speaking in a positive, constructive way out of his own experience. Rather, he is using the particularity of his experience as evidence of his blameworthiness, of how wrong he was. Once he is converted his rendition of selfhood is dry and universalized. The last three chapters after his conversion to Christianity reveal a universal ideal self characterized by unity and sameness and contentment in his proper desire for God, continence. How ironic that the single most influential and loved work of Augustine is the part of his writings that he uses to show how sinful he was!

Further, we see that for Augustine God is the source of this precious unity, both for the world as a whole and for each individual person. Personal unity is not only next to godliness for Augustine, it actually has its one and only source in God. God also provides the unity for a person's disconnected sinful and divisive pre-converted self. As Margaret Miles writes, "the explicit agenda of *The Confessions* is an ordering (also read unification) of experiences and world so that ideas and desires do not contradict one another, but fit—and can be shown to fit—each in its proper place."[52]

Augustine's view of subjectivity provides a final example of his denigration of particularity and multiplicity. It is subjectivity itself that is viewed as problematic. Augustine believes that humans can only love the world and its creatures via the love of God. We must first direct our desire and love toward God. Then through this vertical passion, Christians are enabled to love the world. There is a parallel between this structure in which positive meaning comes to the world and the self only through God as the middle term, and Augustine's interpretation of selfhood. The self knows and loves its own subjectivity only in and through the mediation of God. The self who knows itself by itself is the sinful self, the unconverted self. This self is characterized by multiplicity and plurality. Augustine illustrates his own life as a sinner as the extreme example of this unconverted self. In the mire of particularity demonstrated in the *Confessions*, Augustine illustrates that the particular self is to blame, as "a huge fable,"[53] while God and God's unifying and universalizing effects upon the self after conversion are to be praised.

Desire plays several significant roles both in the quest for unity and in the barriers to it. Proper desire is desire for God; it provides the power and energy necessary for the soul to "blast-off" from the gravity of sin and creatureliness toward the celestial ideal of

---

[52] Margaret Miles, *Delight and Desire* (New York: Crossroads, 1992) 52-53.
[53] Augustine, *Confessions*, 79.

unification with God. Desire for the divine can be seen in contrast to concupiscence, which is improper desire, desire gone astray. Concupiscence not only moves away from the single perfection of adoring God, it moves toward multiplicity itself. Further, the concupiscent will not only desires the multiplicity of the creature above the oneness of the divine; it divides against itself, making itself into a bifurcated will and inconsistent self.

Proper desire, as an expression or emanation from a created good singular will is unified and unifies its subject, for its object is unity itself. Improper desire, on the other hand, not only does not unify, but also divides. The will created by sin is divided and only desires an object that is multiple.

Augustine says that sin/evil is the privation of good. This assertion and all that it means as we have examined above, reveals Augustine's underlying assumptions against multiplicity. He assumes the Neoplatonic prioritization of the One, although with the hierarchy of mind over body (albeit a transformed hierarchy, but still a hierarchy of value). Further, we recognize the seed shells of the Manichean drama of the internal warfare within the human subject between the good and sin. Also present explicitly are Augustine's focused efforts to assert the original goodness of the human self as a whole (body and soul). Augustine's formulation of sin thus far has seemed helpful and even progressive, when taken in the context of the problems with previous formulations.

Sin is the privation of good. Augustine says that everything that is, is good. Yet his doctrine of sin is not that simple. Augustine is still employing a Plotinian hierarchy of value. God is the most valuable, while inert matter is the least valuable. God is intimately associated with Plotinus's the One, and is identified with absolute unity. Humanity is viewed in contrast to this absolute unity. Humanity is a composite of body and soul, and is *ipso facto* less valuable than is God. The world is multiple and thus is also *ipso facto* less valuable than God, and less valuable than humanity. Augustine claims here that both humanity and the world are inherently good *because* God created them. Augustine asserts that God is absolutely good and that God created only good beings.

However, evil and sin come into the picture through humanity's choice to move against itself. All this goodness is only *good* when it is known, loved, desired through God. In other words, in order to love one's neighbor, a person must first love God and then, through God, one can love the neighbor. God's love and mediation is actually what gives everything its "un-sinfulness." So it looks like this:

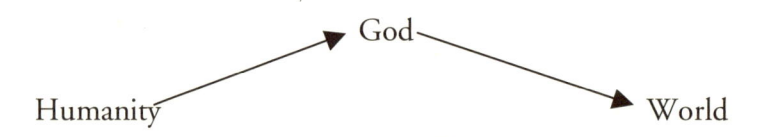

$$\text{Humanity} \longrightarrow \text{God} \longrightarrow \text{World}$$

Sin arises when humanity tries to love anything in itself, without the mediation of God. As the following diagram illustrates:

$$\text{Humanity}\text{---------}\text{World}$$

Sin arises when humanity desires anything other than God's unity. Sin arises when the object of humanity's will is that which is not one. Sin arises when the object of humanity's will is the multiplicity of the world or of the body.

Augustine says that the ontological being of the world is not evil; however, its *form* is.[54] It is the multiformity of the world that creates the consequences of sin: division, disorder, evil. Sin is originally the

---

[54] Here it is apparent that Augustine has not accomplished what he and the line of Christian interpreters of his thought think that he has accomplished. Augustine sought to de-demonize human nature by understanding it as created by God. Specifically he focused on affirming that God created the human body and that God could not have created the cause of evil or sin. Yet we see here that all he does in fact is to divert the focus on the evilness of the nature of the body toward a hatred of the form of multiplicity that exists naturally in the human body.

defection of the will away from the direction of the mind toward the unity of God. The object of the will ought to be the absolute unity of God. This desire for God is continence (the opposite of concupiscence), which would maintain the integral unity of the human person. Unity is associated with continence due to Augustine's belief that the human will has the characteristic of conformity. The will conforms its own structure to that which is its object. Thus, if the will desires God, then the will (along with the rest of the person) becomes *form*atted in conformity with God's will or God's uniformity. This unity of the person is the original form of humanity as God created it. However, it is also the case that if the object of the will is multiple, then the will conforms to this multiplicity. This is exactly how Augustine describes the process of sin. The will, which is created as part of the integral unity of the person, disobeys the soul's own contemplative mind in an act of distraction. Note that Augustine does not describe the disobedience as disobedience of God's command. This distraction, this focus on more than one object, allows multiformity into the human soul. When the will desires that which is not God, by loving that which is multiform, the person's form also then becomes multiple. The unity of the person is so intrinsic to its value that when the will allows this multiplicity into itself, all of humanity suffers the consequences of sin. Since the process of sin is the moving away from unity toward multiplicity, the consequence of sin is that the human will is improperly divided and becomes multiform itself.

What is so powerful and horrible about multiplicity, that it can de*prive* the human will of its *good*ness? I am at a loss here. My only answer must be that it is Augustine's own fearful assumptions concerning multiplicity. Augustine implicitly believes that it is the form of the world's being that is problematic. It is the multiformity of the world and of the body that is in opposition to the absolute unity of God. Augustine believes that unity is good, that goodness is uniform, and that multiplicity is not good because it is not uniform.

A dual desire, ambiguity,[55] and multiplicity arose, and it is in this multiplicity that Augustine finds the serpent of the garden. Augustine says that evil is the privation of good. I have shown that for Augustine, the privation of the good is fundamentally the privation of unity so that sin is defined as privation of the one. Augustine and his legacy thus give Christianity a powerful schematism that inherently distorts multiplicity, particularly in relation to the self.

In the subsequent chapters we will explore conceptualizations of the self that counter this exaltation of singularity and oneness. Kierkegaard gives us an alternative theory of the self as an internal dialectical relationship of polar ontological elements. I then apply this dialectic to his theory of the spheres of existence, as well as to interpreting his pseudonymous authorship, revealing a virtual array of multiple aspects of the self. These parts are positively related to each other in the dialectic of faith. Irigaray also demonstrates an innovative theory of subject-hood that appreciates multiplicity, fluidity, and simultaneity. Irigaray also aids our project with her critique of the unexamined philosophical assumptions that both repress all manner of difference, especially the feminine, and exalt the One and sameness. I draw distinct elements from each author into my new construction of selfhood as a dialectic matrix of multivalent parts. This view promotes awareness of the multiplicity and relationality within a self and opens us to the significance and diversity of external relationships as well.

---

[55] It is interesting to explore ways in which the ambiguous meaning of ambiguity plays on the Manichean devaluation of darkness. Augustine associated ambiguity with sin. Ambiguity can be understood as having more than one desire, *and* ambiguity can also be understood as obfuscation, and opaque dimness, the opposite of clarity and light.

2

Kierkegaard's Multi-Spheres of Living
Introduction

The previous chapter demonstrated the assumption of singularity and the exaltation of oneness in the dominant Western theological and philosophical conceptualizations of human selfhood. It examined Augustine's doctrine of human nature as a paradigmatic example of, and a fundamental influence upon, Western Christian theology of personhood. Deviation from the idealized singular self has signified either mental/psychic sickness, or a result/punishment of sin. Søren Kierkegaard's theological anthropology is quite different from this model. He envisions a multi-tiered self, full of complexities and dynamism.

In the following two chapters on Kierkegaard, I examine the presence of multiplicity within the self in Kierkegaard's thought in three areas: first, through his understanding of the dialectical relationship of the polar factors in human existence; next through his concept of the multiple spheres of existence; and finally, through his employment of various pseudonymous authors. While it may be argued that selfhood and subjectivity are two of the most pronounced themes in Kierkegaard's body of work, he does not explicitly articulate a formal delineation of the self. Rather, we must pull out the implications for his understanding of selfhood from his various writings. The closest Kierkegaard comes to articulating a formal definition of selfhood is in the opening paragraphs of Anti-Climacus's *Sickness Unto Death*, which we will examine in detail below. This chapter describes the three spheres that Kierkegaard discusses and argues that the dialectical character of his understanding of human existence is the fundamental element and the key to unlocking the mysteries of his perception of the synthesis of human existence in three spheres. In the next chapter I analyze his use of pseudonyms in several of his works, as well as his decision in some cases not to use pseudonyms. I will describe the works of the various authors, giving several brief illustrations of Kierkegaard's pseudonyms, and then examine various interpretations of Kierkegaard's pseudonymous authorship. The dialectical nature of Kierkegaard's view of existence is also applied to his employment of these various authors. Finally, I show how Kierkegaard's formulation of the self contributes to a constructive theory of multiplicity within the self.

This current chapter focuses on Kierkegaard's conceptualization of human existence through his notion of multiple spheres of existence and the dialectical factors within the self. First, I briefly describe these three spheres and their relationships to each other as defined by Kierkegaard. Then I critically analyze interpretations of these spheres within current Kierkegaard scholarship, culminating in my own interpretation. I describe Kierkegaard's complex dialectic, starting with his discussion in *Sickness Unto Death* of the dialectical form of the interrelationship of the elements of existence, the finite and the infinite, et al. I argue that Kierkegaard's thought is thoroughly dialectical, relational, and processive. I apply this dialectical form to the form of the relationship of the spheres to each other. The spheres relate to each other dialectically, both objectively in Kierkegaard's conceptualization of existence, and subjectively in the lived religious sphere. By highlighting the spheres' processive nature and progressive development toward greater inclusiveness, I show that Kierkegaard's dialectic is the foundational element in, and the key to unlocking the mysteries of, Kierkegaard's notion of the synthesis of human existence and the spheres. In the next chapter I will argue that his dialectic is also the key to interpreting his employment of pseudonyms.

The contribution to Kierkegaard scholarship here is twofold. First, I am interpreting Kierkegaard's conceptualization of human existence as an unharmonious synthesis of the finite, the infinite, and their relationship to each other. Second, I am applying his dialectical theological anthropology to the relationship of the spheres of existence. In so doing, the relational character and the processive form of his understanding of subjectivity becomes apparent. The contribution to a constructive conception of the self is also twofold. First, in highlighting an aspect of the Western tradition that has been often misinterpreted to fit the normative gaze of oneness, I reveal the presence of voices and viewpoints in which multiplicity and relationship are significant. Second, I direct Kierkegaard's insightful analysis of human subjectivity to a contemporary project of developing a constructive view of the self that accepts the differences and complexities within the person.

Spheres of Existence

Kierkegaard expresses his conception of human existence by demonstrating three stages or spheres of existence, which reflect different modes and models of living. The three distinct spheres, or forms of how to live and how to be related to the facts and processes of one's existence, are the aesthetic, the ethical, and the religious stages. Two of these three spheres also contain two sub spheres, or poles. The aesthetic sphere consists of the immediate pole and the reflective pole.[1] In the religious sphere, the relationship of religiousness A and religiousness B create a mini-dialectic within the religious sphere. The polarity within these spheres, the structure and the content of each of the three spheres, and the dialectical interaction between the spheres indicate one aspect of the complexity of Kierkegaard's view of human selfhood.

---

[1] See Mark C. Taylor, *Kierkegaard's Pseudonymous Authorship* (Princeton NJ: Princeton University Press, 1975) 76-77.

In *Either/Or: A Fragment of Life*, originally published in February 1843, Kierkegaard illustrates the aesthetic way of life and the ethical reply to it.[2] Kierkegaard adopts the style of a literary author of the late eighteenth century, using several pseudonyms to create the experience of the aesthetic and ethical life styles. Victor Eremita, a pseudonymous editor, happened upon a collection of papers in a hidden drawer of an antique secretary. He notes that the papers seem to be in two separate groups, which he forms into two volumes. The first group, denoted by "A," demonstrates the aesthetic sphere, both in content and form. These papers include various essays, diverse in content, purpose, and style, even though they seem to be written by one author to illustrate the disunification and inconsistency that are inherent in the aesthetic realm. The second group of papers is more uniform and is definitely written by one man, who even gives us his name, the pseudonym Judge William, who expounds on the higher value of the ethical way of life. Volume two is written in the form of letters to the author of the first group. This fact is particularly noteworthy, since it sets up the relational form of the spheres of existence and the pseudonyms. They are inherently related to each other.

Kierkegaard illustrates the aesthetic sphere by demonstrating the way an aesthete sees and experiences life. The scattered form of the volume demonstrates the scattered form of the aesthetic self. These essays range from "The Immediate Stages of the Erotic or the Musical Erotic" and "The Diary of the Seducer," to "The Rotation Method" and "The First Love." The aesthetic includes not only pleasure, but also pain, as seen in the essay, "The Unhappiest Man." Only the superficial aspects of pleasure and pain are considered personally, and only for the moment, for their passing interest. He includes a section of witty, brief, unrelated paragraphs, such as:

---

[2] The third, the religious, is present, but only implied in the Judge's sermon.

My observation of life makes no sense at all. I suppose that an evil spirit has put a pair of glasses on my nose, one lens of which magnifies on an immense scale and the other reduces on the same scale.[3]

The form of the aesthetic realm is like a stream that wanders this way and that, reacting to the resistance of the rocks and earth without any intention direction. The analogy is not exact in that the stream may eventually create its own path by carving its way into the earth. This ability is not present for the aesthetic. Instead, the one living in the aesthetic sphere is entirely affected by the external stimuli. It simply flows as the wind blows.

The aesthetic sphere has two phases or poles: the immediate pole and the reflective pole. Mark C. Taylor writes of the dialectic within this sphere as a "microcosm" of the larger Kierkegaardian dialectic of all the spheres. The first mini-sphere within the aesthetic is utter immediacy. It is illustrated by the non-reflective immediate experience of Don Juan, who enjoys the pleasure of any women who are present, and the musical expression of this story in Mozart's Opera, *Don Juan*. A, the pseudonymous author of the aesthetic volume, writes of how easily his sadness evaporates in the moment of music:

> What do I hear—the minuet from *Don Giovanni*. Carry me away, then, you rich, strong tones, to the rings of girls, to the delight of the dance.[4]

He continues in his life of the imagination:

> Mozart's music has certainly been tempting; for where is the young man who has not had a moment in his life when he would have given half his kingdom to be a Don Juan, or

---

[3] Søren Kierkegaard, *Either/Or*, trans. and ed. Howard V. Hong and Edna H. Hong (Princeton NJ: Princeton University Press, 1987) 1:24.
[4] Ibid., 1:41.

perhaps all of it, when he would have given half his lifetime for one year of being Don Juan, or perhaps his whole life? But that was as far as it went.[5]

A argues that in *Don Juan* we have all three pure abstractions, music, the immediate and the indeterminate, brought together in one piece, in one experience. A values immediacy absolutely, claiming that "music always expresses the immediate in its immediacy...the immediate is the indeterminate, and therefore language cannot grasp it."[6]

The second phase of the aesthetic sphere is the reflective pole, which is paradigmatically exemplified in the "Diary of the Seducer." This essay tells of a seducer who is distant and removed in his interest in the girl whom he seduces. The reflective pole is characterized by permanent potential. Reflection here is objective, superficial, and contrived in the imagination. The protagonist of this phase searches for a girl worthy of the game. Once he finds such a girl, he doesn't actually seduce her—he makes no commitments—he simply plays with the possibilities. Johannes the Seducer delights in planning strategy for his game with Cordelia, the girl he has chosen from a distance:

So now begins the first war with Cordelia, in which I retreat and thereby teach her to be victorious as she pursues me. I continually fall back, and in this backward movement I teach her to know through me all the powers of erotic love, its turbulent thoughts, its passion, what longing is, and hope, and impatient expectancy. As I perform this set of steps before her, all this will develop correspondingly in her. It is a triumphal procession...and in this second struggle I shall be victorious as surely as it was an illusion that she was victorious in the first one. The greater the abundance of strength she has, the more interesting for me. The first war is a war of liberation; it is a game.

---

[5] Ibid., 1:104.
[6] Ibid., 1:70.

The second is a war of conquest; it is a life-and-death struggle...Do I love Cordelia? Yes! Sincerely? Yes! Faithfully? Yes—in the esthetic sense...[7]

In an aesthetic sense, he means, in a way that is only valid in the immediate moment of experience, to be forgotten the next instant, when the next girl is to be pursued, manipulated, and discarded. Kierkegaard highlights the duplicity present in Johannes as he both experiences the immediacy of the joys of the seduction but always maintains a safe distance to observe his own external behavior.

Further, this reflective stage also characterizes many philosophers who, according to Kierkegaard, merely reflect upon the realities of other peoples' lives without accounting for the realities of living their own lives. In particular, Kierkegaard refers to Hegel and others who attempt to capture the truth about human existence in a system of stagnant thought that lacks the vibrant dialectic of openness and movement that Kierkegaard believes characterizes existential truth. Note the similarity between Kierkegaard's characterization of speculative philosophy and Johannes the Seducer. Both are removed from actual involvement in life, stuck in the possibilities of the abstract imagination and lack the depth of subjectivity.

The aesthetic sphere as a whole is characterized by its emphasis on the immediate, the immediate moment of the closest external object of immediate stimulation, as in gratification, satisfaction, pleasure, and even sorrow. The aesthetic sphere is "immediate" also in that it lacks concrete mediation and engaged reflection. It does not choose itself or know itself. The one who lives in the aesthetic realm does not reflect upon his/her own life or self. He is unaware of himself and oblivious to the surrounding world, including his own external behavior. The self's immediate experience is determinative, there is no self-examination, or self-reflection, and thus no self-knowledge of any true decisions. The lack of reflective decisiveness

---

[7] Ibid., 1:384-385.

makes the one in this sphere not actually a self, but a chaotic, inconsistent and unpredictable conglomeration of human impulses. There is no genuine selfhood since there is no mediation either by decision and/or by reflection. As Luis Dupré says, "the aesthetic never commits himself, and thus never becomes a self, since the self is essentially a choice, an active relationship to oneself...."[8]

The one in the aesthetic sphere is not yet a self, let alone oneself. In order to develop a self, this sphere must lead into the next one: the ethical, which is characterized by decision. But it won't be an easy transition; as Dupré tells us that the aesthetic sphere "bears within itself the germ of its own destruction."[9] By this Dupré means that the quest for absolute pleasure and comfort in the aesthetic sphere cannot lead to any pleasure and comfort in the long run, for despair and meaninglessness surround the one who by his refusal to choose himself, chooses despair. Dupré continues, "If the aesthete has followed his attitude to its ultimate consequences, there is nothing left for him to choose other than the despair into which he has brought himself."[10] The only way out of this existential despair is *through* the despair. A decision *for* the despair will inadvertently lead one out of this sphere, and into the next one, the ethical sphere. By choosing oneself one brings "an absolute element into his existence: in his commitment to despair he constitutes a relationship to himself."[11] This decision of the person in the aesthetic sphere is like the enzyme necessary for the digestion of the aesthetic pleasures into the ethical nutrients of selfhood.

In the second volume of *Either/Or,* Judge William, who represents the ethical, replies in the form of letters to the aesthetic author. He argues for the superiority of his ethical way of life and

---

[8] Louis Dupré, *Kierkegaard as Theologian, the Dialectic of Christian Existence* (New York: Sheed and Ward, 1963) 42-43.

[9] Ibid., 43.

[10] Ibid.

[11] Ibid.

analyzes how these two spheres differ. The ethical is about maintaining consistent, objective, and reasonable relationships between and amongst people. It is the realm of duty in which proper decisions according to the rules of society are made with commitment and with the assuredness of logical thinking. The ethical sphere demonstrates thoughtful reflection, self-awareness, and careful decisions based on universal norms of society. Here a person's self is "self-made," by her decisions, into a singular, consistent, unified self.

In his first letter/treatise, he argues for "The Aesthetic Validity of Marriage." Marriage, he says, is an honorable estate and therefore in the ethical realm. In fact, he argues, that it is more aesthetically pleasing than the immediate exploits of Don Juan and other seducers. It is in the ethical realm, and not the aesthetic by virtue of the necessity of decisive commitment. Marriage is the height of the expression of ethical existence because in such a relationship one tells all to one's spouse, revealing oneself while also becoming oneself. Kierkegaard's brief evaluation of *Either/Or* in *Concluding Unscientific Postscript* says that the "ethicist has *despaired*; in this despair he has *chosen himself*, in and by this choice he *reveals himself* ('the expression which sharply differentiates between the ethical and the aesthetic is this: it is man's [sic] duty to reveal himself.'…)."[12] Judge William bids the aesthetic author to choose despair, for at least he will have acted decisively. He bids his friend in the aesthetic sphere, "Choose thyself" (obviously playing on the popular phrase "know thyself"). The Judge expands his understanding of the significance of choice, the primary characteristic of the ethical sphere:

What takes precedence in my Either/Or is, then, the ethical. Therefore, the point is still not that of choosing something; the point is not the reality of that which is chosen but the reality of choosing.[13]

---

[12] Søren Kierkegaard, *Concluding Unscientific Postscript*, trans. and ed. Howard V. Hong and Edna H. Hong (Princeton NJ: Princeton University Press, 1972) 227. Emphasis is Kierkegaard's.

[13] Kierkegaard, *Either/Or*, 2:176.

It is *that* you choose, *that* you participate in the becoming of what you are becoming, that is essential for the ethical sphere. Interestedness and commitment are significant characteristics in distinguishing the ethical sphere from the aesthetic sphere. He writes:

> [E]thically the highest pathos is interested pathos, expressed through the active transformation of the individual's entire mode of existence in conformity with the object of his interest; aesthetically the highest pathos is disinterested. When an individual abandons himself to lay hold of something outside of himself, his enthusiasm is aesthetic; when he forsakes everything to save himself, his enthusiasm is ethical.[14]

Note that Kierkegaard's words suggest that the two spheres are both within a single individual, but at different times of his/her life. He does not distinguish the spheres by claiming that they are located within two different individuals; rather, the two different spheres are two different movements within a single individual. I wonder if perhaps Judge William is in fact the author of the first group of papers, at an earlier time in his life.

The difference between the aesthetic and the ethical is given succinctly in the *Concluding Unscientific Postscript*:

> In *Either/Or* the aesthetic standpoint is represented by means of an existential possibility, while the ethicist is existing.[15]

The third sphere, the religious sphere, is primarily concerned with relationality. One's relationships to oneself, to one's decision, and to God, are the determinative questions. Kierkegaard explicitly introduces the religious sphere in *Fear and Trembling*, first published in October 1843, in contrast to the ethical sphere. Later, in *Concluding Unscientific Postscript*, first published in February 1846

---

[14] Kierkegaard, *Concluding Unscientific Postscript*, 350.
[15] Ibid., 262.

under the pseudonym Johannes Climacus, religiousness B is articulated as distinct from religion in general, which is referred to as religiousness A.[16] Also in *Concluding Unscientific Postscript*, Climacus suggests intermediate stages, or borderlands between the stages: irony between the aesthetic and ethical, and humor between the ethical and the religious spheres. Further, there has recently been talk of three subdivisions of the religious sphere, not just two. Richard Schacht argues for religiousness A (Socrates), religiousness B (Christian), and a stage between the two (Abraham).[17] While Merold Westphal also detects a third stage in the religious sphere, but he suggests that it is beyond that of religiousness B.[18]

Kierkegaard demonstrates the religious sphere in contrast to the other two spheres. *Fear and Trembling* is a praise of Abraham as the paradigm of faith. He is contrasted with the knight of infinite resignation, who is the model of ethical and universal norms. Kierkegaard is careful not to conflate the universal and the absolute. One's relationship to the universal is external and the same for all, while a person's relationship with the absolute is particular and individual. The religious sphere is the one most concerned with "the individual," and with the absolute, as he writes:

> Now we reach the paradox. Either the individual as the individual is able to stand in an absolute relation to the absolute (and

---

[16] Although it should also be noted that Kierkegaard begins working out the religious B sphere even before *Concluding Unscientific Postscript* in his Edifying Discourses, but he does not distinguish this sphere by name until *Concluding Unscientific Postscript*.

[17] Richard Schacht, *Hegel and After* (Pittsburgh: University of Pittsburgh Press, 1975).

[18] Merold Westphal, "The Teleological Suspension of Religiousness B." in *Foundations of Kierkegaard's Vision of Community*, eds. George Connell and C. Stephen Evans (Atlantic Highlands NJ : Humanities Press, 1991).

then the ethical is not the highest) /or Abraham is lost—he is neither a tragic hero, nor an aesthetic hero.[19]

The religious sphere includes aspects of both of the other spheres, such as the aesthetics' emphasis on the needs of the particular individual and the careful self-reflection of ethical. The religious person does not make decisions based solely on the universal norms of society, or on the logic of reason, nor on the external relations of humans to each other. But decisions are made. These decisions are often made in "fear and trembling," since there is no external norm or systematic rule to tell an individual what is the "right" decision, only the individual's own faith and discernment.

While the ethical sphere emphasizes *that* one decides, the religious sphere emphasizes *how* one *relates to one's decision.* In *Concluding Unscientific Postscript*, Climacus distinguishes the ethical and the religious spheres in terms of an objective self versus one's subjectivity. The experience of subjectivity is the focal point in this sphere. The *how* of the subject's decision is the emphasis in subjectivity, while the "objective accent falls on WHAT is said."[20] Kierkegaard develops his concept of subjectivity in the context of the problem of the truth of Christianity. This question is not about external facts in evidence, but rather addresses "the mode of the subject's acceptance."[21] Truth, Kierkegaard says, "is subjectivity," meaning that the only absolute decision to be made concerns one's relationship to Christianity, to God (which is truth), and the personal passionate appropriation of this relationship (which is subjectivity). Kierkegaard views subjectivity as the activity of holding the ambiguity and multiplicity of many parts within the self. His indirection emphasizes this ambiguity and multiplicity by evoking subjectivity in his reader.

---

[19] Søren Kierkegaard, *Fear and Trembling,* trans. and ed. Howard V. Hong and Edna H. Hong (Princeton NJ: Princeton University Press, 1970) 122.

[20] Kierkegaard, *Concluding Unscientific Postscript,* 181.

[21] Ibid., 115.

When Kierkegaard says in his *Point of View for My Work as an Author* that all his works are an aesthetic production expressing his religious vocation, he means that he writes all of his works for the purpose of evoking subjectivity within his reader.[22] Subjectivity is a necessary prerequisite for becoming a Christian. He is not primarily concerned with philosophical clarity and the truth of facts as D. Z. Phillips[23] argues; rather, his main concern is to evoke this *subjectivity*.

The double movement of objectivity and subjectivity distinguishes the religious sphere, which is the core of Kierkegaard's dialectic. *Fear and Trembling* gives us a paradigmatic example of this movement of faith in the religious sphere. First, Abraham, the exemplar of faith, must renounce the finite for the sake of the infinite, and then he must return to the finite in love, thus making the dialectical movements of subjectivity.[24]

Note that the primary sources of Kierkegaard's theory of existential spheres, *Either/Or* and *Fear and Trembling*, are dialectical in form and context. Kierkegaard explains the ethical in relationship to the aesthetic and the religious spheres and the religious in relationship to the aesthetic and the ethical. The religious sphere includes characteristics of the aesthetic sphere, such as a focus on the individual and an unmediated truth. But it also shares qualities with the ethical sphere, such as the decisiveness and commitment and becoming oneself.

Interpreting Kierkegaard's Spheres

The most appropriate method of interpreting the relationship and meaning of the spheres of existence is in dispute among

---

[22] Søren Kierkegaard, *The Point of View of My Work as an Author*, trans. Walter Lowrie (New York: Harper Torchbooks, 1962) 6.

[23] D. Z. Phillips, "Authorship and Authenticity: Kierkegaard and Wittgenstein," in *Midwest Studies in Philosophy*, 17 (1992): 186.

[24] Kierkegaard, *Fear and Trembling*.

Kierkegaard scholars. Mark C. Taylor organizes the Kierkegaardian scholarship on the interpretations of the spheres of existence into four major approaches:

(1) Stages in Kierkegaard's own development;
(2) Stages in the development of world history;
(3) Ideal personalities;
(4) Stages in the development of the individual self.[25]

Taylor goes on to provide a sampling of each of these approaches, indicating that the first method is the most common. Josiah Thompson's book, *The Lonely Labyrinth*,[26] is a fitting example here. In this work, Thompson believes that Kierkegaard's philosophy is a symptom of his sickness. He believes that Kierkegaard writes to become healthy, through trying on these various modes of approaching life, in hopes of finding the one most suitable and most healthy for him. The second way of interpreting the spheres is outdated. The third view of the stages is still fairly common. It views the spheres as paradigms for how to live. Kierkegaard's purpose in this view is believed to be simply to put forth the different options and ask the reader to choose. However, says Taylor, if this view is taken alone, it "greatly oversimplifies Kierkegaard's insights."[27] This approach neglects the obvious value given to the development toward the religious sphere in Kierkegaard's thought as a whole. It also neglects the relationship of the spheres to each other present within one person. George Connell's interpretation, which we will examine

---

[25] Mark C. Taylor, *Kierkegaard's Pseudonymous Authorship* (Princeton NJ: Princeton University Press, 1975) 62-63.

[26] Josiah Thompson, *The Lonely Labyrinth: Kierkegaard's Pseudonymous Works* (Carbondale IL: Southern Illinois Press, 1967).

[27] Taylor, *Kierkegaard's Pseudonymous Authorship*, 69.

in detail below, exemplifies this approach while also venturing into the next approach.

Finally, the fourth approach Taylor mentions views the spheres of existence as stages through which one passes along one's maturation toward the highest mode of living—Christianity. This approach is the one with which Taylor personally finds the most cadences. Taylor claims to utilize elements from the third and the fourth group of interpretation in his explication of the complexity of Kierkegaard's view of selfhood and the stages, but he emphasizes the developmental interpretation of the "stages." Taylor uses the words "developmental" and "stages" in his representation of most of the scholarship's approaches to the spheres and consistently throughout his book on Kierkegaard's authorship. He argues that the term "stages," which he uses, is the most helpful term, since "it gives more emphasis to the developmental character of Kierkegaard's dialectic."[28] Taylor's emphasis of the term "stages" and their progressive movement through time to the exclusion of the inter-relational characteristic of these realms of existence is due to Taylor's significant use of the concept of time to focus his analysis of the differences and relationship of the stages. He asserts that Kierkegaard's "arrangement of the stages of existence and the primary characteristics of each stage depend on his conception of time...."[29]

Taylor argues that the various stages of existence are divergent ways of trying to attain equilibrium between the three pairs of existential elements, temporality and eternity, finitude and infinity, and possibility and necessity. Each attempt that fails to attain this equilibrium ends in despair. The more dis-equilibrium, the greater the despair, the greater the dread, and the greater the sin. These attempts toward equilibrium represent the stages and are organized as a developmental process, in which the self becomes more

---

[28] Ibid., 62n.
[29] Ibid., 267.

individuated.[30] The more individuated a person is, the better self one is. The movement from one stage to the next reflects a qualitative development in one's dexterity with the ambiguities of life and a development of individuation. The final stage, Taylor suggests, is the one with the most balanced relationship between these questions of existence.

While Taylor's analysis of Kierkegaard's understanding of the spheres of existence is thorough and more than adequate in most regards, his approach is lacking in its brief treatment of the dialectical relationship of the existential elements and of the stages of subjectivity. I agree with Taylor that the dialectics of the existential elements examined in *Sickness Unto Death* provides the key to understanding the stages or spheres of existence. However, the connection between these elements of existence (finitude and infinite, eternal and temporal, and possibility and necessity) and the spheres of existence is more profound than Taylor suggests. His view examines only the external relationships of the elements and misses the subjective side of the dialectic. He argues that the way a person relates the polarities of the eternal and the temporal to each other determines his or her current sphere or stage of existence. I suggest that the spheres of existence are related to each other in the very same way that the elements of existence are related to each other (and to that relation itself)—dialectically. Taylor's interpretation of Kierkegaard's objective in *Sickness Unto Death* to establish a harmonious and actual equilibrium minimizes the significance of the dialectic in Kierkegaard's view of existence. I suggest the inclusion of both the quantitative and the qualitative dialectics. I will develop this suggestion in greater detail below.

Offering a different perspective, George Connell interprets Kierkegaard's spheres in terms of unity and oneness. He believes that Kierkegaard's "stages of existence" are expressions of distinct types of

---

[30] Ibid., 7.

selves. In this regard his interpretation fits in Taylor's categorization of Kierkegaard scholarship discussed above. In *To Be One Thing*, he argues that "each of the stages, subdivisions of the stages, and intermediate positions in the Kierkegaardian 'phenomenology' may be characterized by its way of accepting or rejecting the imperative of self-unification."[31] Connell believes these stages or selves are distinguished from each other by their relationship to oneness. Furthermore, he argues that Kierkegaard understands human selfhood as that which is made by each individual human's efforts "to be one thing." The goal of human existence, then, is to be a unity, one thing. To attain this goal, a human must "will one thing." In so doing, she makes her will into an essential unity, by conforming it to the will of that which is One, or God. Connell believes that Kierkegaard follows what Jeremy Walker calls "the principle of homogeneity,"[32] which states that a self will conform itself to the "essential character of the object toward which it is directed."[33] Thus, Kierkegaard understands the dynamic of will and unity to be as follows: when a person wills an object, her will becomes conformed to the essential nature of this object. In Connell's eyes, then Kierkegaard believes that a person can be a unity at her essence by willing an object that is essentially a unity itself, one thing.

Unity is the crux of Connell's interpretation of Kierkegaard's spheres of existence. He argues that each sphere is best understood in terms of how one in that sphere responds to this call towards unity. For example, Connell views the aesthete as the type of "self" that is led away from the unity of selfhood by his immediate reaction to whatever is most readily available or captivating at the time. In the aesthetic sphere the person's self is disunified. He is related to the

---

[31] George Connell, *To Be One Thing: Personal Unity in Kierkegaard's Thought* (Macon GA: Mercer, 1985) 37.

[32] Jeremy Walker, *To Will One Thing* (Montreal: McGill-Queens University Press, 1972) 113.

[33] Connell, *To Be One Thing*, xiii

divine imperative to be a unified self in an aesthetic way, as in an immediate, non-reflective, momentary existence. Further, the aesthetic self is not one thing because the object of its will is many different things. (Or one might say it has many different objects of its wills.) Connell considers the existential problem of the aesthete to be that he has a "fundamentally divided personality."[34] He considers the "Diary of the Seducer" as the culmination of the aesthetic sphere because A, the aesthetic pseudonym, writes about Johannes, a second, once more removed pseudonym. The two-tiered structure of the aesthete's experience demonstrates both the immediacy of the stimulus while at the same time, being in a position of external reflective observer. This is articulated explicitly when Johannes writes, "{o}ne ought always to transcend [the moment] a little, so as not only to be baptismal candidate but also priest."[35]

The phase between the ethical sphere and the aesthetic sphere is Irony. Irony is characterized by a synthetic unity, in which the elements of the self are related to each other, but not consciously brought into relation. Connell writes that "the self emerges as a synthesis," yet it is "unposited; that it is, it is only a synthesis of two negatively related moments."[36] This is similar to what Kierkegaard describes in the opening paragraphs of *Sickness Unto Death*, a self that is not yet a true self, but has stopped at a negative unity of the polar elements. Such an entity is not yet a self since it has not related its elements in a positive and intentional way. The imagination of the aesthete is brought to its culmination, which is also its end, as it imagines the possibility of an infinite relation.

The ethical sphere is also understood in terms of its relation to unity. Through a complicated analysis, we see that Kierkegaard's ethical self is a unity of the real and the ideal. While the ironic tries to be a unity, it falls short because it is not concrete. The ethical, on

---

[34] Ibid., 95.
[35] Kierkegaard, *Either/Or*, 1:338, as quoted in Connell, *To Be One Thing*, 95.
[36] Connell, *To Be One Thing*, 37.

the other hand, is thoroughly concrete—real, and thoroughly ideal—the ethical norms. The act of choosing oneself in all one's despair leads the ethical to this unity. This unity is an historical unity because part of the act of choosing oneself is "accepting one's reality. One accepts not only one's present finite aspects (abilities, gender, appearance, nationality, and so forth), but also one's entire past."[37] The past of the self includes mistakes and limitations. Connell describes the unity of the ethical self as achieving this historical character "by positing itself as a synthesis, by fusing time and eternity."[38]

The religious sphere is the final culmination of the quest for personal unity. Connell argues that the absolute commitment demanded by the duty to will one thing is "the first expression of the personal unity of the religious self."[39] Connell understands the passion as the energy that brings or causes unification. The acceptance of one's past becomes understood as repentance of the highest order. And by the singular command to love one's neighbor, the Christian with a single duty satisfies the ethical's multiple commandments. By the continual renewal of faith, the future is committed in an absolute relationship with the eternal. In other words, the "Christian self owes its oneness to its positive unification of its finite and infinite dimensions."[40] For Connell, the Christian commandment is the "command to be one thing," which is a "demand for the integrity of the individual."[41]

Connell highlights the juxtaposition of the aesthetic sphere with what he calls the perfect unity of the religious sphere and argues that this tension in the pseudonymous authorship is an expression of Kierkegaard's own intimate struggle between the temptations of the aesthetic sphere and the religious sphere. We shall examine this in

---

[37] Ibid., 142.
[38] Ibid., 185
[39] Ibid., 160.
[40] Ibid., 185.
[41] Ibid., 190.

greater detail in the next chapter, which focuses on Kierkegaard's pseudonymous authors.

Connell's view is problematic for several reasons. First, it implies that Kierkegaard believes that a truly religious self is self-made. Connell maintains that Christianity is a decision made by the individual to "be one thing." He or she must decide to constitute him/herself as an essential unity by an act of sheer will. On this point Connell misses the utter importance of faith as a gift from God and the paradox of faith, and he implies an indictment of Pelagianism upon Kierkegaard.

Connell's interpretation is also problematic because it places more value on the ethical sphere than on the religious sphere. Connell is correct in asserting that Kierkegaard's plea for selfhood criticizes the multiplicity and ambiguity present in the aesthetic sphere. Connell may point to the second letter/treatise in *Either/Or* B, "Equilibrium Between the Aesthetical and the Ethical in the Composition of Personality," where the Judge analyzes the self of the aesthetic realm:

When an individual considers himself esthetically, he becomes conscious of this self as a complex concretion intrinsically qualified in many ways; but despite all the internal variety, all these together are nevertheless his nature, have equal right to emerge, equal right to demand satisfaction...his self consists of this multiplicity, and he has no self that is higher than this.[42]

This pseudo-self is hopelessly lost in the many-ness of the possibilities with no will to bring him/her into actuality through a decision. An authentic self is chosen in the decisions and responsibilities taken by his/her own self. The "manifold concretion" present in the existence determined by immediacy is blocked out by the decision made for actualization of one of these possibilities. From this indictment, it seems that Kierkegaard devalues multiplicity while

---

[42] Kierkegaard, *Either/Or*, 2:225.

praising unity exclusively. This is not the case as I will show below. Further, Connell misinterprets Kierkegaard in assuming that this characteristic of the ethical sphere carries over into the religious sphere. As I mentioned earlier, the religious sphere shares several unlikely characteristics with the aesthetic sphere, including the emphasis on the individual, but also the value of multiplicity. Kierkegaard actually values multiplicity more highly than the synthetic unity of the ethical sphere, as I demonstrate below.

Another problem in Connell's hermeneutic is his interpretation of the unity of a person's essence or to put it theologically, one's soul. I agree that Kierkegaard is concerned about the essential unity of each individual's soul. Yet I want to make two clarifications concerning this claim. First, "being one thing" is not equal to "being a Christian." One's soul is not necessarily one thing. Kierkegaard writes about "willing one thing" in *Purity of Heart*, but he does not argue that the polar elements of existence are brought together in a synthetic unity, nor does he argue that these elements are related to each other by the sheer force of an individual's will. Connell fails to differentiate Kierkegaard's concern in *Sickness Unto Death* for "willing to become oneself" from Kierkegaard's concern in *Purity of Heart* for "willing one thing." In Connell's view Kierkegaard argues that the human self must "constitute itself as an essential unity in the face of the disruptive action of the world,"[43] by willing one thing, which is willing the Good. This formula from *Purity of Heart* is distinct from the formula of the text on the self, *Sickness Unto Death*, which states, "in willing to be itself, the self rests transparently in the power that established it."[44] Connell has conflated these two formulas. "Willing the good, or one thing" is not the same as "willing to *be*, or to *become*." By replacing Kierkegaard's *willing to becoming* with Connell's *being*, Connell has confused Kierkegaard's understanding of

---

[43] Connell, *To Be One Thing*, xiv-v.
[44] Søren Kierkegaard, *The Sickness Unto Death*, trans. and ed. Howard V. Hong and Edna H. Hong (Princeton NJ: Princeton University Press, 1980) 131.

actuality and possibility and identified willing with a static being. This is a misunderstanding not only of Kierkegaard's primary critique of metaphysics and Danish Lutheran practice, but also of Kierkegaard's purpose in *Purity of Heart*.

In *Purity of Heart*, Kierkegaard names willing one thing as that which opposes the double-mindedness of sin and that which is the essence of being pure of heart. Connell argues that the opposite of "double-mindedness" is willing to be one thing. This is not the best way of interpreting Kierkegaard here. Double-mindedness is described by Kierkegaard not as the state of having more than one part within oneself, but as doing the good for the wrong reasons. It is deceiving oneself into believing that one is doing the good for the sake of the good, when actually one is doing the good out of fear of punishment, or for the reward, or to feel good about oneself. Kierkegaard's discussion of barriers to purity of heart is best understood as taken in the context of searching one's soul for the barriers that inhibits a person from knowing one's self as an individual before God. He writes it for the expressed purpose of preparing a Christian for the sacrament of confession. These barriers can also be understood as beacons that help the one searching to locate those problem areas. The ultimate goal is not to will one thing; the point is to be pure of heart, which means to know oneself wholly as an individual before God. Purity of heart is a religious matter, and the "ethics" discussed in the book are ways to help an individual examine and purify his heart, so that he can become conscious of himself before God. It is prayer of the highest order. Kierkegaard's primary concern in *Purity of Heart* is not willing the good, nor willing to be one thing, but is purity of heart, which is to come to before God, having confessed as fully as possible.

This confused identification between "willing one thing" and "willing to become oneself" leads Connell to miss the processive character in Kierkegaard's view of authentic selfhood. Kierkegaard emphasizes *becoming* oneself, not *being* one thing. This issue is part of

Kierkegaard's philosophical argument with Hegel, which focuses on the mode of truth and being. Kierkegaard reads Hegel as building a vast, interconnected, and perfect System to explain reality. The Spirit is constantly incarnating in human culture in increasingly more accurate and perfect ways. The Germanic Nation is the most perfect and divine like incarnation/concrescence of the Spirit to Hegel's date. Kierkegaard's response in *Concluding Unscientific Postscript* follows:

> Everything said in Hegel's philosophy about process and becoming is illusory. This is why the System lacks an Ethic, and is the reason why it has no answer for the living when the question of becoming is raised in earnest, in the interest of action. In spite of all that Hegel says about process, he does not understand history form the point of view of becoming…It is therefore impossible for a Hegelian to understand himself by means of his philosophy, for his philosophy helps him to understand only that which is past and finished.[45]

Kierkegaard believes that human reality can only be comprehended in the middle of existing, not by reflecting about the fixed principles of the past of human culture while sitting still in the proverbial armchair. He argues that human existence looks quite different from the point of view of the existing individual than it does from the objective eyes of reason and philosophy. He believes that human reality is in the mode of "becoming" not in the fixed mode of "being." He writes that "every moment that a self exists, it is in a process of becoming."[46]

This context of metaphysical concerns helps us understand his theological anthropology: his view of the purpose and nature of human existence. Kierkegaard thinks that Hegelian metaphysics and the Danish Church share the same misguided assumption that reality

---

[45] Kierkegaard, *Concluding Unscientific Postscript*, 272n.
[46] Kierkegaard, *The Sickness Unto Death*, 30.

is fixed. He tells a story about the Danish Christians to illustrate this similarity: The Tame Geese. The Tame Geese waddle to church every Sunday, much like Danish Christians. One of the Ganders preaches about "the lofty destiny the geese had," that the Creator (here the gander paused, for the congregation bowed their head for a moment of pious expression) had deemed the geese the bearers of great flight. For "by the aid of wings they could fly to distant regions, blessed climes, where properly they were at home, for here they were only strangers." And after every such sermon, the geese "waddle" home again, never actualizing, or even seriously considering the truth of this great purpose for their living—flight. Kierkegaard says that this is like the hypocrisy of Christendom.[47] They proclaim that humanity is not yet complete as each individual Christian will come to the stature of Christ, but they do not formulate doctrines and practices toward this task of *becoming* a Christian. In fact, Danish Christendom sees that one is automatically a Christian via a Danish birth. This "monstrous illusion" ignores the truth that one *becomes* a Christian: it is a *task*, and the most difficult task of all, and it is the only task worth pursuing in this human existence.

I also disagree with Connell's view of one of Kierkegaard's primary philosophical and theological points, that truth is subjectivity. He says that Kierkegaard's claim that "Truth is Subjectivity" is an expression of Kierkegaard's "conviction that the self must constitute itself as an essential unity."[48] Connell sees this formula as meaning that a person must be one thing in order to be a self. Kierkegaard's view of the subjectivity of the religious sphere is not a synthetic unity or "one thing." It is not abstract or fixed. It is willing to become who one is, in all the ambiguity of existence. It includes the acknowledgment of both one's guilt as a sinner in despair and one's unique worth as one for whom God died. The

---

[47] Robert Bretall, ed. *Kierkegaard Anthology* (New York: The Modern Library, 1970) 433

[48] Connell, *To Be One Thing*, 9.

subjectivity of the religious sphere is not a systematic unity as Connell claims. Religious existence is characterized by multivalency and movement, holding together the contradictions of existence. It is the constant forth and back motion of the dialectic.

Subjectivity is not individualistic subjectivism; it does not mean that I get to say what I think/believe is right and wrong is therefore right or wrong. Objectivity, for Kierkegaard, is knowledge agreed upon by all reasonable persons, common facts. Agreed upon knowledge is not wrong. What I believe may be wrong. Yet subjectivity is not what I believe, but how I believe it. In this way all of analytical philosophy is anti-Kierkegaardian.[49] Truth is Subjectivity is addressed most directly in *Concluding Unscientific Postscript*, where it refers to the type of knowledge that is existential, such as, what does it mean to die, to be married, to be grateful, to be saved, to be oneself? These questions are not about the facts of existence, commonly answered by any reasonable person. Rather, by subjectivity, he means an individual's moral and religious relationship to the question. It is a question of context. Kierkegaard means by this famous statement, that philosophical theory cannot approach the truth of human being because theory is an abstraction that superimposes its fixed form onto the processive form of actual existence. Actual existence is better characterized as "human becoming" than "human being." Connell's discussion of the divine imperative to "be one thing" does the same thing—it imposes a fixed unity onto something that is in the process of becoming.

Religious existence is characterized by multivalency and movement, in which one holds together the contradictions of existence. It is the constant forth and back motion of the dialectic. Connell's approach to the spheres misses these significant aspects of Kierkegaard's theological anthropology.

---

[49] D. Z. Phillips, "Purity of Heart" (lecture, Claremont Graduate University, February 8, 1994).

The Dialectical relating of the Spheres

The approach I offer here brings together several of these approaches with a fundamental difference: Kierkegaard's spheres of existence are not only an analysis of developmental processes, but rather the spheres are inter-related dialectically in the here and now within the existing individual. My constructive view of Kierkegaard's spheres of existence differs from Taylor's view primarily in its emphasis on the dialectical form of the spheres, as opposed to Taylor's developmental "stages." My interpretation also differs significantly from Connell's contention that the goal of Kierkegaard's religious sphere is to be one thing. Contrarily, I argue that the religious sphere is multivalent, dynamic and relational.

I use Kierkegaard's dialectic as an interpretative framework to elucidate his theory of existential spheres. Focusing on his discussion in *Sickness Unto Death* on the relationship of the three pairs of existential elements that make up the self and also touching on his development of the idea of the dialectic in *Concluding Unscientific Postscript*, I will apply the dialectic to interpreting the spheres of existence.

Kierkegaard's use of the term dialectic is intricate. The term dialectic has an historical and philosophical context that influences Kierkegaard's thought. It is a general philosophical term synonymous with dialogue and debate within the norms of logic, as well as being used in particular ways by Socrates and Hegel. Socrates' dialectical method of asking questions is to elicit the recognition by the dialogue partner that he doesn't really know anything. It is a negative task. Plato employs a polar dialectic that is a "two-fold process involving synthesis...and division."[50] In this movement of thought, ideas are placed together according to their similarities, while at the same time

---

[50] Arthur Krentz, "Kierkegaard's Dialectical Image of Human Existence in the *Concluding Unscientific Postscript to the Philosophical Fragments*," in *Philosophy Today* 41/2 (Summer 1997): 279.

are divided from each other according to their differences. Hegel's dialectic is more one-sided in that it is always synthesizing. For Hegel, the dialectic is the progressive movement of ideas throughout history toward greater and greater conscious awareness of the great idea of the Spirit. Hegel's dialectic has been described as the march of the thesis that meets its opposite, the antithesis, and the two are unified in the synthesis, which then becomes the next thesis to start the process again. While these thinkers influence Kierkegaard's use of the term dialectic, he also develops the term uniquely in his own thought. Most distinctly, he ascribes dialectical meaning to existence, not exclusively to ideas.

The dialectic in Kierkegaard's authorship is a complex web that forms both the structure of the content of his thought, such as the relationship of the existential elements, and also the form of his polemical method, such as the mode of his pseudonymous authorship. His authors are related to each other by name and by argument. He creates a web of interrelated authors/characters who dialogue among themselves. Further, his method is dialectical in that he desires to engage his reader in a conversation.

His existential use of the concept dialectic is expressed most explicitly in both *Sickness Unto Death* and *Concluding Unscientific Postscript.* In *Sickness Unto Death,* Kierkegaard asserts that the human self is constituted by three pairs of irreconcilable elements: the finite and the infinite; the temporal and the eternal; and freedom and necessity. In the midst of this tension, these elements must relate to each other in a conscious and balanced way. The individual cannot fall too much into the finite element, then the infinite element is stifled; neither can she float too much into the infinite element, for then the finite element suffers. A genuine human self is a concrete balance of these two opposite factors. A person that leans too much toward either the infinite or the finite is "disrelated": her balance is off and the relation of these two factors cannot relate itself to itself properly. Despair ensues and she is not a self, as he writes:

> A human being is spirit. But what is spirit? Spirit is the self. But what is the self? The self is a relation that relates itself to itself, or is the relation's relation itself to itself in the relation; the self is not the relation but is the relation's relating itself to itself. A human being is a synthesis of the infinite and the finite, of the temporal and the eternal, of freedom and necessity, in short, a synthesis. A synthesis is a relation between two. Considered this way, a human being is still not a self.[51]

In this passage, Kierkegaard argues that the ontological reality of the self consists in the internal reflexive relating of these conflicting elements. The self is the reflexive relating of the relation of these disparate elements to itself. The dialectic is the form of the relationship of these contradictory elements of existence as they are brought into dialogue with each other. This relation of the disparate parts then, relates to itself in a dynamic and dialectical way. This reflexive relating constitutes an individual. In Walter Lowrie's older translation, Kierkegaard writes, that it is a "dialectical fact that the self is a synthesis [of two factors], one of which is constantly the opposite of the other."[52] Thus, the individual is constituted by the dialectic relationality of the duplicity of elemental realities: finitude and infinity, etcetera. One's genuine inner life is essentially the relating of the relation of the finite and the infinite to itself—the inner element and the transcendent element.

However, Kierkegaard is not done, for this self is such that this synthesis is "established by another."[53] The becoming of oneself is

---

[51] Kierkegaard, *The Sickness Unto Death*, 13.

[52] Søren Kierkegaard, *The Sickness Unto Death*, trans. Walter Lowrie (Princeton NJ: Princeton University Press, 1970) 163. See also Kierkegaard, *The Sickness Unto Death*, trans. and ed. Howard V. Hong and Edna H. Hong, 30. I use Lowrie's translation here because his translation communicates the conflictual relationship of the elements within the dialectic.

[53] Ibid., 13.

willing to become oneself in relation to one's disparate parts, as this relation relates to itself dynamically, *and* in relation to God and God's power. Thus, the "self is the conscious synthesis of infinitude and finitude that relates itself to itself, whose task is to become itself, which can be done only through the relationship to God. To become oneself is to become concrete. But to become concrete is neither to become finite nor to become infinite, for that which is to become concrete is indeed a synthesis."[54]

This theme is continued in *Concluding Unscientific Postscript*, where Climacus affirms that existence is a mixture: "a synthesis of the finite and the infinite, and the existing individual is both infinite and finite."[55] In *Concluding Unscientific Postscript* he emphasizes the impossibility of the task of human existence. He writes of the ideal task: "the simultaneous maintenance of an absolute relationship to the absolute, and a relative relationship to the relative."[56] The key is the relation that must "relate itself to itself" dialectically.[57] Climacus distinguishes two different types of a dialectical method: quantitative, which is objective, and qualitative, which is subjective. Arthur Krentz explains that the subjective dialectic differs from the objective dialectic in that it "emphasizes not the nature of what is known (as does the quantitative dialectic) but, rather, how the 'knower' is related to that which he seeks to know. The shift is from the content of an idea to how one lives the ideas in one's life."[58] In *Concluding Unscientific Postscript*, Climacus develops subjectivity as the ideal form of existence and the form of subjectivity as dialectical—processive and relational.

---

[54] Ibid., 29-30.
[55] Kierkegaard, *Concluding Unscientific Postscript*, 350.
[56] Ibid., 386.
[57] Kierkegaard, *The Sickness Unto Death*, 13. (Hong translation unless otherwise noted.)
[58] Krentz, "Kierkegaard's Dialectical Image," 280.

Further, the relationship of objectivity and subjectivity is also dialectical. Kierkegaard believes that self-consciousness and subjectivity occurs through a dialectic, through the internal dialectic of spirit and matter. Kierkegaard's dialectic of faith is the dialectic of becoming subjective, of becoming oneself before God. Kierkegaard's dialectic of faith views the spirit in the process of becoming subjective/becoming itself through objectifying itself and then returning to subjectivity. The movement from one pole to the other provides the depth of dimension and complexity that is appropriate to the human self. Louis Dupré relates the religious sphere and subjectivity. I am intrigued with Dupré's view of the "trichotomic"[59] dialectic and movement from subjectivity to objectivity, as he elucidates:

> Our relationship with God is necessarily dialectical. The spirit cannot grasp its own essence (subjectivity) without continually objectifying itself; but since the resulting objectivity is not proper to the essence of spirit, spirit must always leave it again to turn back to itself. Objectivity, then, is a necessary pole for the ascent of the spirit. Spirit uses objectivity as the rungs of a ladder to which one clings and from which one loosens one's grasp to pull oneself up.[60]

Kierkegaard's process for becoming subjective, which is the task of becoming authentically oneself, is a dialectic movement between the two poles of subjectivity and objectivity. Dupré's view of this dialectical movement of back and forth is intriguing, but I am wary of his ladder metaphor, since it suggests that one climbs up the ladder, leaving the lower rungs behind and reaches a goal at the top. Kierkegaard's dialectic is a back and forth movement like climbing, but it is more like dancing the walk of life because one must never leave behind one's right foot, even when one is leaning on one's left

---

[59] Louis Dupré, *Kierkegaard as Theologian, the Dialectic of Christian Existence*.
[60] Ibid.

foot. Further, one must be moving and progressing continually. There isn't a top rung that signifies the completion of the task of becoming subjective. Becoming subjective is a continuous process.

Applying this relational dialectic of subjectivity to the spheres of existence reveals a parallel to the relationship of the spheres to each other both externally, or quantitatively, and subjectively, qualitatively. Kierkegaard's view of the spheres of existence is dialectical in two ways. First, the individual moves progressively from the aesthetic to the ethical and then to the religious in a dialectical manner. And secondly, within the religious sphere itself, the aesthetic and the ethical are moving between each other in dialectical relationship.

The significance of the concept of dialectic is also present in Kierkegaard's understanding of the many spheres of existence. The spheres themselves can be analyzed according to how they handle the relation or disrelation of these elements. Further, the relationships between the spheres can also be expressed in terms of the relation of these elements of existence. The spheres can be analyzed according to how the elements of existence are related and how they aren't related in each sphere.

The aesthetic sphere, with its two poles, handles this synthesis of the self by ignoring (or repressing) the presence of two different terms. This is done by either focusing completely on the immediacy of the finite sensuous pleasures, moving from one moment to the next mindlessly, or by being totally absorbed into the experience of infinite possibilities. The aesthetic is concerned only with the immediate and does not have the continuity to focus on more than one of these elements together. The elements are never able to be related to each other, let alone enable the relating of this relation to itself. The aesthete is not conscious of the tension between these two factors. She has escaped from her self, denying the ambiguity at the core of her self through reflecting on the infinite possibilities and never actualizing any of them. This person is in despair and does not even know it. She is in despair at not willing to be oneself.

Contrarily, in the ethical sphere, one begins to be aware of these elements and begins to relate them to each other. One is aware that one is in despair; one has chosen the despair of oneself. A person here acknowledges his finiteness, his limitations and faults. He comes to grips with his history, the facts of his upbringing, the fact that he will someday die. He thinks about himself and his responsibilities. However, the ethical person cannot hold these two elements in a balance either. He is either focused too much on his own natural abilities, such as reason, or on his lack of abilities, and feels guilty that the elements of existence are in disrelationship. He either emphasizes the finiteness of himself and his guilt, or he resigns himself and his finite existence for the sake of the infinite, as we saw in the knight of infinite resignation in *Fear and Trembling*. The despair of the ethical sphere is the despair of willing to be oneself, of which Kierkegaard writes, "is the disrelationship in that self-relation reflects itself infinitely in the relation to the power which establishes it."[61]

In the religious sphere, the tension between these two elements of existence is made conscious. The religious person becomes conscious of herself in the constant movement, dialectical movement of the finite and the infinite. The religious self is willing to become oneself before God. Abraham loves the finite (Isaac) beyond measure, but he gives him up for the absolute. He is not resigned to the demands of the infinite upon him, he still loves the finite. The religious holds the finite and the infinite together in equilibrium. The religious self includes the awareness of her faults and finiteness of the ethical realm. She knows she is guilty, she is a sinner *and* she accepts herself in love anyway. She knows that she is constituted by a Power outside of herself who loves her. In the religious sphere, the self is not

---

[61] Kierkegaard, *The Sickness Unto Death*, 14.

in despair, "by relating to its own self and by willing to be itself the self is grounded transparently in the Power which posited it."[62]

This dialectical structure elucidated in *Sickness Unto Death* is also applicable to interpreting the relationship of the spheres to each other. The elements in existence are oppositional, and yet in the religious sphere they are brought together and held in balance. This dialectical tension is also the glue for understanding how the spheres are related to each other.

These spheres are all present within each whole individual person who is in the religious sphere. The important questions Kierkegaard asks are about the relationship of each of the spheres to each of the others and which sphere is dominant in the various moments of one's life. In speaking of Kierkegaard's spheres of existence, twentieth century theologian Paul Tillich writes that the spheres are "coexisting all the time in ordinary human beings…Man [sic] lives within all of them, but the decisive thing is how they are related to each other and which one is predominant for him"[63]

As I explained earlier, I prefer the term, "spheres" to Taylor's term "stages." While Kierkegaard's view of the spheres of existence is progressive, Taylor's emphasis on "developmental stages" is misleading. It suggests that they are phases that one passes through and then leaves behind. Further, it omits the dialectical relationship between the spheres. Spheres is a better term because it takes the processive and relational natures of the dialectic into account. Openness and freedom of selfhood is so important to Kierkegaard that he refuses to establish a closed linear developmental system. One does not "progress" linearly from the aesthetic sphere, through the ethical sphere, and into the religious sphere, as if it were a fixed time line. Rather, the spheres reflect a spiraling complex movement to greater and greater complexity with each new sphere including the

---

[62] Ibid.

[63] Paul Tillich, *Nineteenth and Twentieth Century Protestant Theology* (New York: Harper and Row Publishers, 1967) 169.

last one, transforming it, and bringing it into the dialectic. The spheres are concentric and overlap with each other to form the dimensions of human existence. They are progressively inclusive of each other and are related to each other.

It does appear that the ethical is in counter-distinction to the aesthetic sphere, given the contradictory characteristics of immediacy and mediation, and the particular and the universal. As Steven L. Ross says, "*Either/Or* confronts the reader with two wholly self-contained and mutually exclusive world views."[64] However, as Judge William's argument for the "Aesthetic Validity of Marriage" and his discussion of "The Balance Between the Aesthetic and the Ethical in the Development of the Personality" indicate, the ethical does not replace the aesthetic, nor does it annihilate the difference. Rather, the ethical takes the aesthetic into itself, thereby including the aesthetic within the ethical. The ethical can even be said to beat the aesthetic at its own game. Marriage, the Judge argues is more aesthetically pleasing than the immediate happiness of Don Juan or the teasing of the seducer. The judge says,

The same aesthetic character which inheres in the first love must, therefore, also inhere in marriage, since the first love is contained in marriage…Marriage has all this too; it is sensual and yet spiritual, but it is more…[65]

Thus, the ethical sphere includes both the ethical sphere itself and aspects of the aesthetic sphere as well. It also hints at the religious sphere, which is to come later. The aesthetic sphere, however, even as it is taken up into the ethical sphere, is not destroyed by its inclusion in the ethical or the religious.

In this vein, I disagree with Dupré's claim discussed earlier, that the aesthetic sphere carries within itself the seed of its own

---

[64] Stephen L. Ross, introduction to *Either/Or* (abridged) by Søren Kierkegaard, ed. Stephen L. Ross, trans. George L. Stengren (New York: Harper and Row, 1986) viii.

[65] Søren Kierkegaard, *Either/Or* (abridged) ed. Stephen L. Ross, trans. George L. Stengren (New York: Harper and Row, 1986) 152.

destruction. He claims that the aesthetic is destroyed, and that the aesthetic sphere is a stage that must be transcended, and in fact, is transcended almost inherently in its own fulfillment of itself. Yet the above quote demonstrates that it is not destroyed, but rather preserved in the ethical sphere. This point is a significant aspect of Kierkegaard's theology of redemption—nothing of the human person is absolutely lost, but rather is transcended and transfigured, and included in the progressive movement toward becoming a Christian. Dupré's way of understanding the aesthetic sphere here, and thus also all the spheres together, neglects the dialectic that Dupré so insightfully brings out in his discussion of the dialectic of faith.

Similar to the inclusion of the aesthetic into the ethical, the religious sphere includes the religious sphere itself, the ethical sphere, and the aesthetic sphere. The movement from the ethical to the religious does not annihilate the ethical, but takes the ethical into itself, preserving it and adding more. For instance, the knight of faith makes a double movement—first he makes the movements of ethics, the movements of infinity, and then he makes the movements of faith. The form of the religious sphere is the dialectical relating of all the spheres of existence. Thus, the religious sphere includes all the spheres. A religious self brings all the spheres together in the dialectic movement of her existence like a spiral of transgressions and regressions—fragmentary ambiguity mixed with fragmentary harmony.

In the highest human existence the self is related to itself dialectically. For instance, in the first part of *Sickness Unto Death*, a self is present only when the elements of existence are related dialectically. In the second part, faith, the opposite of despair, is present only as one realizes that one is both guilty as a sinner and forgiven and loved at the same time. Each state of awareness is dialectically relating to the other. In becoming subjective, one must also relate to oneself dialectically as described above. Finally, then, the religious sphere is a dialectic in which the spheres relate to each other in the walk of existence. The religious self is aware of her faults and finiteness as she knows herself through the ethical realm. She is aware of herself as sinner, but also more than sinner, as one who is saved as well. The subjectivity of the religious sphere is the dialectical interrelationship of the spheres of existence.

The process of becoming subjective and becoming a Christian is becoming what I call *multivalent integration*. The self is the coming together of factors that are in conflict and in opposition to each other. This internal conflict is what causes anxiety/dread of existence. Trying to placate this dread without uncovering the root creates the sickness unto death in its many forms of despair. Despair is not in the number of the parts a self has, nor in its multivalency. Rather, despair is the insistence on singularity and homogeneity of substance. When a self limits itself to one side of the polarity, she falls into despair. Both consciously acknowledging both elements within the self is a necessary prerequisite for willing to become oneself before God. The unity of the self that Kierkegaard desires is not the homogenous one thing of Connell's contention. Rather, it is more precisely articulated as a related connection among the contrary aspects of the becoming human self: a multivalent integration.

In conclusion, I have discussed several ways of understanding Kierkegaard's spheres of existence and offered critiques of three major interpretations. My first critique centered on Taylor's excellent and comprehensive study of Kierkegaard's pseudonymous authorship. object to his preference for the term stages and his emphasis on th developmental structure of the "stages" of existence. I maintain tha the term spheres is a more apt choice because it calls attention t both the dialectical form of the spheres internally and externally, well as the non linear progression and movement from one sphere the next. My primary critique of Connell was his exclusive use of t e lens of unity through which he views the spheres. He is blinded the religious sphere's harmonizing of multivalency and to the triu e movement of the dialectic. I also touched on Dupré's insighful discussion of the dialectic of faith. I suggest that his primry limitation is that he misses the intricate inclusive relationship of the spheres to each other. The spheres progress inclusively, taking the previous one into the present one. I further suggested that Kierkegaard's dialectical structure, so clearly elucidated in *Sickness Unto Death* and in *Concluding Unscientific Postscript,* provides the key insight to interpreting the relationship of the spheres of existence to each other. The polar elements of existence are oppositional, and yet in the faith of the religious sphere they are brought together and held in balance. This dialectical tension is also the glue for understanding how the spheres are related to each other. Each sphere contains the previous sphere and its contents, growing beyond it while not annulling it. This dialectical structure of back and forth of the spheres is the form of the religious sphere and the structure of Christian existence. This inter-relationality governs the dialectical movement between and within the spheres of existence internal to the individual as she moves toward becoming oneself before God. Religiousness B, the ultimate sphere, brings together all the spheres in an integrated whole—integrated in that these conflicting characteristics are connected together in one whole self. This multivalent integration of the self is only possible by "relating itself to itself and in willing to be itself, the self rests transparently in the power which established it."[66] In the next chapter I analyze Kierkegaard's pseudonymity through his dialectic. There I also expand on the implications of Kierkegaard's insights into the self for the construction of a model for a self that is constituted and characterized by multiplicity, dynamic movement, and dialectical relationality.

---

[66] Kierkegaard, *The Sickness Unto Death*, 131.

3

Kierkegaard's Pseudonymity: Multiple Voices of the Self of a Genius

Introduction

The previous chapter elucidated Kierkegaard's spheres of existence and suggested that his dialectic serves as the paradigm for interpreting both his theory of spheres and his view of personhood. This chapter critically examines his employment of pseudonyms, focusing on three common interpretations of Kierkegaard's pseudonymity in the secondary literature. By applying the dialectic of relationality that I delineated in the previous chapter, I offer an intriguing interpretation of the meanings of his use of pseudonyms. Further, I extrapolate from this interpretation the implications for his view of human existence.

Above I argued that Kierkegaard's theory regarding spheres of existence is best understood in light of the reflexive dialectic found in *Sickness Unto Death*. Willing to become oneself before God entails balancing pairs of polar elements (such as the finite and the infinite). Applying this dialectic to the interplay of the spheres of existence yields a view of the fullness of human existence as balancing the complexity of all the spheres of existence. Thus, the fullness of human existence that encompasses the variety of these spheres along with the pairs of existential elements contained within the dialectic reveals the multiplicity of subjectivity (the inner life of the spirit). I concluded that while the duality of the dialectic offers a clear and cutting critique to the privilege ascribed to the One, the presence of the third entity created by the relation of the existential elements, as well as three spheres of existence, offers an even more effective critique against the normative discourse.

Similarly, in this chapter I speculate that his employment of various voices in his authorship reinforces this critique and pushes it beyond two or three different voices/aspects within the self. I argue that the variety of authors, both pseudonymous and non-pseudonymous, can be interpreted in light of Kierkegaard's reflexive dialectic. The complexity and interrelatedness of the authors form a network that further develops the complexity and multiplicity of the fullness of human selfhood. First, I will describe some of the characteristics of the pseudonymous authors and Kierkegaard's use of indirection. Then I address three of the primary interpretations in the secondary literature that critically address the pseudonyms. Further, I argue that these authors are like characters used to evoke a personal identification in the reader. Kierkegaard's style of using vivid details from the perspectives of various characters serves his religious purposes by enabling him to express profound insights into the human psyche and engage the reader in her own internal decision making processes. Kierkegaard wants the reader to enter the dialogues concerning the existential questions raised by the various pseudonymous authors. His style of indirect communication, in particular, his pseudonyms, is designed to evoke subjectivity in his reader. I conclude that his indirection emphasizes this ambiguity and multiplicity by evoking subjectivity in his reader. Here, in applying the reflexive dialectic examined above to the pseudonyms, I further develop my theory that Kierkegaard views subjectivity as the very activity of holding the ambiguity and multiplicity of many parts within the self.

The Pseudonyms

Like the multiplicity of the spheres, the form of Kierkegaard's authorship reveals multiplicity. In some respects his authorship often resembles that of a literary figure of the eighteenth and nineteenth century, rather than that of a philosopher. He employs a variety of pseudonyms. These pseudonymous authors represent different points of view, different spheres of existence, and different aspects or phases of these spheres. In this way, the authors are both illustrative developments of Kierkegaard's concept of the spheres of existence and are shown to be related to each other dialectically in a way reminiscent of the way the factors of existence are related dialectically.

Noteworthy qualities of his pseudonymous authorship include the imaginative and obvious imaginary nature of the made-up names. This indicates that hiding his identity is not his primary purpose. If this were the case, he would have used an innocuous everyday name like Dag Andersen. But he does not choose a single name that can easily be ignored or forgotten. In fact it seems that he deliberately chooses names/words that draw attention to themselves. He uses many different names, some of which are puns, or comic imitations of Latin. For example, Hilarius Bookbinder, is the author/collector of *Stages on Life's Way*, and Constantin Constantius is the author of *Repetition*. The pseudonyms are often particular to a particular book or essay and the pseudonym alludes to the text. For example, *Fear and Trembling*, which is penned by Johannes de Silencio, deals with Abraham's inability to speak about his experience as a knight of faith. Further, Kierkegaard's pseudonyms form a relational context. In some cases he uses the same name for more than one work, as in the case of Johannes Climacus (Joe the Climber), who pens *Philosophical Fragments, Concluding Unscientific Postscript,* and "De Omnibus Dubitandum Est." In addition, he sometimes offers other works by an author with a variation on the name that he has already employed, highlighting the relational context. For instance, Johannes Anti-Climacus is the author of *Sickness Unto Death* and *Training in Christianity*. Here an obvious relationship exists between this author and Johannes Climacus. Some of the relationships between the authors are subtler, such as the fact that Judge William, author of

Either/Or B addresses his essay in the form of letters to the author of *Either/Or* A. These authors sometimes function as characters and parts of the content of the treatise. For instance, Judge William and Constant Constantine appear as characters in *Stages on Life's Way*, as well as authors of their own works. Kierkegaard also presents his works as collections of various other authors as well.

A further complication is that simultaneously with many of his pseudonymous works, Kierkegaard also published edifying discourses and other texts under his own name. For instance, he published *Two Edifying Discourses* in May of 1843, three months after *Either/Or* and four months before *Fear and Trembling* were published. In addition, he published *Three Edifying Discourses* at the same time as *Fear and Trembling*. He does this consciously and intentionally, with an eye to how his authorship as a whole will be understood in the end. As he writes in a book that he wrote to posterity about his authorship, *The Point of View of My Work as an Author*, "the change is simultaneous with the beginning—that is, the duplicity dates from the very start. For the *Two Edifying Discourses* are contemporaneous with *Either/Or*."[1] He is indicating the simultaneity of his different modes of expression.

I suggest that these various authors form a relational matrix that creates, or at least mimics, the structure of authentic selfhood as Kierkegaard interprets it. In this framework I am suggesting that selfhood is a verb, a praxis of bringing together the contradictions and incongruities of the various voices within oneself. It is a progressive and regressive process of discovery, repression, engagement, weaving and acceptance. The pseudonyms reflect the movement of Kierkegaard's authorship in and through various voices, representing the process of becoming oneself before God. This movement is grounded in the same dialectical movement that grounds the spheres

---

[1] Søren Kierkegaard, *The Point of View of My Work as an Author*, trans. Walter Lowrie (New York: Harper Torchbook, 1962) 11.

and the pairs of factors of existence. This provides an extended example of a multiple and related self.

Kierkegaard engages the reader with a multiplicity of pseudonyms, pseudonyms upon pseudonyms even. For example, in his first pseudonymous work, *Either/Or*, the pseudonymous editor (who is already once removed from Kierkegaard) is further removed from the other pseudonymous authors of the text: the aesthetic author(s) in A, and author B, Judge William. And to go even another step, one of the aesthetic authors is an editor himself, claiming to have another's diary in his possession. The pseudonymous editor, Victor Eremita, comments on the peculiarity of being twice removed from a work and yet still being affected by it personally:

And A's reaction does not surprise me, for I, too, who have nothing at all to do with this narrative—indeed, am twice removed from the original author—I, too, sometimes have felt quite strangely uneasy when I have been occupied with these papers in the stillness of the night. It seemed to me as if the seducer himself paced my floor like a shadow, as if he glanced at the papers, as if he fixed his demonic eyes on me, and said, "Well, well, so you want to publish my papers!....."[2]

Kierkegaard notes that an editor/writer even twice removed can be strangely moved by the words and imaged fantasies of an unknown author, here revealing one of his own non-pseudonymous relationships with the bulk of his aesthetic work: strangely moved. It is this emotive state that he hopes to evoke within the reader by placing himself in the position of the reader, thus encouraging him/her to identify with his feelings as the reader/author. Like a literary author Kierkegaard employs his imagination to create/discover in himself characters that not only express aspects of his own personality, but also help him create an evocative experience

---

[2] Søren Kierkegaard, *Either/Or*, trans. and ed. Howard V. Hong and Edna H. Hong (Princeton NJ: Princeton University Press, 1987) 1: 9.

for the reader. These identifications then also engage the reader (as well as the author) in internal dialogue between aspects of the self, encouraging attention and acceptance of the multiplicity and difference within the inner life.

Kierkegaard painstakingly communicates in intricate details the internal experience of being the particular character that Kierkegaard is currently portraying. For instance, in *Fear and Trembling* the reader feels for herself what it feels like to be Abraham. Kierkegaard evokes an immediate experience of the anxiety and shock of what Abraham might have felt as he is commanded to sacrifice his only son. Kierkegaard wants the reader to ask herself: what would I have done in this situation? He accomplishes this by leading the reader through the internal experience of being Abraham. Kierkegaard's talents at creating such realistic sensations are revealed in this text, which takes the reader with Abraham as he painfully climbs each and every step of Mount Moriah toward the altar upon which he will sacrifice his only son. Kierkegaard's words are graphic and direct, enabling the reader to feel as if she were there:

> On the morning of the fourth day, Abraham said not a word but raised his eyes and saw Mount Moriah in the distance. He left the young servants behind and, taking Isaac's hand, went up the mountain alone. But Abraham said to himself, "I will not hide from Isaac where this walk is taking him." He stood still, he laid his hand on Isaac's head in blessing, and Isaac kneeled to receive it. And Abraham's face epitomized fatherliness; his gaze was gentle, his words admonishing. But Isaac could not understand him, his soul could not be uplifted; he clasped Abraham's knees, he pleaded at his feet, he begged for his young life, for his beautiful hopes; he called to mind the joy in Abraham's house, he called to mind the sorrow and the solitude. Then Abraham lifted the boy up and walked on, holding his hand, and his words were full of comfort and

admonition. But Isaac could not understand him. Abraham climbed Mount Moriah, but Isaac did not understand him.[3]

What would it be like to have actually been a witness to this event? What thoughts and feelings might have gone through Abraham's mind? What would I have done in Abraham's situation? Kierkegaard asks and shows the reader how to ask herself such questions. He illustrates four alternative scenarios of what Abraham might have done, or what you might have done in Abraham's sandals. As we have seen above, each scenario demonstrates how easy it is to not be a knight of faith. What would you have done in Abraham's situation? One can almost feel the anxiety as Johannes de Silencio confesses his own struggle with this existential question:

> I wonder if anyone in my generation is able to make the movements of faith?...If I...had been ordered to take such an extraordinary royal journey as the one to Mount Moriah, I know very well what I would have done...I am quite sure that I would have been punctual and all prepared—more than likely...But...The moment I mounted the horse, I would have said to myself: Now all is lost...Neither would I have loved Isaac as Abraham loved him.[4]

Johannes de Silencio reveals that he is not a knight of faith. Kierkegaard employs first person language conversationally, engaging the reader in religious and existential questions in hopes that the reader will recognize and admit his/her own state of faith or lack of faith.

---

[3] Søren Kierkegaard, *Fear and Trembling*, trans. and ed. Howard V. Hong and Edna H. Hong (Princeton NJ: Princeton University Press, 1983) 27.
[4] Ibid., 34-35.

How Are We to Interpret Kierkegaard's Pseudonymous Authorship?

The purpose, authority, and importance of Kierkegaard's decisions to use pseudonyms are much-debated topics in current Kierkegaard scholarship. In *The Point of View of My Work as an Author*, Kierkegaard's own commentary on his vocation written to be published posthumously, he says that he employs aesthetic writing for an ethical effect, all as a part of his religious vocation. His pseudonymous works are "the productions of an aesthetic character, which are an incognito and a deceit in the service of Christianity."[5] Further, he distinguishes three different groups in his authorship as follows:

> The first group of writings represents aesthetic productivity, the last group is exclusively religious: between them, as the turning point, lies the Concluding Postscript.[6]

What does it mean that his entire pseudonymous authorship is an "aesthetic production," as Kierkegaard claims, while at the same time, an expression of his religious vocation? There are several answers given in the secondary literature. I will address three of the most common among perspectives and offer my own critical and constructive answer to this intriguing mystery.

One common understanding of this mystery is given by philosopher of religion D. Z. Phillips, who claims that Kierkegaard's purpose in employing aesthetic means is to debunk the "monstrous illusion" about what it means to be a Christian. Phillips believes that Kierkegaard is particularly concerned with philosophy's contribution to this illusion through its static hold on the becoming self of the existing individual.[7] Representing a second point of view, George

---

[5] Kierkegaard, *The Point of View*, 6.
[6] Ibid., 13.
[7] D. Z. Phillips, "Authorship and Authenticity: Kierkegaard and Wittgenstein,"

Connell views Kierkegaard's life and authorship as driven by the mounting tension between the aesthetic and religious realm in terms of a person's relationship to unity.[8] Lastly, Mark C. Taylor understands Kierkegaard's style of indirect communication as reflecting the reader back upon himself, and thus even his pseudonymous works are an expression of his religious vocation.[9] I will critically analyze these interpretations and build my theory about Kierkegaard's authorship by developing his concept that "truth is subjectivity." Informed by Dupré's reading of Kierkegaard's dialectic of faith, I construct a theory that interprets the pseudonyms as an expression of the multiplicity of the inner life.[10] I conclude that the goal and meaning of Kierkegaard's use of pseudonyms is to evoke subjectivity by engaging the reader in an internal dialogue about being related to God/truth. Further, I argue that this notion of subjectivity, which is tantamount to becoming a Christian, entails tolerating ambiguity, difference, multiplicity, relationality, process, and anxiety within each person, including oneself.

Understood as expressions of the multiplicity of the inner life, which is the fullness of human selfhood, the various spheres and the various pseudonyms are not simply unchosen possibilities, nor are they merely progressive stages. Rather, each of the spheres and the pseudonyms reveals important aspects in Kierkegaard's understanding of human selfhood. Each of these ways of living contributes to the self of a single person.

Midwest Studies in Philosophy, 17 (1992): 177-193.

[8] George Connell, *To Be One Thing: Personal Unity in Kierkegaard's Thought* (Macon GA: Mercer University Press, 1985).

[9] Mark C. Taylor, *Kierkegaard's Pseudonymous Authorship* (Princeton NJ: Princeton University Press, 1975).

[10] Louis Dupré, *Kierkegaard as Theologian, the Dialectic of Christian Existence* (New York: Sheed and Ward, 1963).

Pseudonyms as Clarification of Religious Thinking

In this section I ask the question: what is Kierkegaard's relation to the variety of the pseudonym's voices? I refer to the insights of D. Z. Phillips and C. Stephen Evans and offer my critical analysis of their interpretations. Evans argues that the purpose of Kierkegaard's pseudonyms is to "clarify the role of important concepts in human life."[11] He writes that Kierkegaard "imaginatively constructs and describes existential possibilities, but in the last analysis he does not commit himself."[12] Kierkegaard is engaged in philosophical enquiry, and philosophical enquiry remains a part of the aesthetic realm. Thus, for Evans the variety of the voices of Kierkegaard's authorship reveals nothing positive or insightful, but only serves to show us that the person of Kierkegaard remains in the aesthetic sphere.

Phillips agrees with Evans that Kierkegaard's work is philosophical enquiry, claiming that Johannes Climacus, one of Kierkegaard's most well-known characters, is a philosopher who gives us "an imaginative presentation of the kind of possibility Christianity is. He is not giving a demonstration of the truth of Christianity."[13] But Phillips disagrees with Evans's assertion that this leaves Kierkegaard in the aesthetic realm. Phillips argues that Kierkegaard's philosophical clarification is done for a religious purpose, and thus it does not leave him in the aesthetic realm. Evans might respond that he is not against the value of philosophical enquiry, nor is he denigrating Kierkegaard. He is simply interpreting the author correctly. The issue at the core of this disagreement lies in which author Evans is actually interpreting—Kierkegaard or the pseudonym? The aesthetic sphere does include the reflective pole of philosophical enquiry. Johannes Climacus, no matter how correct his understanding of the system,

---

[11] C. Stephen Evans, *Kierkegaard's Fragments and Postscript* (Atlantic Highlands NJ: Humanities Press, 1983) 22.

[12] Ibid.

[13] D. Z. Phillips, "Critical Notice," *Philosophical Investigations* 9/1 (January 1986).

still remains in the aesthetic sphere, where the reality of the becoming of the individual is misunderstood as a static, knowable, quantifiable entity. The appendix in *Concluding Unscientific Postscript* indicates that Climacus "does not make out that he is a Christian; for he is, to be sure, completely preoccupied with how difficult it must be to become one."[14] The certainty of this perspective separates Climacus from the truth of Kierkegaard's "truth is subjectivity." Becoming authentically subjective is a religious decision. The religious sphere demands intimate personal risk that philosophical enquiry does not.[15] Yet Evans's critical evaluation here is limited to the pseudonym and cannot be applied to Kierkegaard himself. Climacus' perspective does not and cannot reflect Kierkegaard's personal spiritual/faith stance. The subjectivity of the religious sphere is not discernable from the outside, and especially not from the writings of one or many authors who are dissociated from the actual author in question. The question that must be examined in greater detail is "what has Climacus to do with Kierkegaard?"

For Phillips, Kierkegaard's relation to the pseudonymous authors is a constructive employment of imagined embodiments of various perspectives on the truth. In Phillips's understanding Kierkegaard uses these pseudonyms for the sake of making a philosophical point—a clarification of what is religious living and what is not religious living. But it is not a demonstration of religious living. And according to Evans, this is an aesthetic purpose.

Neither Phillips nor Evans, nor I, can judge whether or not Kierkegaard himself is in the religious sphere. No one but Kierkegaard knows. And he himself claims that his writings are for a religious purpose in his analysis of his work as an author, as he writes:

---

[14] Søren Kierkegaard, *Concluding Unscientific Postscript to Philosophical Fragments*, trans. and ed. Howard V. Hong and Edna H. Hong (Princeton NJ: Princeton University Press, 1992) 1:545.

[15] Ibid., 1:53-55.

[B]ut I know also with God that this very work of mine as an author was the prompting of an irresistible inward impulse.[16]

However, I will say that this sounds more like a religious calling than an artistic expression. He even makes this stipulation explicitly when he says "I cannot explain my work as an author wholly…this in part because I cannot make public my God-relationship."[17] A knight of faith cannot be recognized from the externals in his life, and certainly not from a representative of himself mediated through the medium of writing.

As the central point in D. Z. Phillips's analysis of Kierkegaard's authorship, he argues that the purpose of the pseudonyms is to clear up the "Monstrous Illusion" in the religious thinking in Denmark of Kierkegaard's day. This fallacy is the commonly held misunderstanding that being a Christian is as simple as being born a Dane. Phillips argues that the purpose of Kierkegaard's authorship is in "depicting aesthetic, ethical, and religious perspectives, challenging people about the meaning of their own lives."[18] Kierkegaard wants to clear up this misunderstanding by clarifying their thinking. He shows his readers a mirror of themselves, gets them to recognize themselves, and then lowers the boom—"your way of living is in fact the aesthetic sphere or the ethical sphere. It is not the religious sphere as you had mistakenly believed." In Phillips's argument Kierkegaard believes that people are confused about what it means to be(come) a Christian. Some people mistakenly think that the values espoused by what Kierkegaard calls the aesthetic sphere, such as beauty or sublime music, are actually the values of the religious. Others believe that religion is living by ethical commands. Kierkegaard demonstrates

---

[16] Kierkegaard, *The Point of View*, 7.
[17] Ibid., 9.
[18] Phillips, "Authorship and Authenticity," 186.

the actual truth of these different viewpoints by offering a mirror. He illustrates the aesthetic sphere and hopes that those confusing the religious with the aesthetic will recognize themselves in this literary mirror created by his employment of pseudonyms. He hopes that most of the readers, once conscious of their confusion, will change their lives in order to rectify their error.

In summary, D. Z. Phillips believes that Kierkegaard uses indirection to illustrate three different modes of living for the purpose of clarifying the true nature of religious thinking. The aesthetic and the ethical modes of interpreting life/living stand in contradistinction to the religious mode of living. Kierkegaard believes that many Danes (and others, perhaps) who believe that they are living as Christians are actually deceiving themselves about their lives. By illustrating these other non-Christian modes of existence through pseudonymous authors in counter-distinction with the true mode of Christian existence, articulated through works with Kierkegaard's own name attached as author, Kierkegaard hopes both to meet persons where they are and show them that they are not where they think they are. Thus, the variety of voices serves to reach a variety of confused thinking. However, the pseudonyms have only a negative function in that it shows people what Christianity is not and, by implication, what they are not.

I agree with Phillips that one of Kierkegaard's primary intentions is clarification of what it means to live in the religious sphere. I push beyond Phillips's argument in asserting that Kierkegaard also wants to help those in the other spheres find their way toward the religious sphere by examining and changing their mode of existence. Kierkegaard notices that many writers of his day promise to make things easier, and thus there is nothing left for him to do but make things more difficult. I believe that this statement is referring to the "illusion" that being a Christian is easy, as easy as whatever you are doing now, either in the aesthetic mode or the ethical dimension. It is whatever you were born to do. Kierkegaard says that the point of his authorship is a polemic against, "the monstrous illusion we call Christendom, or against the illusion that in such a land as ours all are Christians of a sort."[19] Instead, Kierkegaard believes that becoming a Christian is the most difficult of tasks; and so he seeks to make things more difficult, but not more difficult than they actually are. He writes:

> My intention is to make it difficult to become a Christian, yet not more difficult than it is, and not difficult for the obtuse and easy for the brainy, but qualitatively and essentially difficult for every human being...[20]

Up to this point Phillips and I generally agree. But now here is where we separate. Phillips argues that Kierkegaard's goal is exclusively to clarify the obfuscation of Danish belief. Clarity of thought is his only conscious purpose, Phillips says, and anything else would indicate Kierkegaard's own confusion, since religious decisions can only be made by the individual himself. Kierkegaard can do nothing to create a leap of faith in another's soul. Phillips does admit, however, that perhaps Kierkegaard does hope that those readers who are living in the aesthetic sphere might change their lives once he has revealed their theological confusion, but Kierkegaard can accomplish nothing beyond providing a mirror to show their confused thinking. Phillips asserts that Kierkegaard's use of pseudonyms is limited to highlighting what Christianity is not, which will then clarify the actual distinctions between these different modes of interpreting reality (the spheres).

This is a common way of interpreting the pseudonyms. But I believe that this is not the extent of Kierkegaard's purpose, nor is it the extent of the insights Kierkegaard offers for understanding the nature and process of the human situation, particularly concerning the various spheres of existence and the various pseudonyms.

---

[19] Kierkegaard, *The Point of View*, 6.
[20] Kierkegaard, *Concluding Unscientific Postscript*, 1:557.

Kierkegaard's religious goal is under the pseudonymous poetry like the presence of Christ is under the bread in a Catholic mass. As Kierkegaard writes in his journals, "My task has continually been to provide the existential-corrective by poetically presenting the ideals and inciting the people about the established order."[21] He is passionate about affecting his readers (especially Regina) and engaging them in a religious quest toward salvation. His writing is the means by which he affects his reader.

The pseudonymous authors enable Kierkegaard to employ a method of indirect discourse that is appropriate in matters of the soul. Indirect discourse is speaking with symbols instead of direct language. Directly confronting a person about the properness of his/her personal mode of religiosity does not help that individual transform his/her mode of living into a truly Christian one. Religious communication is indirect and symbolic and thus must use indirect communication for this religious project. Pseudonyms make use of connotations from different authors and different types of authors. The major difference between my conclusion and Phillips's view centers on the unique characteristic of indirection. Phillips believes that Kierkegaard is simply clarifying thinking about the values and characteristics that make up the truly religious mode of living, writing that "through the disinterested elucidations of his pseudonymous works, [Kierkegaard] was hoping to awaken others to an understanding which he possessed, but which they lacked."[22] However, mere clarification of the distinctions between these distinct modes of interpreting life could be done directly. For instance, Kierkegaard could have set forth a philosophical argument demonstrating that the ethical norms are not identical to the values of faith. He could have stated the values of each mode of living and explicitly and directly contrasted them. He could have made similar

---

[21] Søren Kierkegaard, *Journals and Papers*, trans. and ed. Howard V. Hong and Edna H. Hong (Bloomington IN: Indiana University Press, 1967) 1:331.

[22] Phillips, "Authorship and Authenticity," 190.

analyses of the differences between an aesthetic approach and a religious sensibility. Applying Oakum's Razor would instruct him to use the most simple and most direct method in communicating his points. But he does not. He employs complicated and mysterious means because they are the most, if not the only, effective method to evoke an existential decision in the reader. If luring a person toward making a personal decision for involvement in one of these modes and away from another were the purpose, it would be necessary to employ indirect means. Kierkegaard is intentional in going to such excessive lengths in using indirection, multiple authors, and deceptive means in publishing.

Phillips's way of interpreting Kierkegaard's theory of the multi-spheres of existence and his employment of pseudonymous authorship also limits the applicability of Kierkegaard's insights about human existence to persons who are fully submerged in one or the other spheres of "non-Christian" existence. This view would eliminate the relevance of Kierkegaard's thinking on the human self in general. For if Kierkegaard is simply speaking to those who are confused about their mode of living, and are actually in either the aesthetic sphere or the ethical sphere but have mistaken the respective spheres for Christianity, then these works have nothing to say to those who are not in any of these errors. Further, this conclusion implies that Kierkegaard has nothing to say to those who are not intent upon becoming a genuine Christian, nor is he speaking of the structure of human existence at all. He is simply arguing for a certain understanding of Christianity that he believes to be correct and against interpretations that he thinks are wrong. Moreover, the spheres of existence would be understood not as spheres of existence at all, but rather as groups of mistaken thinking. All of these implications are problematic. Kierkegaard could have communicated this merely clarifying "truth" without the elaborate means of pseudonyms. It is more likely that Kierkegaard is up to something much more. His various spheres and various pseudonyms are intended to communicate something substantive and effective about selfhood. Phillips's view does not account for the dialectic, a most important aspect of Kierkegaard's thought.

In summary, Phillips argues that Kierkegaard uses aesthetic works/modes of writing for a decisive purpose: to evoke clarification in his readers. The purpose of pseudonymous philosophers is to show that philosophical theory does not get to the truth. By utilizing the pseudonyms, Kierkegaard shows what the truth is not. This is a negative critique then of philosophy's ability to aid the religious project. Philosophy can not get you to the truth if truth is subjectivity, nor the truth of religious living, but it can tell you that what you think is the truth is in fact not the truth. Phillips's conclusion is that Kierkegaard's pseudonyms illustrate that the philosophical approaches don't know what truth is. Yet he stops there. This interpretation assumes that there were many persons in Copenhagen who might recognize themselves in Johannes Climacus' complex philosophical obfuscation. I don't believe that Kierkegaard thinks this is actually the case. Kierkegaard's purpose in using pseudonyms is not explained fully by Phillips's argument.

I agree that Kierkegaard's work may be emulating and correcting Kant's critiques of reason and religion, but Kierkegaard's use of pseudonyms also reveals a positive truth and is not merely a critique on what theory does not know. The positive character of truth is found in the relating of the authors to and with each other through the dialectic in a similar way as the spheres are related. Truth is the process of becoming oneself; it is the inter-relationality of oneself with oneself; truth is subjectivity. This will be developed below.

The question underlying this issue of Kierkegaard's pseudonymous authorship is perhaps "how far can the religious truth be shared?" How can faith be shared? Luther argues that Christians should speak about their faith—to witness to others and each other. But can there be an inter-subjective experience? I think Kierkegaard believes that faith cannot be communicated directly. It cannot use the direct mediation of language. How would you go about trying to communicate the emotion of an intense inner experience? Tell a story that evokes those same feelings? Show colors or have people do something similar in their body to what you did when you had your experience? Put people in a similar or corresponding situation? We shall return to this question/issue later.

Unity as the driving force of Kierkegaard's Authorship

George Connell views unity as the focus of Kierkegaard's authorship as a whole. Although Connell's book focuses on the quest for unity in Kierkegaard's understanding of selfhood developed primarily from his theory of spheres of existence, his claims have implications for interpreting Kierkegaard's use of pseudonyms. He does make a few direct statements relevant to the pseudonyms, but I will mostly extrapolate from his analysis in general. I have chosen to address his framework of interpreting Kierkegaard because his emphasis on oneness of self is one of the primary positions against my interpretation of Kierkegaard. In the previous chapter we saw Connell arguing that Kierkegaard understands human selfhood in terms of unity. A self is made by each individual's efforts "to be one thing." Connell follows the progress of Kierkegaard's authorship historically, starting with his early journal entries, marking a particular entry as the key for understanding both the authorship and Kierkegaard. He quotes a journal entry from Kierkegaard's time in Gilleleje (1830) in which Kierkegaard writes:

> What really matters is to find a purpose, to see what it really is that God wills that I shall do; the crucial thing is to find a truth which is truth for me, to find the idea for which I am willing to live and die.[23]

---

[23] Kierkegaard, *Journals and Papers*, quoted in Connell, *To Be One Thing*, 15.

Connell takes this entry as the quest for truth and unity that shapes Kierkegaard's theory of existence as well as his authorship. I concur with his position that Kierkegaard's authorship as a whole corresponds to his personal preoccupation with selfhood and subjectivity—his own as well as a theoretical understanding. However, I am critical of his use of unity as the organizing principle of Kierkegaard's authorship. Using the same framework of interpretation concerning the spheres of existence, Connell views the pseudonymous authorship as the literary expression of the differences between the aesthetic sphere and the religious sphere. Kierkegaard's theme of unity as a divine imperative to be one thing drives his authorship across and through these "stages" in the development of authentic subjectivity. The overall purpose of his authorship is the religious development of the human soul. Connell interprets Kierkegaard's claim that "Truth is Subjectivity" as an expression of Kierkegaard's "conviction that the self must constitute itself as an essential unity."[24] He reinforces this argument that Kierkegaard's authorship is most intimately concerned with his own personal unity by highlighting the fact that Kierkegaard's own literary critique of Hans Christian Andersen focuses on the other famous Dane's lack of personal unity. Connell writes that "Kierkegaard concludes that Andersen is unable to produce an organically unified work of art because he lacks a life-view, and is, therefore, disunified in his personal experience."[25] This lack of personal unity in the author is the basis of Kierkegaard's primary critique of Andersen's novels. Kierkegaard asserts the "unity of works of art to be essentially if not immediately connected with the unity of the artist as a person."[26] There are intriguing implications to be drawn from the knowledge that Kierkegaard judges Andersen as a failed author because of the presumed lack of a unified personal life-view. This insight is

---

[24] Connell, *To Be One Thing*, 9.
[25] Ibid., 22.
[26] Ibid., 37.

particularly interesting when we reflect upon the spheres in terms of how each is related to the state of unity.

I have already addressed most of my critiques of Connell's argument that Kierkegaard's conceptualization of ideal selfhood is to be one thing in the previous chapter. Allow me to apply that analysis to his conclusion that a personal struggle for unity is the best interpretative framework for Kierkegaard's pseudonymous authorship. Connell's interpretation is problematic on three counts. The first follows from his conflation of Kierkegaard's claim that purity of heart is "willing one thing," on the one hand, with his contention that an authentic self as "willing to be itself, the self rests transparently in the power that established it,"[27] on the other. Connell creates a new formula, "To Be One Thing," and views it as corresponding to the new commandment for Christians—the duty to love. This new formula is problematic because it does not take into account Kierkegaard's two separate formulae nor the thoroughgoing dialectic in Kierkegaard's authorship. For Connell, Kierkegaard's imperative is to be one thing throughout and through his authorship. However, as I discussed in the previous chapter, Kierkegaard's formulae are distinct. Conflating them confuses the terms unity with oneness and collapses Kierkegaard's insightful distinction between theoretical knowledge and existential truth. Connell highlights this distinction himself, in his research into the origin and development of Kierkegaard's careful analysis of these two types of truth. Connell very helpfully draws out an important influence upon Kierkegaard's practical existential meaning of truth. Sibbern, one of Kierkegaard's teachers of Hegel while in graduate school in Denmark, makes an explicit connection between the sort of unity found in a theoretical system of knowledge and the sort of personal unity seen in a self. Sibbern sees this connection as problematic only in terms of how the

---

[27] Søren Kierkegaard, *The Sickness Unto Death*, trans. and ed. Howard V. Hong and Edna H. Hong (Princeton NJ: Princeton University Press, 1980) 131.

latter can hinder the former, which is the true and noble pursuit: truth for truth's (knowledge's) sake. Kierkegaard's sharp reaction to this attempt to instill a disembodied devotion to abstract truth is found through out his entire authorship as he proclaims that Truth is Subjectivity.

Connell's analysis includes Kierkegaard's concern for the existing individual as a correlate to the critical claim that the *modus operandi* of a system of knowledge is a different sort of operation than the mode of the existing individual. He agrees that this difference is a fundamental difference. Theoretical knowledge is fixed, non-processive, and abstract, abstracted from the reality of life. It is really only a probability game based on past observations. Philosophy, like any science, can only predict the present or future of a phenomenon from analyzing its past behavior via statistical probabilities. Contrarily, an actual existing individual is always in the process of becoming. These two sorts of modalities are so contrary that the first cannot fully understand the realities of the second. Objective knowledge cannot get one to the truth about one's self, nor to personal unity of oneself; only subjectivity can lead one to the truth about existing. Yet what Connell does not address is that this process of living is ambiguous and relational. Kierkegaard emphasizes this difference between thinking about existence and the actual experience of living. This difference is found in the structure of experience, as Kierkegaard writes that living "separates, and holds the various moments of existence discretely apart."[28] Lived religious life is not being one thing. It is bringing several particular variant realities into relation with each other, while maintaining the tension between them. Kierkegaard writes in his journal that the three great ideas of life (despair, doubt, and aesthetic pleasure) must be brought into

---

[28] Kierkegaard, *Concluding Unscientific Postscript to Philosophical Fragments*, trans. and ed. Walter Lowrie (Princeton NJ: Princeton University Press, 1941) 107. See also: Kierkegaard, *Concluding Unscientific Postscript*, 1: 118: "Existence is the spacing that holds apart…"

concrete mediation together in one life, "mediated and embraced in life by the single individual, not until then do the moral and religious appear."[29] This integration presupposes multiplicity. Life is characterized by ambiguity, multiplicity, and dialectical relationality, not a singular oneness or "one thing." Only scientific or theoretical knowledge could be reduced to one thing.

Connell's emphasis on Kierkegaard's consummate concern for the existing individual in his quest for personal unity of the self follows from this, but his understanding of personal unity as "being one thing" is wrongheaded. He traces the various ways of existing in Kierkegaard's schema using the manner each tries to be "one thing." This approach offers insights into the failures of the various spheres and transitions between the spheres. The culmination of Kierkegaard's authorship in Connell's framework is the Christian self. Writing reflectively on the progression of his thesis, Connell says that as his study:

> ...progressed from the ironic to the ethical to the immanent religious and finally to the Christian self, it became apparent that each form's characteristic expression of oneness overcomes the fatal weakness of its predecessor's form of oneness. Thus, only with the Christian self is the demand for oneness fully met.[30]

Here Connell reinforces his view that oneness is the ultimate goal of subjectivity and of Christianity in Kierkegaard's authorship. The essential difference between religiousness B (the Christian self) and all the other ways of living concerns the form of oneness of self. I agree that Kierkegaard attends to this structure of subjectivity. But I argue that the problem in the various ways of living that are not Christian is in "trying to be one thing" on one's own power and will.

---

[29] Kierkegaard, *Journals and Papers*, 1:795, quoted in Connell, *To Be One Thing*, 47.

[30] Connell, *To Be One Thing*, 192.

The unity of the religious sphere is a complex of tensions and ambiguous relationships within the self and with one's neighbors. This leads me to the second problem, which is the definition of unity as singular and as "being one thing." Unity necessarily implies more than one thing. To have union with another, there must be both one and another. Otherwise there is no unity, just singularity and oneness.

In summary, Connell's arguments that Kierkegaard's entire authorship is founded on his quest for personal unity are wrongheaded in the following ways. First, his formula "willing to be one thing" conflates two separate Kierkegaardian formulae, willing one thing and willing to become oneself, into a false formulae: to be one thing. Further, this conflation entails confusing Kierkegaard's emphasis on the subjectivity of existential truth with the static fixed state of abstract theory, reducing the complexity and ambiguity of Kierkegaard's insight about the spheres of existence and faith to sameness and clarity of reason and thought. And lastly, Connell's identification between the unity and one thing leads to a false and reductionist view of Kierkegaard's term subjectivity.

Pseudonyms as Mirrors, Reflecting the Reader Toward Herself

Mark C. Taylor offers the most comprehensive and insightful analysis of Kierkegaard's authorship, arguing that the purpose of pseudonyms is to evoke introspection in his readers. The pseudonyms, he says, push the reader to reflect upon him/herself instead of the author, since the pseudonymous author would be unknown while Kierkegaard and his personality might be known. Further, his past writings might enter into the reader's interpretation while reading and influence the reader's thinking, while an unknown would have no reputation, making the work to stand alone and forcing the reader to reflect back upon his/her own life. Kierkegaard employs various authors "to engage his reader in a Socratic dialogue that will issue in a more profound self-awareness and a more complete realization of selfhood."[31] Recall that D. Z. Phillips argued that Kierkegaard's goal is to clarify Danish thinking and stopped there. The first aspect of Phillips's goal is in accord with Taylor's understanding here, yet Taylor's view is expanded and extended. For Taylor, Kierkegaard's intention includes transforming the ways people live as well as the ways they think. He suggests that "the most important aspect of his writings is the change that they occasion in the lives of his readers."[32]

Kierkegaard hopes that the intimate details revealed by the various pseudonyms will enable the reader to become involved in the show by identifying with the subjectivity of the character in the book or the pseudonymous author. He uses pseudonyms so that he can construct characters and authors rich with experiences and opinions that will engage various types of readers. This way he is not limited to his own particular experiences or his particular type of self.

Taylor agrees that Kierkegaard is providing guidance for the reader's edification through establishing various authors exemplifying different types of selfhood:

> By developing an edifying philosophy, Kierkegaard attempted to call people back to themselves by providing the occasion for the self-consciousness necessary for autonomous individuality…In his aesthetic authorship, he creates contrasting personae who project imaginary worlds. Each of the pseudonymous texts embodies a different form of life. The style of writing reflects the style of life and vice versa.[33]

A variety of pseudonyms can reveal intimate details of a variety of different persons' lives, not just Kierkegaard's own, for the sake of evoking a subjective effect from persons at different stages along life's

---

[31] Taylor, *Kierkegaard's Pseudonymous Authorship*, 343.
[32] Ibid.
[33] Mark C. Taylor, *Imagologies: Media Philosophy* (New York: Routledge, 1994) 2-3.

way. For instance, in the "Diary of the Seducer" we read the diary of an aesthetic person with a peek into his inner life. Kierkegaard emphasizes the vivid real-life experience in hopes of evoking identification with this character, which he hopes will in turn evoke a personal evaluation of the reader's own subjectivity and her own location in one or many of the spheres. In other words, Kierkegaard wants the reader to ask herself which sphere is dominant in her inner life and grapple with her own answers.

Thus, Taylor argues that Kierkegaard's pseudonyms are effective in inciting the reader's involvement in the conversation because the pseudonyms focus the reader's attention away from the author and onto the reader herself: "[T]he movement of the pseudonymous works is always away from the author and toward the reader. In writing the pseudonymous works, Kierkegaard seeks to withdraw his own person as far as possible from his works."[34]

This is a helpful conclusion about Kierkegaard's motive in utilizing pseudonyms, since it highlights Kierkegaard's concern with affecting the life of his reader. And Taylor's analysis is intriguing on many points, yet it does not account for all the variables. Taylor says that the pseudonyms function to draw the reader's attention away from the author—to get the reader to ignore the author. However, Kierkegaard's choices for pseudonyms are quite distracting—Hilarius Bookbinder, Johannes the Seducer, Anti-Climacus. The characters that Kierkegaard creates to "edit" and "author" his books are quite full of personality—they steal the show, so to speak. It seems more likely that Kierkegaard highlights the pseudonymous authors in order to direct the reader to the overall form of each work. Further, the names of the authors also suggest the relationship of the authors to each other in the grand dialectic that makes up Kierkegaard's authorship. He may be trying to distance his person from his writings, but Kierkegaard is not trying to hide the identity of the

---

[34] Taylor, *Pseudonymous Authorship*, 58.

pseudonymous authors. He chooses pseudonyms that definitely create an image of the author. These images are obviously not in the likeness of Kierkegaard himself; rather, they are fantastic characters/authors. This interpretation fits with the idea that Kierkegaard wants to create various types of authors, which he believes will make it easier for various types of persons to identify with them. He wants to reach persons in each of the spheres. He speaks to this strategy of his pseudonymous authorship when he writes:

> [I]f real success is to attend the effort to bring a man to a definite position, one must first of all take pains to find him where he is and begin there...In order to help another effectively I must understand more than he—yet first of all surely I must understand what he understands. If I do not know that, my greater understanding will be of no help to him.[35]

Taylor's assertion that the pseudonyms serve to direct the reader's attention away from Kierkegaard's own personal life is insightful.[36] I agree with Taylor's argument here and want to develop it further.

Kierkegaard as filmmaker/director

Allow a heuristic analogy. Kierkegaard is a bit like a nineteenth century filmmaker, with some of the same purposes as a filmmaker. He is like Oliver Stone, who creates a subjective experience in order to make a comment on our society in hopes of impacting individuals

---

[35] Kierkegaard, *The Point of View*, 27.
[36] Yet I also wonder if Kierkegaard is not also, and even primarily, creating different personae that hide the character of the actual author from himself, not just other readers. It is not only others that he seeks to engage, but himself as well. His practice of reading aloud to himself sermons and discourses that he had written supports this possibility.

in such a way that they will change their values, or like Francis Ford Coppola, who directed *Apocalypse Now*. In his self-analysis of the film, Ford Coppola says, "*Apocalypse Now* is not a film about Vietnam, it is Vietnam."[37] I believe Coppola is referring to his employment of incongruity in the film to effect incongruity in the spectator's experience. In this film he places familiar occurrences in alien environments. For instance, he shows surfboarding on a beach that is being attacked by mortar fire. He engages these contradictory elements as a technique to communicate the experience of the American soldier's experience of illogic and contradiction in the war in Vietnam. He wants the viewer to experience the anxiety and radical contradiction that the veteran experienced. He wants the viewer to ask, what would I have felt in that situation?

Kierkegaard could have said the same thing about his aesthetic works, for instance, *Either/Or* A is not an essay about the aesthetic sphere; it is the aesthetic sphere. I mean that reading the essays of author A is becoming an aesthete, for a time. The pseudonymous editor, the authors, the vagueness of how many authors contributed, the general format of the text, and the literary style are all significant aspects of the way Kierkegaard communicates his intention. C. Stephen Evans posits a similar idea in saying, "the pseudonymous characters do not merely tell us about the existence-spheres. They live out those spheres, within the realms of the imagination, naturally, not as actual fact."[38] I agree that the reader lives out the spheres as an internal effect that Kierkegaard hopes to generate within the reader. The first volume of *Either/Or* is written in the form of multiple author-styles, contents, and positions. The lengths of the entries range from one line to fifty pages; the styles fluctuate from stories, to essays, to arguments, to diary entries; the tones vary from

---

[37] Opening quote from the film, *Hearts of Darkness*, a film about the epoch making of *Apocalypse Now*. *Hearts of Darkness: A Filmmaker's Apocalypse,* directed by Fax Bahr and George Hickenlooper (Hollywood CA: Paramount Pictures, 1991).

[38] C. Stephen Evans, *Fragments and Postscript*, 14.

comedy to sorrow and unemotional; the content includes music, seduction, martyrdom and wisdom. There is no clear, singular connecting theme to provide a natural organization to the papers called A. This disunited form is a major aspect of what Kierkegaard communicates. He gives the reader a taste of being an aesthete. The reader may ask: are all these various essays and one-liners actually from one author? Kierkegaard uses the assortment of differences in his pseudonymous authors to create an experience of the discontinuity of the aesthete's pseudo-subjectivity.

Paying attention to the form of what Kierkegaard is doing in his authorship is a fruitful approach to grasping his meaning. This focus is indicated in the monogram to *Fear and Trembling*. In it he writes "What Tarquinius Superbus spoke in his garden with the poppies was understood by his son but not by the messenger."[39] The story to which this monogram refers tells that the king communicated indirectly to his son by walking in the garden and lobbing off the heads of the tallest poppies indicating that the son should kill the highest leaders under him. The king and the son knew to attend to the form or what was being done because the words were either a cover or misdirection. Perhaps Kierkegaard is communicating to his readers that we should pay attention to what he is doing and the form of his writing, not just the content of his works. And the form of Kierkegaard's writing is viewed best from the standpoint of the authorship as a whole. From the distance of a filmmaker, the characters and story lines come together in a way that gives the whole film its meaning. Merold Westphal highlights Kierkegaard's own understanding of his pseudonymous authorships as likened to the production of a play or novel. Kierkegaard says, "all poetic creativity would *eo ipso* be made impossible or meaningless and intolerable if

---

[39] Kierkegaard, *Fear and Trembling* trans. Walter Lowrie, 21. See also Kierkegaard, *Fear and Trembling,* trans. and ed. Howard V. Hong and Edna H. Hong, 3: "What Tarquinius Superbus said in the garden by means of the poppies, the son understood but the messenger did not."

the lines [spoken by such characters] were supposed to be the producer's own words."[40] Westphal suggests that Kierkegaard does not have a mysterious or devious purpose for using pseudonyms, but is simply differentiating himself as the producer of the texts. He sees the pseudonyms as a part of Kierkegaard's "deliberate attempt to disappear."[41] Kierkegaard, like a film maker, doesn't want the viewer/reader to be distracted by the presence of the director, but to become absorbed in the subjective experiences happening on the screen and in the story.

Kierkegaard's *The Point of View of My Work as an Author* declares that he employs aesthetic writing for an ethical effect all as a part of his religious vocation:

> How far a so-called aesthetic public has found or may find enjoyment in reading...the productions of an aesthetic character, which are an incognito and a deceit in the service of Christianity, is naturally a matter of indifference to me; for I am a religious writer. Supposing that such a reader understands perfectly and appraises critically the individual aesthetic productions, he will nevertheless totally misunderstand me, in as much as he does not understand the religious totality in my whole work as an author. Suppose, then, that another understands my works in the totality of their religious reference but does not understand a single one of the aesthetic productions contained in them—I would say that this lack of understanding is not an essential lack.[42]

He describes his purpose in writing as "a religious author to employ aesthetics...."[43] Kierkegaard wants to communicate with the

---

[40] Quoted in Merold Westphal, *Becoming a Self* (West Lafayette IN: Purdue University Press, 1996) 7-8.
[41] Westphal, *Becoming a Self*, 4.
[42] Kierkegaard, *The Point of View*, 6.
[43] Ibid., 17.

aesthetic on the aesthetics' own level, in terms of an aesthetic context of values and perspectives.[44] Kierkegaard wants to reach persons who are in the aesthetic and ethical spheres, and evoke within these readers existential awareness and process. He wants them to move toward becoming subjective. He feels that it is his religious vocation to communicate with persons not yet living in the religious spheres. He realizes that speaking directly about religious values will not affect that which he hopes to effect. He must understand what is understood by the person within which he wants to effect this change. He writes aesthetically to meet the aesthete where she is and push her toward a leap—a leap of subjectivity.

The Dialectic of Multiple Voices and Internal Relation

In this section I continue to build on the insights and interpretations above and upon my critiques of these thinkers in arguing that the processive form of truth and of subjectivity as revealed in the dialectical character of his thought is the hinge pin upon which his understanding of subjectivity hangs. If we examine the authorship as a whole, we note that he writes under a variety of pen names including his own name, which might suggest a discontinuity. Yet he also writes a single text that addresses his view of the unifying point, a single goal, of all of the texts of his authorship. The best way to interpret his authorship is to take it as a whole, together and with special attention to the form of what he is doing (vis-à-vis Tarquinius) and the effects that he hopes to have (to communicate the religious meaning of the beautiful object of his aesthetic skill). The form of Kierkegaard's work, which is an important aspect of his meaning, can be seen best when special attention is paid to the interplay of these fictional writers. Kierkegaard's concept of dialectical subjectivity as elucidated in the

---

[44] This is like Paul Tillich's answering theology, which sees God as coming to humanity where humanity is to solve the real problems of being human.

previous chapter gives a clue to understanding the relational form of his authorship. His purpose in employing pseudonymous authors is to illustrate that truth is subjectivity. The subjectivity aspect of this equation is revealed in his discussion and illustrations of the spheres and in the dialectic of their relating. The truth aspect of this equation is revealed by his employment of pseudonyms to illustrate that truth cannot be communicated in direct theories, but only in the dialectic perspective that allows for the inter-relationality and the processive becoming that is characteristic of Kierkegaard's dialectic. The dynamic and relational nature of this dialectic becomes obvious when we shift our attention away from what the content says and toward how it is said, highlighting the form and interplay of the authorship.

The connecting element of all of Kierkegaard's works is a revolution in theological anthropology. Religious selfhood is the foundation of every word he writes. His Christian psychology is about how a self can and should hold together multiple forces, truths, and concerns. Take Abraham, for example, who must join his love for the finite in Isaac with the divine command to sacrifice Isaac all within the context of the ethical/universal demands upon him. Abraham does not erase one for the other. He follows the divine command, but this action does not annul his fatherly love. Both are held together in tension. This paradigm illustrates the type of unity Kierkegaard advocates. This unity is not blended into a "milkshake" in one person. More like a stir-fry, this unity of self is constituted by the dialectic of multivalency. The aspects are distinguished from each other, yet they affect each other in their relationship.

His employment of pseudonyms demonstrates the non-univocality of his work, his thought, and his concept of selfhood. The self is the reflexive relation of the various spheres, pseudonyms, and ontological elements. There is a direct correlation between this dialectic and the one that is discussed in *Sickness Unto Death*: it's "the relation's relating itself to itself."[45] This profound insight is the essential storyline that runs through all of Kierkegaard's writings. The divergence between the dialectic of "the philosopher" and Kierkegaard's dialectic is found in Kierkegaard's unyielding belief that human reality is not like abstracted theory. Human reality is not yet what it is to become, whereas theory is fixed and systematically unified. Hegel's mistake, thinks Kierkegaard, is not internal to the otherwise brilliant and creative system, but is in the application of this system to signify human reality. It does not capture spirit. The answers it gives are not adequate to the real questions of existence. They are like the elaborate mansion in the sky that is perfectly constructed and quite beautiful to gaze upon but is utterly impractical because there is no way inside. A person cannot live in this systematic mansion. Human reality is becoming. The mode of human selfhood is processive and relational. This mode is so qualitatively different from the mode of systematic thought that the theory cannot capture it or even understand it.

Kierkegaard's vision of human existence, expressed throughout his authorship, pseudonymous and non-pseudonymous, is a vision of movements and relationships within a person's inner life. This inner life is subjectivity, which signifies both the internality of the person and one's relationship to God and the objective facts of one's life. A person's inner life is qualified by the nature of the form of the relationship he/she has with that which is external to the self. We might even say that an individual's inner life is the form of his/her relationship to that which is external to the self. Objectivity is looking at the self from the outside, while subjectivity is looking at it from within.

While other scholars have offered creative and helpful interpretations of Kierkegaard's pseudonyms, highlighting this dialectical context offers the most intriguing and insightful way of

---

[45] Kierkegaard, *The Sickness Unto Death*, 13.

understanding it. D. Z. Phillips, for instance, argues that Kierkegaard utilizes the variety of pseudonymous authors to illustrate the futility of the various philosophical approaches to the truth.[46] This establishes a negative or critical point, namely that the variety of theoretical approaches to the truth does not and cannot get to the truth. I agree that Kierkegaard believes theoretic approaches to the truth fail. But they fail not because of the variety, but because abstract methods can only produce abstract knowledge. To know anything true about actual reality, such as human existence or divine reality, one cannot rely upon a theoretical mode. Theoretical modes are abstractions from the constant flux of reality. Instead, Kierkegaard proposes that "truth is subjectivity." Subjectivity is the form of infinite passion for eternal happiness. Applying his dialectic to understanding selfhood reveals that the nature of concrete human reality is such that it is always in the process of becoming. Being is not fixed or static; rather, its very ontological reality is movement. Existence is not being; it is becoming. Thus, Phillips's interpretation of the pseudonymous authorship as a negative critique of this misapplication of an abstract theoretical knowledge is only part of the Kierkegaardian story. I believe Kierkegaard's purpose is a positive articulation of what and how truth is. This positive articulation of truth by Kierkegaard is indirect and only discerned by standing back and looking at the works of art at a distance. The dialectic of the authors in the context of each other is this positive expression of truth. This context is not directly expressed, but is indirectly implied in Kierkegaard's thought.

When Kierkegaard's works are read together as a whole and the interrelationship of the various authors are highlighted, then his authorship reveals its religious nature by which it also reflects the truth. This truth can be known and is known as the reader interacts

---

[46] Scholars have focused exclusively on the question why does Kierkegaard use pseudonyms. I wonder if we should assume the pseudonyms and ask why Kierkegaard bothers with the writings to which he ascribes his real name.

with each of the authors and allows them to interact with each other. The authors reveal the truth when their various perspectives are taken together as a unity of conflicting elements and conflicting approaches. It is only in this mode of dialectic, that the pseudonymous authors' truth is revealed. In the preface to "Purity of Heart" Kierkegaard tells a parable that expresses this idea. He writes of an artisan who cannot weave the religious meaning into the threads of the altar cloth she sews, for the religious "meaning is in the beholder and the beholder's understanding when, faced with himself and his own self."[47] It is the interaction between the believer and God through the art of the cloth. I could make a similar insight about Kierkegaard as artisan: the religious meaning of his authorship cannot be directly written into the letters, but is found in the reader and the reader's understanding when faced with his/her own self. It is the interaction of the believer/reader and God through the works as a whole. Kierkegaard wants the reader to forget the author of the text and his part in the midst of this existential interaction just as the needlewoman is forgotten.

The developing of a person's subjectivity toward its full becoming is the self. This definition is not to be confused with notions of the empowerment of the self, such as the Army's propaganda, "be all that you can be." Nor is it merely a popular psychology motto that directly advocates the achievement of one's full potential, complete with peak experiences and positive thinking. Rather, Kierkegaard believes becoming a self is the activity of practicing spiritual discipline. It is the becoming of the relation of dipolar elements. One element is grounded in human natural experience, while the other element is constituted beyond the human herself. Both elements must be acknowledged and held together consciously and with a relational equilibrium. This relational

---

[47] Søren Kierkegaard, *Upbuilding Discourses in Various Spirits*, trans. and ed. Howard V. Hong and Edna H. Hong (Princeton, NJ: Princeton University Press, 1993) 5.

equilibrium is only possible in self-conscious relation with God. Kierkegaard's writings on selfhood are indirect communications for the desired purpose of evoking a process toward subjectivity in which a person can become aware of these existential elements and be motivated to relate them together in a balanced way, all toward becoming oneself and becoming a Christian. Kierkegaard is articulating a theological or spiritual process of becoming a Christian. This process is the most difficult of all things, he says. Becoming a Christian entails becoming subjective, a process that does not correspond to emotional or psychological maturation, but rather is spiritual maturation spoken of in the New Testament.[48]

For Kierkegaard, self-consciousness and subjectivity occur through an internal dialectic of spirit and matter. This dialectic of faith is the dialectic of becoming subjective, of becoming oneself before God. Recall that in Kierkegaard's dialectic of faith the spirit is in the process of becoming subjective through objectifying itself and then returning to subjectivity. Dupré's elucidation of this dialectic and movement from subjectivity to objectivity is particularly intriguing, and I suggest that the pseudonyms represent objectifications of Kierkegaard's persona.[49] Perhaps they function as means by which he can attain subjectivity, observing them and then returning back to himself. Perhaps Kierkegaard is modeling the process of subjectivity in demonstrating this method of becoming oneself so that others can follow his method toward their own subjectivity.

This dialectic is the key to understanding the intent, effect and structure of Kierkegaard's authorship. It provides the structure and form of his authorship as a whole, for his pseudonymous authorship, his theory of spheres of existence, and for his conceptualization of selfhood. This section integrates my interpretation of Kierkegaard's

---

[48] See, for example, Ephesians 4:13, Hebrews 6:1, and Colossians 4:12.

[49] Dupré, *Kierkegaard as Theologian*, 124.

pseudonymous authorship with my arguments in the previous chapter in which I applied the dialectic to the spheres of existence, concluding in an integrated interpretation of his conceptualization of selfhood. The spheres of existence viewed under this dialectic create a form for the reader to objectify her spirit so that she can then return to the heightened subjectivity of becoming oneself. Kierkegaard equips the reader, who is on her way to becoming subjective in and through his authorship. Kierkegaard's process for becoming oneself, which is becoming subjective, is a dialectic movement between the two poles of subjectivity and objectivity. This dialectic is the paradigm underlying Kierkegaard's authorship—its content, its form, and its purpose. It informs the reason he writes, how he articulates, and what he communicates. He writes not merely in an attempt to enter an engaging philosophical conversation about truth, faith, subjectivity, etcetera, with the Danish readers of his day. Rather, he writes by a sense of calling, almost coercive in its unrelenting demand on the time and energy of his short life. He self-consciously writes to express his spirit in objective words, thus providing the objective pole of his dialectic of becoming subjective, of spirit becoming itself.

Perhaps his authorship also functions to unite Kierkegaard's own various inner parts/voices by objectifying these elements of his subjectivity so that he can reintegrate them at a higher immediacy into his spirit. These are parts of his personality and mind that he knows only through his imagination and with the pseudonyms gives physical voice and reality to them. Following the dialectic structure of Kierkegaard's understanding of faith's movement, the process is as follows: spirit posits itself objectively and then returns to subjectivity changed. Viewing Kierkegaard's own authorship as following the structure of this dialectic, we can see that his spirit posits itself objectively in the words and ideas of the characters and sphere of his pseudonymous authorship. Then his spirit returns to subjectivity when he reads his objectified thoughts. This return occurs through Kierkegaard's use of a highly experiential form and technique geared toward evoking subjectivity in his reader, which in this case is him. Viewing Kierkegaard's pseudonymous authorship as the objectification of his spirit so that he can then return it to the heightened subjectivity of becoming oneself takes seriously his dialectic and yields a complex view of subjectivity—his and ours.

He asks for the use of the imagination from his reader. The imagination, that would enable humans to fly if they would only use it, instead of waddling home after the sermon, like the "Tame Geese" in his delightful parody of Hans Christian Andersen's story. If the reader will employ his imagination, Kierkegaard will create for him the experience of another's perspective of subjectivity. This experience, while not efficacious by itself, is a catalyst toward experiencing and engaging one's own subjectivity.

The aesthetic form of Kierkegaard's pseudonymous works serves to hook the reader into his imagination. Kierkegaard meets his reader where he lives and gets him to identify with the characters in his writings. The intended effect of the aesthetic means that Kierkegaard employs in his pseudonymous works is to evoke subjectivity. He enables and even manipulates his reader to see herself in the character—to notice where the character ends up and to evaluate what sort of existential relationship the reader has with this character. In other words, the reader asks herself: what form of existence is dominant in my own life? In reflecting upon her own sphere of existence, the reader clarifies whether or not she is living as one in the religious sphere or only thinks that she has been, and now realizes that she is actually living in the aesthetic sphere or the ethical sphere. She is shown what she must do to truly be in the religious sphere, or rather, more Kierkegardianly, how she must do it—in subjectivity. He is trying to communicate a subjective experience, or an experience of subjectivity. He knows that it can't be done directly, and so he uses his creativity to experiment on how to share or even approximate subjectivity. He writes with a literary style, hiding his own authorial identity.

Kierkegaard's concerns do not stop with this clarification of thinking; rather, Kierkegaard's indirection seeks to manipulate his individual reader's lifestyle and sphere of existence, moving her (and moving her toward Christianity). Kierkegaard's aesthetic works are prerequisites for entering the religious sphere. Before being able to live religiously, an individual must become subjective—self-conscious.[50] But how can another's subjectivity be enabled? Only through indirect discourse is religious persuasion possible. As I mentioned above, indirect discourse is speaking with symbols instead of direct clear words. As Tillich reminds us, symbols participate in the reality they represent and are efficacious for those who participate in the symbol.[51] Kierkegaard's indirection utilizes the efficacy of the symbolic mode of communication. He unlocks dimensions of reality and of the reader's soul that would otherwise be closed.[52]

George Pattison posits the idea that Kierkegaard's authorship is an attempt at making Regina, his absent lover, present as his dialogue partner.[53] Perhaps his authorship is actually an attempt to give all the characters of his imagination life, presence, and in a sense "objective reality." And in so doing, he provides an aid to his reader in her attempt to posit herself objectively and return to her higher, reflective subjectivity. In addition, Kierkegaard posits his own spirit objectively, so that he can then return to the higher immediacy of subjectivity given in Dupré's analysis of the dialectic of faith.

The pseudonymous authorship is also a way in which Kierkegaard brings together all the spheres. The spheres and the pseudonyms are explicitly connected in *The Point of View of My Work as an Author*. Kierkegaard's pseudonymous authorship is an aesthetic form, and its effect is religious: "the productions of an aesthetic character,

---

[50] Friedrich Schleiermacher argues for this prerequisite also.
[51] Paul Tillich, *Dynamics of Faith* (New York: Perennial Classics, 2001) 42.
[52] Ibid.
[53] George Pattison, speech, Kierkegaard Society Dinner at the annual American Academy of Religion meeting (Philadelphia PA, 1994).

which are an incognito and a deceit in the service of Christianity."[54] Kierkegaard is saying that his authorship is both aesthetic and religious at the same time. This authorship is like the self, his own self and the self of his reader: multiple and internally related to itself. The authorship as a whole is complex, multivalent, full of contradictions and relationships. The different authors are related to each other like the spheres are related to each other—dialectically and internally—within Kierkegaard himself and within the reader. The whole of Kierkegaard's writing is in the form of a dialogue among and between the various authors and the reader. The authors engage each other and the reader. The authorship is in the service of the religious; it bonds all three spheres of existence in an intricate dance of coming together and separating. The authorship is structured like the subjectivity of the religious sphere, which is structured in terms of the dialectic in *Sickness Unto Death*. Kierkegaard claims that truth must give precedence to the truth of the existing individual, which "is a synthesis of the infinite and the finite, and the existing individual is both infinite and finite."[55] This dialectic is the contradictory elements of existence brought into dialogue with each other. The human consists of several pairs of non-harmonious elements in existence brought into dialogue with each other. The human consists of these two fundamentally different states: the infinite and the finite. These two elements are in relation to each other, but cannot be reduced one to the other. Neither can the relation of these elements be reduced to a singularity. The self is not the stagnant relation, but is the relating itself. The form of subjectivity is thus processive, dialectical, and relational. The pseudonyms are structured in this way and are related to each other dialectically. Further, the pseudonyms are implicitly and explicitly related to the spheres. Explicitly in Kierkegaard's articulation, and

---

[54] Kierkegaard, *The Point of View*, 6.

[55] Kierkegaard, *Concluding Unscientific Postscript*, trans. and ed. Howard V. Hong and Edna H. Hong, 1:350.

implicitly in that they share the same dialectical structure. All of these dimensions of Kierkegaard's thought point to a conceptualization of selfhood as processive, dialectical, relational, and multiple.

In conclusion, I have argued that this "multi-sphered" conception of human selfhood in the context of a dialectic relationality among the elements of existence provides the structure for Kierkegaard's whole authorship, including both his pseudonymous works and those written under his own name. Although most scholars divide Kierkegaard's pseudonymous authorship from his genuine works, I have argued that both sets of works, and every word of every work, all have the same purpose: to articulate and communicate that "Truth is Subjectivity." He could not have written any fewer words and still communicated the same profundity of truth. Kierkegaard himself acknowledges this integrity to his work. Bretall tells us that in *The Point of View for my Work as an Author*, Kierkegaard "tells us that the whole of his authorship centers about this one question." And this question is: what is it to become a Christian?[56] The answer is found in his writings, in the content, the form, the development, and the dialectic movement of the words and the works, the authors and the themes.

I have pulled out many implications for Kierkegaard's understanding of selfhood. The reality of human existence is a constant process of becoming. The human self moves, or rather the self is the moving itself. It is a dialectic structured by sets of two poles: the finite and the infinite,[57] which are constantly moving and reflexively relating. It is propelled by the tension of maintaining the active relationship of these two poles. The elements are related in a polar way—neither can be lost or absorbed into the other without

---

[56] Robert Bretall, ed. *A Kierkegaard Anthology* (New York: The Modern Library, 1970) xxii.

[57] I have chosen only one set, the finite and infinite to illustrate the workings for the sake of clarity.

dire consequences. The first pole is the earthly existence of the particular individual, the temporal. The second is the transcendent pole of the infinite, the eternal. It is by the dialectical relationship of these poles that Kierkegaard says the human is constituted outside of itself.

Life for the authentic and earnest individual consists of walking in this tension, with one foot in the finite and the other in the infinite, stepping on and on through the decisions one makes toward becoming oneself. This dialectic of Kierkegaard is the "walk of life."

Kierkegaard sees pure aesthetic existence as the possibility of ignoring the second pole and of living in the moment without awareness or attention to either the transcendent constitution of oneself or to the process of becoming that is essential to full human existence. This person, says Kierkegaard, is in despair at not willing to be oneself.[58] She/he refuses to participate in the decisions necessary for becoming who one is to become and has stalled his/her spiritual development in an immediate and abstracted posture. Likewise, ignoring the first pole and hopping through existence in the pole of infinite resignation leaves one stuck in the ethical realm, without a passionate relation to the absolute. This person is in despair and knows she is in despair and is resigned to it. And then there is the third sphere, the religious sphere, which requires both feet to take a running leap into faith.

Kierkegaard elucidates on this theme throughout his authorship. Becoming oneself means becoming subjective, which entails becoming aware of one's inner life and participating in the decisions of living throughout this hike upon the uneven terrain, which is the task of becoming a Christian.

Kierkegaard's reinterpretation and transformation of theological anthropology subverts the embedded assumptions of oneness and

---

[58] See Kierkegaard, *The Sickness Unto Death,* trans. and ed. Howard V. Hong and Edna H. Hong.

uniformity in the traditional philosophical theories about selfhood. It enables us to think of variety and conflict as appropriate elements of the human self that are innate, natural and not a result of sin or sickness.

I have pulled out the implications of Kierkegaard's thought, his literary style of pseudonyms, his use of indirection, and his religious purposes as they relate to selfhood. I have highlighted his explicit accounts of what it means to be a self. Then I have woven these interpretations together into a complex, yet coherent "Kierkegaardian" theory of selfhood. This conceptualization is multifaceted itself and demonstrates not only the viability of a theory of selfhood that includes multiplicity and internal relationality, but also the superiority of such a view. Now I want to weave a new conceptualization of selfhood, using some of the threads of this dialectic of relationality and other threads of Irigaray's constructive insights into the importance of multiplicity and difference, into a more adequate and effective theory of selfhood that enables multiplicity and relationality.

4

Irigaray's Critique of the Economy of the Same

In the last chapters we have examined how Kierkegaard's conceptualization of the self differs from the patriarchal proclivity toward uniformity of selfhood. Kierkegaard posits a three-tiered structure to individual existence, consisting in the aesthetic sphere, the ethical sphere, and the religious sphere. Then he employs various and sometimes contradictory pseudonymous authors to entice his readers to identify with these author(s), which, in turn, manipulates the reader to identify with these various viewpoints representing the three spheres of existence. His authorship culminates in bringing these variegated views together, while holding them in tension without collapsing any of them into the other, or a common synthesis, or into a universal singularity. And lastly and most importantly for our project here, we have seen that these various spheres and pseudonyms are voices of human existence that are interrelated to and with each other, internally as well as externally. Kierkegaard's dialectic of faith is the overall structure of this relationality. He says, "the progress of becoming must be an infinite moving away from itself in the infinitizing of the self, and an infinite coming back to itself in the finitizing process."[1] The subject must posit itself or "project" itself into objectivity. Once the subject recognizes itself reflexively as this object, it also becomes aware that objectivity is not the proper mode of the spirit, and so it returns to

---

[1] Søren Kierkegaard, *The Sickness Unto Death*, trans. and ed. Howard V. Hong and Edna H. Hong (Princeton NJ: Princeton University Press, 1980) 30.

subjectivity. Yet returning it brings with it something of the objectivity it has now become.[2] This dialectical movement is the movement of the spheres within each person; it is also the movement of Kierkegaard's authorship itself. The pseudonyms that make up his authorship are related to each other and are best interpreted in light of this dialectical network.

I will return to this dialectical structure later in my constructive endeavor. The dialectical nature of the relationship of the polar elements that constitute the self and give form to the interplay of the spheres of existence and between Kierkegaard's pseudonyms is one of the core insights that I employ in my constructive conceptualization of multiplicity of selfhood. I also employ his notion of reflexivity of the relating of the parts to each other and to the whole in my constructive work below.

Kierkegaard's theological anthropology offers an alternative to the normative conceptualization of the self that is found in the Western philosophical and theological traditions. He is critical of the thought of particular thinkers and the general trends in these traditions, that define human existence as static, completed, and able to be systematized. Yet his critiques are not thorough going in scope or depth, nor is that his intention. While Kierkegaard's context and geographical location places him on the northern boundary of the Germanic-Anglo continental tradition, his thinking is still shaped by the patterns and configurations of Western discourse. He does not question the embedded assumptions upon which this tradition is built. Irigaray, however, does challenge and critique these assumptions directly in scope, depth and intention. She scours the tradition both past and present for its problematic assumptions.

Awareness of this alternative viewpoint within the tradition indicates the complexity and richness within the Western

---

[2] Louis Dupré, *Kierkegaard as Theologian, the Dialectic of Christian Existence* (New York: Sheed and Ward, 1963).

philosophical discourse. It gives us a stronghold in both our critique of the embedded assumptions about singularity and selfhood as well as enabling greater continuity in our conversations about what it means to be a self. It is a strategy that serves the current endeavor well by maintaining the lines of continuity within the history of the tradition. Alternative viewpoints have not been totally absent or completely repressed, giving us access to the language and insights that have come before us, and also giving us dependable shoulders upon which to stand so that we can see further.

I seek to construct a theory of multiple selfhood that utilizes and integrates Kierkegaard's insights into the dynamic reflexively-relational understanding of subjectivity on the one hand, with the insights of Irigaray's recovery of the lost feminine as multiple genuinely different, and embodied on the other.

The following two chapters explicate Irigaray's vantage point on the issue of multiplicity of self. We begin with her critique of the unspoken assumptions within Western discourse that inhibit multiplicity and difference. She not only critiques the dominant metaphysics that has constructed and maintained an emphasis on oneness and uniformity, she also offers a feminist reconstruction of selfhood that enables multiplicity. Her constructive work highlights plurality, fluidity, difference and the self's connection with the body, elements which are lacking in Kierkegaard's analysis.

Irigaray is primarily interested in enabling genuine feminine difference that can be known by women and expressed in the culture as a whole. She critiques the dominant discourse as phallocentric—male-centered, made for men, by men, and of men. In this system women are oppressed and the feminine itself is repressed. She employs several terms for this system including phallocentrism, phallogocentricism and phallocraticism. According to Elizabeth Grosz in *Jacques Lacan: A Feminist Introduction*, "phallocentrism" refers to both the "over-valuation of the male sex organ" as well as to the "continuing submersion of women's autonomy in the norms, ideals, and models devised by men."[3] Phallogocentricism is a collusion between phallocentrism and logocentrism, which claims a central or transcendental signifier or guarantee for all meanings.[4] It also indicates a hierarchical dichotomy between the signifier and the signified. In other words, it is the tendency in Western thought to view words as more important than that to which they refer. I will also employ Irigaray's term "phallocratic" when discussing male-centered/male-dominated systems, institutions, and politics.

Irigaray's critical work contributes to my critical analysis of the exultation of oneness implicit in Western thought through her explicit articulation of that which has been unspoken, either because it is assumed as normative (phallocentric presuppositions) or because it has been repressed and has no language by which to communicate (the lost feminine).

While her work is distinct from mine in that it exclusively addresses women and the feminine, her critique is a helpful foundation for my analysis of the embedded assumptions in the dominant discourse concerning oneness. Here I explicate her creative and fecund methods for getting at the hidden assumptions in Western discourse and the fruits of her analysis. Then I pull out the implications for my own critique and apply them to my discussion of theological anthropology from a feminist perspective. Her insights help us to address the three primary problems with the exaltation of oneness addressed in the introduction of this book.

In this chapter I explore Irigaray's challenge to Western discourse, especially her critique and employment of Sigmund Freud and Jacques Lacan, and apply them to my analysis of the embedded assumptions concerning theories of the self. In the next chapter I address Irigaray's constructive work, highlighting her strategies

---

[3] Elizabeth Grosz, *Jacques Lacan: A Feminist Introduction* (New York: Routledge, 1990) 174.

[4] See Jacques Derrida, *Of Grammatology*, trans. Gayatri Chakravorty Spivak (Baltimore: Johns Hopkins University Press, 1974) 49.

toward enabling and encouraging genuine sexual difference. She explores several characteristics and forms that are most conducive to the feminine, such as fluidity, multiplicity, bodily connection, and permeability. My critical analysis of the current dominant theories of selfhood focus on the embedded assumptions concerning oneness and sameness. Irigaray's analysis focuses on the phallocentrism of the current dominant discourse and its repression of the feminine. Our analyses dovetail in focusing on the detrimental repression of difference and highlighting the beneficial possibilities of multiplicity.

Brief Introduction to Irigaray

Like Kierkegaard, Luce Irigaray is a complex thinker who is unable to be categorized into one discipline. She began her academic career as a linguist, writing about the differences between women and men with regards to language. She is also a psychoanalyst, trained in Lacan's school, *École Freudienne de Paris,* and a literary theorist. She is what Margaret Whitford describes as a *"feminist philosopher* with the emphasis on *both* terms."[5] Her philosophical project is twofold: to critically examine the theoretical presuppositions that undergird Western discourse, and to give voice to that which had been oppressed and repressed into cultural unconsciousness. Her attention is primarily focused on those assumptions and claims about women and the feminine. Her goal is to allow genuine feminine symbols, language, and subjectivity to exist and be explicitly expressed, enabling women and society to experience, think, and speak genuine sexual difference. Her method is akin to a psychoanalyst's approach of uncovering the unspoken logic that governs the way the analysand, or patient, interprets reality and behaves socially. She applies these techniques to her "analysis" of Western society and discourse. Sticking with the metaphor, like a psychoanalyst, she seeks to elicit

---

[5] Margaret Whitford, *Philosophy in the Feminine* (New York City: Routledge, 1991) 3.

the overt expression of that which has been repressed. She both critiques the masquerade of phallocentrism's hegemonic claims to the one singular truth and highlights constructive images and symbols of feminine subjectivity. Both her critical and constructive work functions like the work of a psychoanalyst by examining unconscious resistances, highlighting that which has been repressed, and helping to construct a new self, a rediscovered, uncovered and transformed subject-hood for women.

Irigaray's writings are not systematic or organized in a linear fashion. This form is part of her approach and message. This style and the fact that much of her texts in English have been made available in compilations of articles and essays originally written at different times and contexts, makes grasping her insights difficult at times. To combat this obstacle, I am pulling out and organizing some of her insights in a more systematic configuration. However, please keep in mind that this structure is imposed upon Irigaray's thought for our heuristic purposes. To be clear, I do not think that this structure is an improvement upon Irigaray, quite the opposite. It lessens the creativity and efficaciousness of her work, making it more difficult to appreciate the full impact of her radicality by adding a step between the immediate experience of the fragmentation of syntax and language and the pluralization of discourse. Yet I think that stating her points in this more familiar format is helpful in the process of analyzing her work for my purposes as long as the reader is exposed to her own words and syntax in the form of direct quotes. And so with this caveat let's proceed to Irigaray.

Sexual {In}Difference

We have reached a paradigm shift, she proclaims, a new age in which sexual difference is the foremost question. "Sexual difference is one of the major philosophical issues, if not the issue, of our age," is the beginning claim in *The Ethics of Sexual Difference*.[6] Genuine sexual difference has not existed publicly before now. The ecology of phallocentric discourse has prevailed. This discourse is characterized by its exclusive construction by the male, for the male, and about the male. In contrast to this economy of the Same, Irigaray seeks to build completely new foundations for a society of difference. Everything must be re-evaluated. Attempts at simply equalizing economic and political power and other concerns of women's struggles for liberation will only lead back to an economy which values sameness unless the entire system is restructured. A revolution is needed "to reinterpret everything concerning the relations between the subject and discourse, the subject and the world, the subject and the cosmic, the microcosmic and the macrocosmic."[7]

Unlike many liberal political feminists, Irigaray does not try to erase sexual difference into a world of equality with men. Working toward such equality reinforces the belief that the male is the standard to which women should be equal. This endeavor could lead women into becoming just like men, which would entail women loosing or never finding that which is uniquely feminine. To "suppress sexual difference is to invite genocide" of women.[8] Rather than this approach, Irigaray seeks to elucidate a theory of genuine specificity and autonomy of women's sexuality. Unlike other French feminists, she is not interested in dissolving personal identity that is based on sex. Rather, Irigaray wishes to establish for women, an identity of one's own, on women's own terms and from women's own foundation.

She starts with the claim that Western culture, society and discourse is patriarchal. She highlights the way that patriarchy not

---

[6] Luce Irigaray, "Sexual Difference," in *The Ethics of Sexual Difference* (Ithaca NY: Cornell University Press, 1993) 5.

[7] Ibid., 6.

[8] Luce Irigaray, "Equal or Different?" in *The Irigaray Reader*, ed. Margaret Whitford (Malden MA: Blackwell Publishers, 1991) 32.

only oppresses women, but also represses the feminine itself. Women are not in a position to be aware of their own feminine self, their own feminine modes of experiencing, of knowing, of thinking, of writing, of speaking, of desiring, of loving, of having sexual and sensuous pleasure, put generally—of being. The feminine has been repressed in women's own individual consciousness, as well as for the whole society.

With this repression of the feminine all types of genuine difference are repressed as well. This repression has led to what she labels "the *economy of the Same*," which is an overarching system that governs the laws of operation of all aspects of existence: personal, social, and political. It is a "project of diversion, deflection, reduction of the other in the Same,"[9] and gives "*a priori* value to Sameness."[10] The economy of the Same is an embedded and systemic institution that operates overtly as well as having become so much apart of our ideology that it is also effective below our awareness.

Irigaray's project to enable a society of genuine sexual difference entails both critique and construction. She critiques the phallocentric discourse that led to the economy of the Same and also discerns of and builds up the qualities and forms of genuine feminine difference. Her techniques intertwine philosophical analysis of psychoanalysis and psychoanalysis of philosophy, paying special attention to the structure and function of language and to that which is unspoken. Both philosophy and psychoanalysis focus on the "process of interpretive rereading."[11] Psychoanalysis's techniques of examining the underside of operations reveal the assumed structures of phallocentric discourse itself. Beginning by evaluating the power of discourse, she says, "it is indeed precisely philosophical discourse that

---

[9] Luce Irigaray, "The Power of Discourse and the Subordination of the Feminine," in *This Sex Which is Not One* (Ithaca NY: Cornell University Press, 1985) 74.

[10] Ibid.,72.

[11] Ibid., 75.

we have to challenge and disrupt."[12] Irigaray discovers that phallocentric discourse derives its power, its *"position of mastery"*[13] from its ability and desire to "eradicate the difference between the sexes"[14] and *"reduce all others to the economy of the Same."*[15] The logic of the Same is based on the claim that *the one* is an absolute norm. The repression of sexual difference produces and perpetuates the economy of the Same in which all difference is repressed and all those who are different are oppressed.

Irigaray's analysis reveals the gender associations embedded in Western discourse's exclusive construction of the logic of the Same. She also demonstrates the problematic and disturbing results of the emphasis upon the One. She sees a direct correspondence between the derivative status of woman as "the other" in Western discourse and the elimination/extermination of any and all real difference in discourse and culture. In a society with "others" as aliens who are not real, being different from the normative *one* means depreciation and possible extermination. The one is to the other as male is to female. She claims a clear correspondence between male experience (and sexuality) as it is theorized in psychoanalysis, and the dominant philosophical proclivity toward the one. Femininity is defined in Western thought as a lack, a lack of the penis, a lack of access to the phallus and its power, a lack of active desire, a lack or void that must be filled if the woman is to have any status, identity or satisfaction.

This present establishment, "the economy of the Same," is a phallocentric construct based on the exclusive and inflated value of the phallus. Phallocentric identity is an identity that is centered upon the phallus, and is built upon that which it represses—the feminine. According to Lacan, whom we will examine in depth below, the phallus is identified with *the one* and functions in Western discourse

---

[12] Ibid., 74.
[13] Ibid., 73.
[14] Ibid., 74.
[15] Ibid., 73.

as the master signifier. As master signifier, the phallus is the chief standard by which all other words and concepts take their meaning. The problem with the economy of the Same is not only its foundation, which is this exclusive emphasis on the phallus, but also its effect, which is to exclude, repress, reduce, and destroy difference, especially sexual difference, but also all difference. Within this phallocentric interpretive framework male experience is dominated by a focus on his one penis and his need and desire for another (such as hand or vagina) to stimulate him. Irigaray explicitly shows the positive correlation between male characteristics and what philosophy has construed as the central organizing "*a priori*" principle of truth and value: the One. Likewise she lays out the correlation between what is named as "feminine" characteristics and what philosophy has named as other, as not valuable, and as absence. Phallocentric discourse has limited nearly all expressions of truth, value, and reality to that which conforms to the models of the one, the good, God, unity, and uniformity.

Irigaray's project is to encourage the expression of genuine sexual difference, both on the societal front and with individuals. She believes that the difference between men and women is real, large, and irreducible. However, this "genuine" difference has been obliterated by patriarchy in at least two ways. Phallocentric discourse is the construction of exclusively male experience expression and desire. Women as *subjects* and *thinkers* about the nature and structure of reality are excluded. Second, phallocentric discourse exploits the feminine and women, forcing them into constrained models and positions like a flat mirror upon which the narcissism of maleness is reflected in reverse. Woman and the feminine have become a dumping ground for all the negative characteristics of humanity. Those characters which males want to disavow have been projected upon women and the feminine.

Irigaray evaluates the history of ideas to discern the necessary conditions for the possibility of phallocentric discourse's reign. She finds that the dominant discourse constructs a coherent singular norm of truth and value, an economy of the Same. This emphasis on oneness posits itself by repressing everything else, actually depending upon the repression of the other and the projection of its own negative reflection. It is a binary system that actually functions as a monism of positive reality and its negative opposite.

In *Speculum of the Other Woman* she critically analyzes several classical and contemporary figures of phallocentric discourse whose theories have founded the assumptions about and conceptualizations of the so-called feminine. Her choice of the term speculum indicates a variety of connotations. A "speculum" is an instrument for looking inside the woman, the other. Irigaray seeks to open up what has been closed and hidden and peer inside. It makes a play on the preference for visual stimuli and metaphors in most of the cultural discourse—the specular economy represents a masculine bias, she says. Also she is making a play on "speculative" philosophy and her own fluid methodology of speculating on possibilities for genuine feminine expressions. Beginning with Freud, and working her way "backward" in history to Plato, she evaluates Western thought's explicit and implicit de-valuing of the feminine.

Irigaray utilizes psychoanalysis to deconstruct Western discourse's economy of the Same, "psycho"-analyzing the philosophical assumptions of Western culture's values that lie unquestioned, as she writes:

> This process of interpretive rereading has always been a psycho-analytic undertaking as well. That is why we need to pay attention to the way the unconscious works in each philosophy, and perhaps in philosophy in general. We need to listen (psycho)analytically to its procedures of repression, to the structuration of language that shores up its representations,

separating the true from the false, the meaningful from the meaningless, and so forth.[16]

Here she calls us to evaluate what Western philosophers have repressed and ignored and wanted us not to see or think about. She directs our attention to what they have hidden, and what dynamics and forces lie under their conscious attempts to concoct a coherent uniform narrative of their lives and times.

Freud is particularly pertinent to her analysis of patriarchy. She suggests that Freud actually demonstrates that Western thought is blind to sexual difference. Like many great inventions and innovations, his discovery occurred quite accidentally and even without Freud's conscious awareness of this idea, or of its importance. In studying sexuality Freud stumbled upon an assumption rooted deep within Western thought that has shaped the operations of all of Western discourse even as it remained hidden. This supposition is that it is "*sexual indifference that underlies the truth of any science, the logic of every discourse.*"[17] In other words, Freud, and most other scientists, philosophers, thinkers, do not see two sexes that are different from each other. Rather, the masculine is assumed as a representative for all humanity. And the feminine, if mentioned at all, is "always described in terms of deficiency or atrophy."[18]

Studying Freud's prescriptive description of female ego development, she explicates the philosophical and cultural assumptions that lie at the core of Freud's inception of "the science of Psycho-Analysis," and finds that they are explicitly biased against women and the feminine. Freud's theories reveal many assumptions that are deeply ingrained in Western culture's understanding of the feminine. The most telling examples are found in Freud's discussion of feminine sexual development, the little girl's resolution of the Oedipal

---

[16] Ibid., 75.
[17] Ibid., 69.
[18] Ibid.

complex, and her movement toward becoming a woman. Freud tells us quite matter-of-factly, that the little girl is really a little man. The little girl's psycho-sexual development is far more complicated (and confused) than the little boy's parallel development.[19] The boy needs to accomplish three straightforward tasks in order to resolve the Oedipal complex: first, sublimate his specific choice of love-object, Father's "mother"; second, sublimate his murderous jealousy toward his father; and finally and mostly, just wait. The little boy holds on to the gender of his first love object and simply waits until he grows up and can have a "mother" of his own. The boy also maintains the form of his desire as aggressive and active. He also holds on to the primary erogenous zone of his body where he experiences sexual pleasure, his singular penis.

The little girl, on the other hand, has to change all three of these aspects of her sexuality if she is to even hope to mature and become a woman. As an immature female, Freud tells us that she is like the male: her mother is her first love object; she actively and aggressively desires her; and she focuses her sexual pleasure upon an external organ, her clitoris and the activity of stimulating herself. To come into her femininity, she must renounce the favored zone of sexual pleasure, the clitoris, for the vacuum of the vagina. Secondly, she must also give up her mother as her love object and take her father, repress her love for a female, for the sake of needing a male (but then wait like the little boy until her adulthood). Additionally, she must repress her active and aggressive desire and become a passive participant in sex. The only desire proper to her as a "woman" is the desire to be desired. She can not desire her object in an active or aggressive way. (According to Freud, active desire is a form of sexuality that is inherently masculine and a woman who actively desired her partner would be only mimicking the masculine reality—a male homosexual in the case of a woman who aggressively desired a

---

[19] Just who is confused about it here is ambiguous—the little girl or Freud?

male, and a male heterosexual in the case of a woman who actively desired another woman.) Freud is not even trying to hide his phallocentrism here. It's obvious the little girl is a little man; her clitoral activity is phallic. Further, any form of masturbation is noted by Freud as "masculine activity."[20] Irigaray says of Freud's view of becoming a woman, "the task will consist mainly in recognizing and accepting her atrophied member."[21]

Irigaray's method in *Speculum of the Other Woman* is to simply show us what Freud says, and he convicts himself along with the rest of Western discourse. Freud's view of femininity corresponds to his view of feminine sexuality. The little girl is constituted as a subject by her penis envy, which Freud identifies as the same as "the discovery of the inferiority of the clitoris."[22] This penis envy has several significant negative affects upon the girl as she matures into womanhood. Her attitude to the external reality of men is marked by jealousy, since she is jealous of both what the man has and of the greater affection he receives from Mother because he has what she doesn't. She also develops a natural sense of inferiority and adapts the universal masculine contempt held for women because of the "inferiority of the clitoris." Further, she must disavow her closeness with her mother, since her mother has rejected her for the sake of the penis. These affects continue to be detriments for her as she matures toward womanhood. According to Freud, the ego is comprised of one's identifications, the internalization or introjection of those whom we once loved but from whom we have now withdrawn our emotional

---

[20] Sigmund Freud, "Anatomical Distinction Between the Sexes," in *The Standard Edition of the Complete Psychological Works of Sigmund Freud*, trans. and ed. James Strachey (London: Hogarth Press, 1957) 8:190.

[21] Luce Irigaray, *Speculum of the Other Woman*, trans. Gillian C. Gill (Ithaca NY: Cornell University Press, 1985) 22.

[22] Freud, "Anatomical Distinction Between the Sexes," 8:190.

investment.[23] As the ego develops then for the woman, it is filled with the detrimental affects of the loss of her first love object, the active mode of her desire, and of the pleasure of her own body—in short, her self-abandonment.

Irigaray notes the contribution of Freud's definition of women in terms of penis-envy to maintaining the phallocentric economy of the Same: "If women had desires other than 'penis-envy', this would call into question the unity, the uniqueness, the simplicity of the mirror charged with sending man's image back to him—albeit inverted."[24] Freud's characterization of femininity is really an assertion of masculinity:

> Freud does not see two sexes whose differences are articulated in the act of intercourse, and more generally speaking, in the imaginary and symbolic processes that regulate the workings of a society and a culture. The 'feminine' is always described in terms of deficiency or atrophy, as the other side of the sex that alone holds a monopoly on value: the male sex. Hence the all too well-known 'penis envy.' How can we accept the idea that woman's entire sexual development is governed by her lack of, and thus by her longing for, jealousy of, and demand for, the male organ? Does this mean that woman's sexual evolution can never be characterized with reference to the female sex itself?[25]

Irigaray also shows that the woman's role, as constructed in the phallocentric production of "Reality: Male and Female," is to act as the reverse image of masculine characteristics and identity. This role insures the male players of their singular truth and of the righteousness of their singular self. The repression of the feminine

---

[23] See Sigmund Freud, "Mourning and Melancholia," in *The Standard Edition of the Complete Psychological Works of Sigmund Freud*, vol. 14.

[24] Irigaray, *Speculum of the Other Woman*, 51.

[25] Irigaray, "The Power of Discourse and the Subordination of the Feminine," 69.

enables patriarchy's love affair with the Same (itself). It enables patriarchy to create everything in man's own idealized image—as one.

Sex difference, or should I say, the *lack of* sex difference, is predicated upon the difference between having a penis and envying one. The woman is defined according to her relationship to the penis, and not according to her relationship to her own sex organs. Irigaray's analysis reveals that Freud's theories about how a little girl becomes a woman are parallel to his description of melancholia, the depressive form of what would be mourning if it were healthy. Following Freud's theory, Irigaray points out that:

> After the little girl discovers her own castration and that of her mother—her 'object,' the narcissistic representative of all her instincts—she would have no recourse other than melancholia....the libinal economy of the little girl...crosschecks with the symptoms of melancholia: —profoundly painful dejection, —abrogation of interest in the outside world, —loss of the capacity for love, —inhibition of all activity, & —fall in self-esteem.[26]

Irigaray understands that Freud is describing the norms of society, he is not creating these structures, "he merely accounts for them." However, his and Lacan's uncritical articulation of them is problematic and violates Freud's own principles of evaluation. Psychoanalysis's stated method is to search out the unconscious dynamics underneath the conscious behavior and feelings. For Freud the goal of therapy is to "bring the unconscious part of the self with its unconscious ideation into consciousness with the release...of the unconscious strangulated affect."[27] He seeks to bring the unconscious workings of this analysis to conscious awareness. Yet when it comes

---

[26] Irigaray, *Speculum of the Other Woman*, 66-67.

[27] Jerome David Levin, *Theories of the Self* (Philadelphia: Hemisphere Publishing Corporation, 1992) 93.

to women, he simply affirms these unconscious societal biases. As Irigaray tells us, "Freud is enmeshed in a power structure and an ideology of the patriarchal type" which leads to "internal contradictions in his theory."[28]

For instance, Freud's methodology in constructing his theories of women and of feminine sexuality violates his own "science" of psychoanalysis. This is true in at least three ways. First of all, Freud uses a different methodology in his study of women than he does in his study of men. He doesn't theorize his view of feminine sexuality and development through his observations of healthy women, as he does with men. With men his theories of male sexuality and development are a mixture of scientific observations and literary allusions. However, when he turns to theorizing about women, he merely derives a theory from his previous conceptualization of male sexuality using two criteria: 1) how a woman is or is not like a male, and 2) how a woman's being fulfills male needs. Woman is defined by the fact that she has no penis and by how she provides an envelope or sheath for man's pleasure. Irigaray shows that Freud develops a positive theory of male development and from this theory derives a negative or reverse theory of female sexuality and development. Further, Freud's theoretic gymnastics for womanhood are not only unscientific; they are not in continuity with psychoanalysis. Freud violates his own principles of psychoanalysis to examine the unconscious and repressed dynamics operating in any given analysis. Freud does not uncover his own preconceptions about what it is to be feminine. This oversight negatively affects his attempts to muddle through a theory to explain how a little girl develops into an adult feminine subject. Instead, he gives a formula of how she originally behaves like a little man. Therefore, Irigaray, stating the obvious, reveals that for Western discourse, "there never is (or ever will be) a

---

[28] Irigaray, "The Power of Discourse and the Subordination of the Feminine," 70.

little girl."[29] Freud's conclusions certainly do not follow the accepted philosophical principle called Occam's Razor that an explanation for a phenomenon ought to be the most simple possible and then progress to more complexity as it explains anomalies. Rather, it appears here that Freud starts with the complex theory of male sexuality and makes it more convoluted to fit women into it. He does not employ the scientific method of empirical observation of women to hypothesize an appropriate theory to interpret and understand feminine sexuality. According to Freud's thinking, a woman is only desirable to a man in so far as she is like his mother. Irigaray says that this configuration makes it impossible to resolve the Oedipal complex in both the man's birth family and in his marriage and children family. This is the case because the man can never really grow up and be free to choose his own mate. Neither is he in a position to behave like a father to his children, since his wife is really his "mother" as well as theirs.

Further, his theory of women is impractical, as well. The steps that a little girl is to go through on her road to resolving the Oedipal complex and maturing into a woman is so complex and confusing that no little girl would do them naturally, not even if she had a manual.

Freud is stating explicitly what is implicitly assumed. His theories are descriptive of that which is assumed in common understanding. Irigaray's point is that not only are Freud's models of feminine sexuality phallocentric, but all models of feminine sexuality given in Western thought are phallocentric. Freud's disjunctive theory of feminine sexuality begins with a focus on the clitoral activity of the little girl, which Freud names as phallic activity and a phallic organ. Then he suggests that a mature woman moves to vaginal orgasms, which he defines as the opposite of a phallic organ. Since he identifies a clitoris as a "little penis" and all active sexuality

---

[29] Irigaray, *Speculum of the Other Woman*, 48.

as phallic, then it is no wonder that he names the little girl's desire as penis envy and her maturation as renouncing her active desire for her mother. Irigaray warns that feminists cannot focus on the clitoral activity to find true femininity. Exclusive focus on either clitoral activity or vaginal passivity, are both phallocentric views. Neither theory offers an adequate feminine understanding. Any model of feminine sexuality that focuses on either clitoral or vaginal dimensions are constructed phallocentrically. Irigaray asks "for what sexuality, apart from the phallic, is being offered?"[30] None is the answer in the common discourse. This issue reflects my own embedded assumption. It seemed clear that the clitoris and the activity of stimulating it, which are portrayed as active, aggressively desirous, and focused on external stimulation, were closer to the "truth" of women's sexuality than Freud's second track of passivity. Yet Irigaray reveals to us that this bias is also a phallocentrically constructed viewpoint. Irigaray says, "Female sexuality has always been conceptualized on the basis of masculine parameters."[31] Female pleasure needs to be conceptualized in a way that is not limited to either of these foci, but opened to more than what has previously been theorized. Irigaray seeks to represent female sexuality in a positive way, making the *radical* claim that we need non-masculine terms, metaphors, experiences, and ideas to imagine and express and experience genuinely female pleasure.

Jacques Lacan is another prevalent representative figure in the psychoanalytic philosophical context of Irigaray's scholarship. A French psychoanalyst whose intellectual popularity began in the late 1960s as he embarked upon what he calls a "return to Freud" for French psychoanalysts, Lacan's thought has been influential not only for would-be analysts, but also, for other thinkers who use his theories to challenge our philosophical assumptions about language

---

[30] Irigaray, *Speculum of the Other Woman*, 62.
[31] Luce Irigaray, "This Sex Which Is Not One," in *This Sex Which Is Not One*, 23.

and subjectivity. Like many contemporary French feminists, Irigaray studied with him at the *École Freudienne de Paris*. There are four areas of Lacan's work that are of particular interest for Irigaray and our examination of her thought: 1) Lacan's employment of psychoanalysis philosophically; 2) his transformation of Freud's focus on the biological penis to the linguistically symbolic phallus and his subsequent focus on the phallus as the central symbol of all symbols and meaning making; 3) his theory of ego development as fundamentally narcissistic, and 4) the function of the Mirror phase in this development. We will address them in the order just mentioned.

The first point is straight forward. Lacan employs psychoanalysis philosophically to challenge the values and norms of society and individuals, and particularly the primacy of consciousness. Lacan believes that the unconscious of philosophy is the "unconscious of representative consciousness itself."[32] Irigaray is influenced by this insight to use the theories of psychoanalysis philosophically, and she takes this analogy further by using the methods of psychoanalysis to analyze philosophy and discourse as if they themselves were analysands—patients to be healed.

Lacan views his "return to Freud" as a valiant effort to pull Freud out of a biological determinism that reveals the symbolic relevance of his theories. (Although some, including Irigaray, might rephrase Lacan's appropriation of Freud as a "dis-embodying" of Freud's theories.) Lacan finds Freud's theories profoundly insightful when they are applied to the development and acquisition of language and language's relationship to the unconscious, instead of being viewed strictly as concerned with the body and sexuality. This is not entirely out of character for Freud since he also saw the significance of language and its innate relation to the unconscious. For instance, some of his earliest work analyzes how language

---

[32] Mikkel Borch-Jacobsen, *The Emotional Tie* (Stanford CA: Stanford University Press, 1993) 158.

expresses the unconscious in such phenomena as slips of the tongue. Freud focused upon the unconscious and sexuality in understanding individual selfhood; Lacan sees Freud's analysis of both the unconscious and sexuality as deeper expressions of language and society. While Freud focused upon the power of the physical penis in individual development and then in the society's collective reaction to the repressed desires and fears associated with individual's formative experiences, Lacan asserts the symbolic power of the phallus and its prominent role in the formulation of language and the operation of culture. As Grosz says, "for Lacan, subjectivity and sexuality are functions of the material play of a language regulated by the symbolic order."[33] And the phallus is the master signifier of the entire symbolic order. As the master signifier, the phallus is the norm by which all are judged and understood. Eilberg-Schwartz understands Lacan to be saying that "the phallus is the symbol of the effect that language has on the development of human subjectivity."[34] It is the power of meaning, creating the dichotomy of syntax: subject versus object. This symbol then provides this dichotomous structure to subjectivity, gender, language, and ontology itself. Syntax, language, subjectivity, ego development, sexuality, and the unconscious are all structured analogously: according to the binary opposition of having access to a phallus and its power on the one side, and not having access to a phallus (power) on the other. The dichotomies go as follows: phallus/no phallus; subject/object (not subject); one/not one; penis/penis-envy; good/bad (not good); spirit/matter (not spirit); presence/absence; male/female, etcetera. There are those who have access to the phallus, on the one hand, and those who do not, except the derived power through a male. The phallus is what divides the sexes and what determines their relationship to each other. The psychological differences between

---

[33] Elizabeth Grosz, *Sexual Subversions* (Syndey: Allen and Unwin, 1989) 20.
[34] Howard Eilberg-Schwartz, *God's Phallus* (Boston: Beacon Press, 1994) 28.

men and women are not the direct result of their biological differences, but come from the meaning ascribed to these differences.

Sexual difference is created and viewed according to this dichotomy. The male is defined as the subject which is one because he, having a penis, the one organ of pleasure and privilege, has direct access to the phallus, while the female, not having a penis (or having a not-penis), is defined as the object, or the "not one." He has presence and she "has" absence. The male sex is constructed according to its relation to the phallus—it owns the phallus, or at least believes that it does by virtue of its penis, and thus the male is the subject of all discourse. The female sex is also constructed in terms of its relationship to the phallus. It does not have a phallus and is defined as a lack. Thus, the female also is the not-subject of all discourse; she is defined by Lacan as this subject which is not one. Irigaray makes a pun on Lacan's claim for the title of one of her most famous essays and books, "This Sex Which is Not One."[35] In this essay she sees Lacan as revealing the common bias that women's "sexual organ, which is not *one* organ, is counted as *none*."[36]

The third area of interest in Lacan for Irigaray is his linguistic appropriation of Freud's theories of ego development, in which the child's ego is formed by the child's identification with its image in the mirror. It is from these points where she develops her clarity on the function of projection of maleness and repression of the feminine. The child's ego develops by seeing itself in its relations with others. The process utilizes the imagination, or as Lacan refers to it, the imaginary. The imaginary is the way the child constructs the world and those around the ego; it makes them appear to be like the ego itself. The process by which the child's ego is formed includes the employment of the imaginary projection of the child's self onto everything else.[37] Otherness is changed into sameness in such a way

---

[35] Irigaray, *This Sex Which Is Not One*.
[36] Irigaray, "This Sex Which Is Not One," 26. Emphasis is Irigaray's.
[37] Lacan says child; he really means the boy child. Yet he does not tell us how the

that otherness is not perceived. Only the projected self is perceived. That which appears too different from the Same is ignored/not able to be seen. This is the narcissistic ego of Freud's later thought. Most scholars of Freud, particularly American ego psychologists, typically ignore this later contradictory view of the ego, in favor of the earlier, "realistic" ego.[38] In the American view, therapy seeks to build up the patient's ego and self-esteem. The ego is rational and seeks rational and harmonious resolution and compromise between the irrational and socially unacceptable urges of the id, such as sex and violence and child-like needs, on the one hand, and the rational and expected behavior of authority.

Contrarily, Lacan and many French psychoanalysts adopt Freud's later and less developed view of the narcissistic ego, which redirects its libidinal energy back from an external object and onto a part of its own body, narcissistically creating itself. This approach does not seek therapeutic results for the patient; it is not concerned with strengthening or weakening the ego. Rather, it utilizes frustration, seeking to subvert, render ambiguous, and resist the ego's conscious ideals. This narcissistic ego is an "entirely fluid, mobile, amorphous series of identifications, internalizations of images/ perceptions, invested with libidinal cathexes."[39]

Adopting this view of the ego enables Lacan to suggest his "Mirror phase" in contrasting parallel to Freud's Oedipal stage. As this narcissistic ego projects itself onto external objects, it projects its own libidinal energy outward onto others and imagines that these projected energy deposits are actually something other than itself. The narcissistic ego can project its positive parts or its negative parts.

---

girl child does this.

[38] This significant difference between the typical American view of Freud and the French psychoanalysis's understanding explains in part why American feminists have difficulty in appreciating the contributions of French feminists like Luce Irigaray.

[39] Elizabeth Grosz, *Jacques Lacan: A Femininst Introduction* (New York: Routledge, 1991) 28.

This self is constituted only in its experience of pleasure or pain in its relations with others. Others are not truly other, but are projections of parts of the ego itself. Freud refers to this ego as like "the body of an amoeba," which relates to external objects only through incorporating the object into itself and allowing its own boundaries to be reshaped by this foreign object, which is now part of its self (a little like the process of eating).[40] This ability and tendency of the ego to project its own image onto others and then re-appropriate its own image as if it were the other is the same process by which the child enters Lacan's Mirror phase, where the child is able to create his differentiated subjectivity.[41] With Irigarayian spectacles, one can see that this process reveals just how society is exclusively male and mother-othering. Irigaray's analysis shows how women, particularly in the form of mothers, are defined as the opposite or reverse of the male little boy's narcissistic ego. This process continues into societal dimensions.

Lacan's Mirror phase parallels and contrasts Freud's Oedipal stage in another way as well. Prior to each phase is a pre-phase--pre-Mirror, or pre-Oedipal. Freud's pre-Oedipal stage is characterized by the child's desire and absolute demand for the mother and by his castration anxiety. The male child feels conflicted between his desire and his anxiety. The Oedipal stage, or phallic phase, is the resolution of the Oedipal complex by which the child represses his desire for his

---

[40] Sigmund Freud, "On Narcissism: An Introduction," in *The Standard Edition of the Complete Psychological Works of Sigmund Freud,* 14:75, quoted in Elizabeth Grosz, *Jacques Lacan: A Feminist Introduction,* 29.

[41] This process of projecting, or alienating, one's own self onto an object which can then be re-appropriated by the self to give the self self-consciousness is paralleled in Marx's analysis of how self-consciousness can occur through work. However, the worker is alienated from himself because this projection of himself, which is his cathected libidinal energy, is alienated from himself by the capitalist boss, who then keeps the energy and power and money for himself, his profit. This is why the exploited worker is deprived of himself. It is not just that he is not paid enough. Feuerbach might also be a connecting thinker between Marx and Freud.

mother, and thereby his anxiety and fear of his father can be abated, allowing him to identify fully with his father. This resolution enables the conflict to disappear and the *unity of identification* to be experienced.

While Lacan's pre-Mirror phase parallels Freud's pre-Oedipal stage, there are several points of difference. Both indicate two significant characteristics. First, the subject who is not yet a subject perceives itself as fragmented. He is not a unified subject, as Lacan says in "Aggressivity in Psychoanalysis," the "images on the fragmented body [are the] images of castration, mutilation, dismemberment, dislocation, evisceration, devouring, bursting open of the body."[42] Secondly, this phase is also associated with the non-reflective identification with and desire for the mother.

Lacan's pre-Mirror phase is characterized not by psychic conflict but by cognitive and bodily dissonance. The child experiences his body as fragmentary and disconnected, an aggregate or conglomeration of separate parts. He feels that he is not in control of his own body, nor his reality. There is no experience of unity of body or self. As the infant matures, different parts of his body develop at different rates. At one point the child feels its right hand more fully and as more adept than his feet or toes. This creates what Lacan refers to as the child's experience of "the body-in-bits-and-pieces."[43] Lacan believes that the child forms a "unity" or identity with the mother and cannot yet see itself as separate from her or from his environment. The child has no self-boundaries.

The Mirror phase, beginning around 6 months of age and lasting until around 18 months or so, is the primary stage in the development of subjectivity and of language. It marks the child's simultaneous recognition of itself as a whole totality—a "one" in and of itself, and the recognition that it is distinguished from the world.

---

[42] Jacques Lacan, *Écrites, A Selection* (London: Touistock, 1977) 11.
[43] Ibid., 4-5.

Irigraray's Critique of the Economy of the Same   161

The world is not the child's own and the child is not the world. Here the mother becomes other, outside of the child's control. And thus the child experiences a loss—a lack. This "lack" mode of being is associated with the experience of fragmentation. Experiencing itself as fragmentary and lacking is assuaged by the "new" recognition of its image as whole in the mirror. The child, from now on, seeks a stable reassurance of its wholeness through identification with this image: the One. This occurs originally through what Lacan calls the "imaginary," by which the child projects an identificatory image of himself as a whole unity onto all external relations that he has. The mirror is the paradigmatic experience of this, but the child experiences this play of the imaginary in other situations as well. As the child matures, Lacan believes that the subject places language and the symbolic in the role of the mirror image to fill this lack.

Lacan describes the development of discourse in human children in conjunction with the child's differentiation from its mother. Paralleling yet contrasting, Freud's discussions of sexuality and repression of the child's unaccepted desires to have the parent, Lacan argues that language itself is structured like the unconscious. And since the child's relationship to the unconscious creates the child's relation to the symbolic order, all of which are determined by the child's possession of a penis, he differentiates himself from the other/mother through the power and reign of the phallus, which then in turn acts as the major catalyst of ordered speech. Thus, language is phallocentric. Lacan's discussions of ego development, sexuality, and language are truly only applicable to male development. For Lacan men are subjects who are "one," and women are subjects which are "not one." Lacan believes that women cannot speak themselves, for they do not and can not have direct access to the phallus, which is the only way into the symbolic order and, thus, language. This is what he means when he says, "Women don't know what they are saying, that's the whole difference between them and me."[44] For Lacan, like Freud, women are identified as an ego/self by their lack of a phallus. They are defined negatively, as something that they are not, rather than as some positive reality that they actually are. Irigaray turns this negative definition into a positive reality. The feminine, she writes, does not "obey Lacan's model of 'not all' to which the One is necessary. There is something of One, but something escapes it, resists it...rebelling against all laws."[45] In *This Sex Which is Not One*, she redefines this Lacanian "not one" of the feminine to say that feminine sexuality is "always at least double...is plural."[46] This positive reality is where Irigaray's constructive work takes off, as we shall see later, and is characterized by this not one, this plurality.

Irigaray psychoanalyzes psychoanalysis itself. She questions its unconscious, what it has repressed: the feminine. She seeks, like a psychoanalyst, to bring out that which has been repressed into the light of consciousness. She has to work through psychoanalysis's own resistance. Subversively, she seeks to enable the "return of the repressed," that which bubbles up from the unconscious to threaten the "ego" of phallocentrism. Irigaray reverses the repression of the feminine on two fronts: in psychoanalysis and other phallocentric discourse, and in individual women themselves.

This brings us to a fundamental problem with both Freud's Oedipal stage and Lacan's Mirror phase with regards to female development of subjectivity. Women cannot develop an identity and subject-hood through these male constructed structures. She can only become a "masculine" subject. Irigaray scolds psychoanalysis, and Lacan in particular, on this point, accusing their theories of

---

[44] Jacques Lacan, *The Seminar XX, Encore: On Feminine Sexuality, the Limits of Love and Knowledge*, ed. Jacques-Alain Miller, trans. Bruce Fink (New York: W.W. Norton and Co., 1998) quoted in Luce Irigaray "Cosi' Fan Tutti," in *This Sex Which Is Not One* (Ithaca NY: Cornell University Press, 1985) 86.

[45] Luce Irigaray, "The Poverty of Psychoanalysis," in *The Irigaray Reader*, 97.

[46] Irigaray, "This Sex Which Is Not One," 28.

forcing "the evolution of little girls' desire to fit in with the schemata that explain the evolution of little boys' desire."[47] To address this deficiency Irigaray argues that women symbolically "re-enter" the pre-Oedipal/pre-Mirror stage, in such a way that women's unique positive reality could be valued and accepted. By regressing from an imperfectly resolved Oedipal complex, back to the fragmentation described by Lacan, women could effect a bursting open of the pre-Oedipal body, so that women can re-develop a feminine counterpoint to Freud's/Lacan's Oedipal/Mirror stage. Such a counterpoint would allow for and encourage genuine feminine difference from the very start of public discursivity and private subjectivity. This is a task of her constructive work and will be addressed in the next chapter.

Irigaray uses the theories of Lacan toward developing a strategic method that gives the feminine a voice, an avenue down which women can develop their own discourse and also their own experiences and theories of the self, as well as to become/discover their own self. Deconstructing psychoanalysis, she reveals the sexist, unscientific, and mistaken assumptions implicit and explicit in psychoanalysis's phallocentric construction of feminine sexuality. She reacts to this psychoanalytic thought by both affirming the descriptive insights, and critiquing the prescriptive claims that value and define women only in terms of men. First, she might say "*non—* Lacan and Freud, female children must develop distinctly in terms of something positive: the vagina, the two pairs of labia, the clitoris, and much more." Women's subjectivity should be theorized in relation to women's bodies and in terms of presence, not in terms of lack and absence. To maintain a theory that ignores the role women's own bodies in the maturation process of women is not only scientifically irresponsible, but also is unethical and contributes to the injustice of sexism. With such a starting place, women would also develop their

---

[47] Irigaray, "The Poverty of Psychoanalysis," 91.

own linguistic structure and connotations. Further, Irigaray's analysis sees that the singularity of the phallus is instrumental in the character of singularity that is present in male-centered, patriarchal constructions of reality and society. This is made explicit in the subsequent construction and craving for a single, monistic, authoritative answer in the phallocentric culture and in the exclusive and hierarchical nature of the phallocentric view and use of language and societal norms. Thus, women's construction of discourse and societal norms might be shaped more by the multitude of sexual parts, experiences, tools, embodiments. Further women's constructions would be more inclusive, less hierarchical, and structured with many diverse and different authorities, multiple in their valuation of society and in the structure of women's grammar and discourse. Discourse is a paradigmatic phenomenon symbolizing society in general. It is used here metaphorically to represent culture, as well as literally in expressing the unqualified dependence that our society has upon discourse.

She is critical of Lacan and Freud's prescriptive worth, yet their descriptive value is quite insightful and helpful to her feminist project. Lacan's ideas do reflect the current situation of women. She may say, "*oui*, Lacan, you have accurately described the situation in current discourse—the masculine experience of ego development has been normative for all, male and female." Women have assimilated this cultural assumption even as unreflective babies. To be a "subject," a self with a differentiated ego, who participates in the construction and construal of discourse, is to be identified with the male. Women have been defined according to what they lack. The comprehensive consequence of such patriarchal polemics has been that the feminine has been almost completely repressed in our society. Lacan and other past and present male psychoanalytical thinkers can be helpful for the women's movement because they describe clearly this tendency to identify that which is positive and conscious in the individual's development and also in the evolution of society and culture strictly with the male and his characteristics.

Irigaray's analysis of Freud and Lacan's theories reveals how Western society believes women should act and, in fact, the way they must behave in order to gain value and acceptance. Women have access to the symbolic realm in only one of two ways. Either a woman abdicates her difference from maleness and assumes a cover of sameness, or she must be content with a derivative access to language, power and meaning through her husband, son, or father. In other words, either she becomes like a male, or acquiesces her autonomy to a male family member. Irigaray agrees that this is actually the way women are in society and the way that the idea of feminine functions in Western culture. However, she believes that it does not mean to suggest that it should continue to function as such or that such a description of femininity has any biological or innate basis. In fact, her indictment against psychoanalysis is upon the prescriptive use of their theories. She uses these theories to show the way things have functioned as part of her critique of the problematic nature of the dominant discourse.

Irigaray pulls out an embedded correspondence between Western discourse and male sexuality (as male sexuality is expressed culturally and described in psychoanalysis). As she says in "Woman's Exile":

> All Western discourse presents a certain isomorphism with the masculine sex; the privilege of unity, form of the self, of the visible, of the specularisable, of the erection (which is the becoming of the form).[48]

This marvelous insight is the core of her critical analysis of all of Western philosophy. She exposes the connection between philosophy's constructions of value and truth, on the one hand, and

---

[48] Luce Irigaray, "Women's Exile," *Ideology and Consciousness* 1 (1977): 64.

their correspondence with Freud and Lacan's descriptions of normative male sexuality and development, on the other. Likewise there is a correspondence between the way female sexuality has been theorized and the way that otherness and difference function in society in general.

This is not a claim for a direct correlation between male anatomy and Western sameness, but rather Irigaray is referring to morphology. Morphology is the study of the structure and form of an animal or word. Irigaray's careful emphasis on morphology indicates that the structure and meaning given to male sexuality and its privilege in this culture is what is at issue. Morphology points us to the socially constructed male body and its meaning and function for our current culture. In other words, there is no biological determination that males must project sameness and singleness onto the entire world, nor is there an anatomical determination that males must experience their sexuality and their selves as singular and phallocentric. But in this culture with its meaning and power ascribed to the phallus as described so clearly in psychoanalysis, this emphasis upon oneness and its correspondence to male sexuality is clear.

The exclusivity and uniformity of phallocentric discourse are correlated. Since the male attains subject-hood, according to Lacanian psychoanalysis, by first identifying himself with everything external to himself and then, in his imaginary, recreating everything that is external to himself (including and especially Mother) in his own image, he creates a world in which everything is either just like him or is exactly the opposite of him. All other external objects and characteristics are ignored and excluded.

This childhood construction of himself, his mother (women in general), his father (a bigger perfect image of himself), and the rest of the world are projected into language and the structure of consciousness itself. This projection is part of the maturation process itself and becomes hard wired into his cognitive structure and remains effective in his collective adult existence: culturally, politically, economically, socially, psychologically, and religiously. Thus, the problem of gender and language is not merely that many languages ascribe gender to words, nor that a few words are biased in favor of men, although these facts are certainly significant. Rather, it is the entire structure of language itself that contains and maintains the bias against the feminine. Irigaray elaborates upon the fact and nature of "gender markers show how one sex, how the world, has been forced to submit to the other."[49] She goes on to focus on how "the laws of syntax in French reveal the power wielded by one sex over another."[50] The masculine gender is attributed to all the most valued entities, such as God, the sun, etc., because "man gives his own gender to the universe as he intends to give his name to his children and his possessions."[51]

Language serves as the symbolic substitute for the child's imaginary. The imaginary is a pre-linguistic moment in the formation of the ego whereby the child "imagines" or sees images of him/herself as whole and real. The image of the wholeness seen in the mirror is reflected back to the child and she/he begins to develop a unified sense of her as a differentiated and whole being. When the child overcomes the Oedipal complex, he breaks the maternal bonds of connection and identification and adopts the paternal rules of the realm of symbolic meanings, which enable him to control his environment (so the child believes). This analysis shows the psychology of the male leads to a proclivity toward uniformity—the monistic interpretation of himself and the world. Everything he wants to be (like his father, who has control over the environment, knows everything and, most of all, has the mother) is given ontological status—it is real. All the characteristics and forms that are not like

---

[49] Luce Irigaray, *Sexes and Genealogies*, trans. Gillian C. Gill (New York: Columbia University Press, 1993) 173.
[50] Ibid.
[51] Ibid.

his childhood images of his father, including the qualities and forms of others, especially Mother, as well as certain qualities of himself, are banished. These qualities are either turned into the reverse image of the privileged qualities, or they are made invisible—either way, neither represents genuine difference. These dynamics are particularly evident in the characterization of female as the "opposite sex." Characteristics associated with femininity are viewed as opposites from those associated with masculinity, such as weak and strong, or active and passive. When examined deliberately, it is obvious that female and feminine characteristics are not in actuality "opposite" from male and masculine qualities. The self in this schema is turned into a monistic expression of the privileged values. Thus, conformity to uniformity of the self is established. The acquisition of language reinforces it and enables it to thrive. Phallocentric culture rewards it.

Irigaray points out the parallel between Lacan's articulation of the ego development of the male child and the dynamics that undergird Western discourse. Just as the child needs to project himself onto the external objects in his environment and then either reclaims them as like him and, thus, valuable or disowns them and blames the object of his projection for this bad characteristic, Western discourse uses language to project onto the feminine its own characteristics, experiences, hopes and fears. Then the male-dominated discourse names qualities as either good—in which case it claims them for itself as masculine (or higher and human)—or bad—in which case it distances itself from them, viewing them as feminine (or part of a lower animal nature). In this way discourse itself becomes phallocentric, oppressive to women, and repressive to the feminine.

Her recognition of Feuerbach's influence in Lacan's theory and her appropriation of it highlights the human propensity to see himself in all external realities. Man creates the world and those around him in his own image. Irigaray writes, "the feminine is defined as the necessary complement to the operation of male sexuality, and more often, as a negative image that provides male sexuality with an unfailing phallic self representation."[52] Woman is named as a hole of the same proportions of internal depth as the male is named as extension, symbolically as well as literally. Western philosophy has created the world in its own idealized image—a coherent singularity. Further, to uphold this mendacity, Western philosophy not only blocks out anything that questions it, but also creates a reverse image—an anti-matter if you will—to balance out its assertions of absolute and singular truth. Thus, the economy of the Same emerges unquestioned. Metaphysically, the One depends upon the other; maleness as an essential category depends upon a category called not-maleness. The One is limited and circumscribed by that which is named the other. Without the other, the One would not know where it stopped and started. The One is the static presence known by its differentiation from the fluidity, multiplicity, and absence of the other. Uncovering the origin of the Western emphasis on oneness and sameness calls into question the assumed *a priori* status of its claims.

Irigaray also utilizes Marx in her evaluation of the economy of the Same. The term "economy" here serves both to express a general system of relations and operations, as well as to evoke the more specific meaning associated with Marx and his critique of capitalist practices. She articulates a connection between class struggle and sexual exploitation. She uses Marx and Engel's analysis of commodity capitalism and its evil exploitation of the worker and applies it to her evaluation of the function of women in phallocentric culture. She writes:

> Marx's analysis of commodities as the elementary form of capitalist wealth can thus be understood as an interpretation of the status of woman in so-called patriarchal societies. The organization of such societies, and the operation of the

---

[52] Irigaray, "The Power of Discourse and the Subordination of the Feminine," 70.

symbolic system on which this organization is based—a symbolic system whose instrument and representative is the proper name: the name of the father, the name of God—contain in a nuclear form the developments that Marx defines as characteristic of a capitalist regime...[53]

Women's role in society parallels the role of commodities in commodity capitalism. Both are objects of exchange on the market. Their value is determined by men's desire. She writes:

Woman is traditionally a use-value for man, an exchange value among men; in other words, a commodity...whose price will be established, in terms of the standard of their work and of their need/desire, by 'subjects': workers, merchants, consumers.[54]

Women have functioned in society as objects of male possession: men control women's bodies as the means of re-production; men project their own undesired characteristics onto women in the construction of their narcissistic egos; men construct their fantasies of the feminine to meet their needs. Men relate to each other through the commoditization of women as Irigaray says "woman has value on the market by virtue of a single quality: that of being a product of man's 'labor'."[55] Women are objects and means for men to use toward their own ends.

This economy of the Same, which is dependent upon the exchange of women, is a strictly "ho(m) m-o-sexual" society, in which "man begets man as his own likeness," and "wives, daughters, and sisters have value only in that they serve as the possibility of, and potential benefit in, relations among men."[56] Women are the means

---

[53] Luce Irigaray, "Women on the Market," in *This Sex Which Is Not One*, 172-3.
[54] Irigaray, "This Sex Which Is Not One," 31.
[55] Irigaray, "Women on the Market," 175.
[56] Ibid., 171-2.

through which men relate to each other. She says this "circulation of women among men is what establishes the operations of…patriarchal society."[57] Men don't actually relate to women, for genuine femininity is invisible in the normative discourse; they relate to each other through women.

In conclusion, then, let me sum up Irigaray's critical insights. Irigaray's essential goal is to "secure a place for the feminine within sexual difference"[58] In her view the current situation has no space for genuine difference between male and female. She believes the origin of this problem is found paradigmatically in psychoanalytical theories about female development and sexuality. This implicit indifference in Western culture and language manifests itself overtly in the oppression of women and the repression of the feminine. The feminine has been defined in masculine terms and according to women's relevance for men, and thus the feminine has no positive attributes of her own. The so-called difference between the (opposite) sexes is actually a subordination of "the other to the same."[59] The systems of meaning making such as language and symbols have "always operated 'within' systems that are representative, self-representative of the masculine subject."[60] In other words, the current economy, the economy of the Same, is a system of the male, by the male, and for the male.

Irigaray's analysis also helps to reveal the explicit and disturbing correspondence between Augustine's definition of evil and Freud's definition of female. Augustine's formulation of sin and evil represents the dominant view of evil in Western theology and continues to have tremendous effect on most forms of Christianity's thinking. Recall that Augustine defines evil as the privation of good. Evil does not have ontological status in and of itself, but only derivative status from

---

[57] Ibid., 184.
[58] Irigaray, "This Sex Which Is Not One," 159.
[59] Ibid.,159.
[60] Ibid.

the good it corrupts. The human body is not evil, says Augustine, nor is the will that becomes divided, but rather the sin of evil is the turning away from the higher good that it could have done or willed. Evil is the privation of good. Movement toward God or toward the One is good. Movement away from God or away from the One is sin.

In a way that parallels Augustine's derivative definition of evil, Freud defines women in derivative terms. The feminine is defined as the lack of the male organ. She is constituted by her envy of that which she does not have—the penis. For a little girl to become a woman, she must repress her aggressive desire to have her mother, and repress her active sexual behavior of masturbating her external organ, her clitoris. A mature healthy woman, according to Freud, desires only to be desired. She is defined as a sheath or envelope for his penis. Lacan also utilized this Freudian structure: woman is defined as lacking a penis, as a lack of the phallus, as a privation of the phallus, as a subject which is not one, as a privation of the One, as a privation of the good, as evil.

Women and the feminine have been placed symbolically in the position of evil for they have been defined as a deprivation of the One. Femaleness is defined as a privation of maleness. This definition of femaleness as a lack, or privation of the penis reveals a parallel between the way Western discourse views women and the way it views evil. This parallel can be noted not only in the position of the feminine, but also according to the function of the feminine in Western culture. Feminine characteristics and form are associated with sin and inadequacy. The multiplicity of the feminine, as suggested by Irigaray corresponds with that which Augustine views as sin: the multiformity of the divided will.

Instead of merely attacking the male-privilege of the normative discourse, as many American and liberal feminists have done, Irigaray enables us to think about the very structure of the system of value differently. Instead of trying to create a connection between the privileged One and femininity in order to give women access to power, she builds up the historical and philosophical identification between the One and maleness making her readers aware of the constructed correspondence between the phallus and the One. Male-centered thought has constructed the world in terms of his childhood imaginary, which consists of narcissistic reflections of the male self and rejections of the other (the feminine). Irigaray reveals that women as *speaking subjects* have been excluded from this construction. They have not been able to contribute significantly to its creation, nor are women as subjects even accounted for in this phallocentric world. Women have been included in this world only as objects, screens and vessels to be filled and used by male projections.

Her insights are particularly helpful for my project of bringing to the surface those embedded assumptions that exalt oneness and reward sameness. My project is broader in application in that I do not limit my critique to gender and sexual differences, but open it to the issue of difference in general. And my project is more specific in scope in that I am concerned with the deleterious affects of these assumptions upon theories and concepts of selfhood. Irigaray's ideas help me to address several harmful implications that are associated with the economy of the Same. First of all, Irigaray has shown that the exaltation of oneness and sameness in Western discourse is a projection of the phallocentric imaginary arising from the process of ego development of male children and has become inscribed in the structure of language. Thus, it is neither an *a priori* truth, nor an accurate interpretative framework for understanding reality. Further, she has demonstrated the corrupt and biased character of what she calls the economy of the Same. It is based exclusively on the experience and needs of those men with power. Maintaining it benefits them to the detriment of women and the feminine. My analysis adds that this economy of the Same is detrimental to all who do not fit in to phallocentrism's normative model of being. Women are not the only victims of this economy of the Same. All types of difference and diversity are repressed. The problem in my eyes is more extensive than the repression of women and the feminine. The exaltation of the One and the Same blinds us to the rich diversity in ourselves and in the world. It is an embedded assumption that colors the way we view and don't view reality.

With Irigaray's analysis, it is clear that this economy of the Same passes itself off as reality and yet it is not. This proclivity toward the Same erases and inhibits real differences. Irigaray's analysis also makes clear that the only type of value available to persons that are different from the dominant principle is derivative value. All value is derived from one's similarity to the One. Both the value ascribed to the other and the ontological reality of this constructed other are derived from the value and power of the normative reality. The ontological reality of the real other (not that which is constructed by phallocentric discourse) is made invisible and remains unknown in this economy.

A second significant problem with the emphasis on oneness is that it retards our ability to be internally related to ourselves. Removing the value of difference diminishes differences within persons as well as between them. The self is forced to reduce its multiplicity to singularity, leaving no opportunity for the parts of a person to be related, since the parts are squeezed into a singularity. When the parts resist being shackled, dissonance results, shifting the focus from the dynamic and mutual relating of the parts of the self to the disparity between the parts. In this situation, a singular dominant part wins out and silences the others as well as relationality within the self. A reflexive relating of parts within each self is an essential dynamic in the becoming of a relational self. Not only is the reality of a relational self suppressed, but also any understanding of selfhood as a relational matrix is suppressed. In order for a relational process to flourish, the differences within the self must be respected and encouraged to flourish. Kierkegaard's understanding of the self as a dialectical and reflexive process of relating promotes such flourishing. This limitation leads to the third issue discussed in the introduction, which is the alienation of difference—all difference between persons, and particularly sexual differences. There is less acceptance and appreciation of difference in culture and community in general. This xenophobia contributes to the wrongful reduction of all deviations from the norm, such as racial, cultural, class-wise, and sexual orientation, into a singular difference. I call this the *impoverishment of diversity*. If a second story or an alternative viewpoint is accepted at all, all differences are reduced into one type of deviation from the norm. So that racial differences between persons are viewed in a way similar to religious differences and so on. The complexity of persons and their attributes are truncated. This economy of the Same even erases the genuine differences between and among differences. Sexual difference is a different sort of difference from the so-called norm than is racial difference, which is a different sort of difference than is cultural difference, etcetera.[61] This truncation is problematic because reality is much more rich and diverse. An example of this reduction of difference to sameness occurred recently in the experience of one of my colleagues. She is an African American woman who attended *Fiesta*, a celebration of Hispanic heritage. A public television program aired with a still photo of her in a series of photos of other individuals, all named, including her, as Hispanic. Perhaps this was an honest error, but it is more likely that the economy of the Same is at work here. Any variation from the "white" norm is often lumped together and viewed in a similar vein by the majority discourse. Luce Irigaray's analysis of Western discourse demonstrates the connection between this reduction of all difference to sameness and the repression of women and the feminine. Her critique attacks this attenuation and opens women and culture to the acceptance and appreciation of all genuine difference.

---

[61] See Ellen Armour, *Subverting the Race Gender Divide: Deconstruction, Feminist Theology, and the Problem of Difference* (Chicago: The University of Chicago Press, 1999).

Irigaray's analysis reveals the problematic nature of any system of thought, legislation, intercourse, and value that view and define women solely in terms of male morphology and characteristics. Given Irigaray's critique, major changes are needed in all cultural norms and institutions including politics, economics, erotic relations, theological and philosophical assertions, etcetera, but most especially, language itself. We need theories and experiences of women and women's sexuality that are based on positive characteristics of women. Irigaray's constructive thought moves toward re-formulating women's sexuality. She discerns several "feminine" characteristics. These characteristics do not represent an essential norm of a static form of femininity that all women must fit into or live up to. Rather, Irigaray focuses our attention upon the types of characteristics and forms that have been repressed by phallocentric discourse, such as fluidity, multiplicity, both at once-ness, etcetera. She believes that phallocentrism has repressed these characteristics and forms because they are feminine. Women are invited to explore whether or not these qualities fit our authentic experience. Irigaray's constructive project helps to combat the claim of universal sameness by demonstrating the presence of women's experience of multiplicity. The next chapter will examine her constructive insights toward a theory of subjectivity for women that is genuinely different from both the normative theory of the masculine subject and its phallocentric fabrication of the feminine.

5

Irigaray's Embodied Feminine Subject

In this chapter I explore the ingenious ways in which Luce Irigaray utilizes her skills as a philosopher and a psychoanalyst in a project that combines her critical insights and her constructive work in a creative and strategic manner. Irigaray's goal is the liberation of women from the insipid phallocentrism of Western culture. She is committed to empowering women to name their own reality, their own bodily experience, their own form and syntax. Irigaray's work is political; the avenue of her choice of activism is discourse. She not only critiques the phallocentric discourse, but also engages in constructive work toward facilitating genuine feminine difference. This chapter highlights four of the methods that she employs in her constructive endeavor as well as the conclusions that she draws about feminine difference from each of these methods. Several of her primary methods draw from her experience and wisdom as a psychoanalyst, and she applies these psychoanalytic techniques to the current philosophical discourse. Her methods include highlighting that which has been repressed, employing insights from metonyms of the feminine body and sexuality, using a psychoanalytical technique called mimesis as political activism, and developing a feminine syntax and grammatical structure to language. I will also address her conclusions about the feminine and pull out the implications of her investigation for my work in reconstructing selfhood, and I will conclude with a section that examines the similarities and differences between her work and Kierkegaard's thought.

The previous chapter focused on Irigaray's critique of phallocentrism and the economy of the Same. She understands women's positions under the current phallocentric economy as oppressed, and searches for that which is genuinely feminine in women. She demonstrated the correspondence between the male morphology/sexuality as expressed by Freud and Lacan and the structure of Western discourse in general. Further, we saw parallels between Freud's theory of narcissistic ego formation and the structure and process of the formation of phallocentric discourse. The little boy projects himself onto everything around him, especially his mother (and women in general), and thus creates all in his own image. Her critical appropriation of Lacan argues that the very structure of Western language is formed from exclusively male experience and exclusively benefits phallocratic culture, communication, and thought. Further, she shows that the assertions of masculinity as positive are built upon its negative projections onto the feminine. For example, masculine is seen as active and strong, while feminine indicates passive or receptive and weak. The female is constructed as the opposite of the male.

For centuries the dominant discourse has defined "woman" in terms of those things that it does not want to claim in itself—things like passivity, subjectivity, immanence, and sensuality. As defined by men, then, woman as "other" has not really been Other. Rather, she has been an "other" man; she has been the lack, which is only the flip-side of his presence, the "hole" whose *raison d'etre* is to be filled by him who sees himself as "whole." Real sexual difference has not existed; rather, man has defined himself in terms of an "other" which is the Same as man, so that what man has been engaged in all along has been what Irigaray calls "ho(m)mo-sexuality."[1] This complex can be understood as a system that enables men to relate to other men

---

[1] Her analysis also is suggestive as to why gay men who act as "Drag Queens" are feared and ridiculed in such an economy, for they are only *acting* out the phallocentric constructed images for this "other which is not one" and reveal to the dominant male society the pretend nature of their projections. In this way they are engaging in mimesis.

through women.[2] Women function, as we have seen, as mere commodities that are exchanged between men, so that men might jockey for honor, power, and money. Women are primarily symbolized (and thus function in the symbolic order) as intermediating objects, which enable male-to-male interactions. Irigaray argues that it is precisely this power of the dominant discourse to reduce all others to the economy of the Same, to reduce women to mere reflective pawns for male social intercourse, that has allowed it to maintain its position of mastery for centuries.[3]

Her psychoanalysis of Western discourse shows that there is a correlation or even an identity between that which is unconscious (since Western culture has repressed it) and the feminine. Her constructive work elicits the characteristics and forms of the feminine. Her critical methods enable her to search for the feminine that the phallocentric discourse has repressed. In this way, she simultaneously proposes likely candidates for the lost feminine and subverts patriarchy by highlighting what phallocentric culture denies, thus disrupting its balanced harmony. The male subject's positive reality depends upon the repression of the feminine and the projection onto women as negative and derivative. While her critique focuses on the phallocratic discourse and its sexism and exclusivity, her critique also reveals much about the content of this dominant discourse. Her critique has uncovered the Western over-emphasis on the One, which has led to a reduction of all others and otherness to the Same. Difference is devalued and ignored, especially sexual difference. Her ultimate goal is to encourage a world of genuine sexual difference.

As we shall see, she uses these techniques in her constructive endeavors as well. The critical and constructive functions in Irigaray's

---

[2] See Luce Irigaray, "Commodities Among Themselves," in *This Sex Which Is Not One,* trans. Catherine Porter (Ithaca NY: Cornell University Press, 1985) 192n.

[3] Luce Irigaray, "The Power of Discourse and the Subordination of the Feminine," in *This Sex Which Is Not One,* 74.

critique of the form and content of patriarchy's values come together as two sides of the same coin. Her critical analysis leads to and enables her constructive work. By marking out what has been named as male or female in the dominant discourse and highlighting that which has been repressed, she can locate possible candidates for the genuine feminine. She uses her training in psychoanalysis, her skill in philosophy, and her feminist sensibilities to listen for the voices that have been repressed and to accept and reevaluate the qualities that have been repressed. Highlighting those characteristics and forms that have been repressed is a strategy of both her constructive work and her critical work. Because this action subverts the phallocentric norms by giving articulation to that which patriarchy has denied and repressed, it disrupts the game of patriarchy. She throws a proverbial wrench into the machine of women's destruction.

Continuing to employ psychoanalysis philosophically, she approaches the presenting problem of patriarchal society as if it were a patient. If the problem in society is that women are oppressed and the feminine in repressed, Irigaray suggests that a return of the repressed will enable the feminine to rise to consciousness in individuals and in society in general. Her treatment plan is to uncover that which has been repressed and return it to consciousness. In psychoanalysis the earlier stages of development are extremely important. Further, sexuality, desire, and bodily experience play paramount roles in the development of ego and identity. As a feminist, she is also concerned with the way that gender is addressed or not addressed. In the previous chapter we saw that the descriptions Freud and Lacan give of early childhood development and their impact upon ego and identity indicate that society is thoroughly embedded in phallocentric norms. The cultural discourse, the way reality is interpreted, and even language itself are all governed exclusively by and through male experience and needs. The results of her critical analysis show that women have gone through these early childhood stages, which are governed by the symbolic order, in terms of their relation to the phallus or penis and not in terms of their own genitalia or experience. Women need to transverse these early stages anew symbolically—only this time transit through these phases in terms of their relation to feminine sexuality, female morphology, and women's bodily experience. Irigaray thus directs women to attend to the body and particularly to the morphology of female sexuality. She invites us to join her thought experiment by pulling out the implications of these sex organs and the nature of women's desire for what they could indicate about the nature of the feminine. She is searching for the virginal in the sense of that which is "untouched, uncorrupted, unmarred" by the phallus and phallocentrism. What sort of feminine subject arises from a schema for ego development taken from women's experience, women's bodies, and women's desire?

The first step is to elicit a discursive "return of the repressed." The "return of the repressed" is a psychoanalytic term representing the continual and unwanted effects of the repressed energy, feelings, memories of unpleasant, painful, or otherwise undesired events, often from childhood. Psychotherapy operates on the premise that that which has been repressed does not simply disappear, but continues to affect the way a person feels, thinks, and behaves consciously. The analyst seeks to elicit a "return of the repressed" in the controlled and safe space of therapy so that the fixated energy can be released and the unresolved conflicts and feelings can be addressed directly and hopefully resolved by integrating that which has been repressed into the conscious person. In using the term philosophically Irigaray plays psychoanalyst to the dominant phallocentric discourse and society as analysand. The problem in society and discourse can be addressed in a way similar to the work of psychoanalysis. Irigaray is the analyst; society and dominant discourse is the analysand; the oppression of women is the overt problem; the repression of the feminine is the diagnosis; the phallocentric discourse is the resistance, since it consciously articulates that there is no problem. Irigaray listens for the glitches and "slips" in the phallo-philosophy and phallo-speech that indicate the return of the repressed. This is a Freudian technique—to look for the glitches in the patient's speech. Parapraxia, or Freudian slips, such as "saying one thing when you really mean your mother," indicate the presence and character of that which has been repressed. The goal of this analysis is to bring to consciousness that which has been repressed so that it can be accepted in a direct way, and thus society will be healed and genuine feminine difference can flourish. Irigaray seeks to restore the repressed feminine to the surface and include it in conscious society with its own integrity, thus enabling a world of difference.

Deploying the fruits of her critical work, she looks for possibilities for the feminine in what phallocentric culture has repressed, erased, denied, and rendered invisible. She transfers the techniques of psychoanalysis, which seek to uncover the unconscious of an individual, onto her analysis of philosophical unconscious assumptions.[4] She highlights the unconscious of phallocentric discourse to see the possible positive characteristics, forms, and origination of the feminine. This technique yields several candidates for feminine characteristics and form. Multiplicity and multiformity of selfhood, fluidity, non-specular (such as tactile), partial openness, and simultaneity (both-at-once) are some of the most likely forms of experience and expression of the feminine. Later we'll see her exploration of these possibilities poetically and experimentally, looking to the female body and morphology, and especially sexuality, to discover the origin of the feminine. Women's sexual and bodily experience provides new ways of understanding the *jouissance*, or the pleasure, of the feminine. Women's sexuality is also a fecund recourse for metaphors for feminine discursive knowledge. Her emphasis on

---

[4] Luce Irigaray, *Parler n'est jamais neutre*, trans. Margaret Whitford (Paris: Minuit, 1985) 55.

feminine sexuality focuses on both the morphology of female sex organs and the nature of feminine desire itself.

In *The Ethics of Sexual Difference*,[5] Irigaray goes beyond the critique of phallocentric Western thought that she illuminates in *Speculum*, and attempts to grasp the utopian mode of thought necessary to found a society based on recognition of sexual difference. As elaborated in the previous chapter, the current phallo-culture renders genuine relations between the sexes impossible. The so-called difference/opposition between the sexes is based on theories that have exclusively used male experience. Irigaray refuses to accept the idea of the phallus as the transcendental signifier of sexual difference and suggests that primary female identity be linked to actual women's experiences, beginning with little girls' feelings of possessing internal sexual organs, as well as external organs. This approach enables her to conceptualize sexual difference in a series of metaphors of mucus membranes, lips, envelopes, angels, and children. We will explore the implications of her analysis for a constructive theory of feminine subjectivity below.

Irigaray's critical and constructive work enables women to search for a genuine feminine self for themselves. Irigaray's critical analysis reveals that phallocentric discourse has defined maleness and femaleness in the dominant discourse exclusively in terms of a dichotomy between the penis/phallus and the not-penis/phallus. Anything that does not fit into this dichotomous structure is repressed. Examining that which is neither "male" nor what has been defined as "female" in this dichotomous structure, offers clues as to what the feminine might truly *be*. Here is one important way in which her critique of Western discourse, especially of psychoanalysis, is useful for her and my own constructive analysis. By marking out the qualities that society calls male and female, Irigaray shows us how

---

[5] Luce Irigaray, *The Ethics of Sexual Difference* (Ithaca NY: Cornell University Press, 1993).

to recognize the genuine feminine. Irigaray's constructive analysis explores those spaces that are associated with neither male characteristics, nor the stereotypes of female characteristics. This critical exposé leads the way for the constructive task of women discovering their own positive expression and experience of femaleness.

This work is strategic in two significant ways. First, bringing to the surface that which has been repressed subverts the norms and structures of phallocratic thinking, eliciting a return of that which has been repressed and wrecking havoc on the phallocentric structures. This could also allow for the space needed to think differently about the feminine and other aspects of reality as well. Second, since she believes that phallocentric discourse feeds off of the repression of the feminine, the most likely hideaway for genuine characteristics of femininity is in what patriarchy has and continues to disregard and hide. For instance, phallocentric philosophy upholds oneness as normative and the standard for health and holiness. It denigrates multi-formity and associates it with sin and sickness, death and decomposing. Irigaray believes that this devaluing of multi-formity is constructed to cover over certain positive characteristics and forms of the genuine feminine. Phallocentric discourse functions to render unintelligible any theories about the self as multiple, relational and different.

Irigaray is not asserting a definition of woman, or even a theory of femininity as some of her critics have suggested. Rather, she offers possibilities of feminine form and character from that which patriarchy has denied; while at the same time, her critique exploits the opportunity to subvert the power of phallocentrism. With this technique Irigaray uses her critique of Western discourse's phallocentrism to create constructive possibilities for models of feminine subject-hood and discourse that resist the uniformity of the economy of the Same. As mentioned above, one significant characteristic Irigaray highlights that has been repressed and ignored in the discursive reign of oneness, is multiplicity or multi-formity of self. Irigaray identifies the dominance of the monolog model of selfhood with phallocentrism and phallocratism. In other words, phallocentrism represses the feminine and all types of difference. In her endeavor to liberate what has been repressed in this patriarchal society, she searches for the reality of the feminine. Just what the feminine is, is not readily discernable, and certainly not definitely definable. The feminine is open to discovery and suggestions. The question is where and how to discover the feminine. Irigaray's constructive work is thus a thought experiment, in which she ingeniously discerns several possibilities for the characteristics and forms of the feminine. Her critical work sets the stage for her thought experiment in which she invites us to let down our tired old assumptions about what it means to be a self and to try on the many-colored cloak of a feminine self. Let me emphasize this caveat. The results of her creative work here are suggested possibilities, not claims of essential definition.

Irigaray's critiques of rationality, discourse, subjectivity, and identity are not efforts on her part to dissolve rationality, discourse, subjectivity, and identity. Nor is she suggesting that women are or should be irrational, non-discursive, non-subjects, or without identity. Rather, she is suggesting that women be a part of restructuring rationality, discourse, subjectivity, and identity, so that these phallocratic institutions and structures are no longer funded by the repression of the feminine. Institutions of society should serve to enable genuine sexual difference. Her project is to restructure the constitution of rational subject-hood through a feminine imaginary. She mimics phallocentric philosophy in order to displace its normative center.

Irigaray is responding to the Western acceptance of the Aristotelian metaphysical tenet that woman does not have access to her own essence, to her own desire, to her own language, to her own speech, to subjectivity. Irigaray's assertions of women's own language, subjectivity, imaginary, and sexuality subverts the normative structure of cultural and discursive norms and opens the way to female subjecthood. How can women access our true feminine self/identity? The most direct access is through mysticism, in which the borders between body and soul are disrupted. The genuine feminine could be known outside of the assigned sexual (in)difference in phallocentric discourse. Amy Hollywood's analysis of mysticism interprets Irigaray as suggesting that the "two sexes must be fully articulated in their difference before the dissolution of that difference in ecstatic unity can be dissolved."[6] However, Irigaray also believes that other overt paths can be found. One way is through her philosophization of a therapeutic technique—mimesis, which is imitation to excess of the problematic behavior. She seeks to employ this imitation politically to subvert the dominant structure.

The objective of Irigaray's deconstructive discourse is to try to bring sexual *difference* into play, without bringing gender hierarchy. That is, to allow women to escape the Same which defines them as its "other" so that they might be free to define themselves as that which is really Other and authentically different. Since a real Other has never been permitted to speak and does not have its own language, Irigaray realizes that women will have to use the language which is available to them, for they have no other choice at present. However, her eventual hope is to allow a "feminine syntax" to emerge from within the male discourse.

Mimesis

One method she employs in this endeavor is her indirect method of mimesis, "in which the woman deliberately assumes and exaggerates the feminine style and posture assigned to her within this

---

[6] Amy Hollywood, *Sensible Ecstasy: Mysticism, Sexual Difference, and the Demands of History* (Chicago: University of Chicago Press, 2002) 188. See also Luce Irigaray, *The Ethics of Sexual Difference.*

discourse in order to uncover the mechanisms by which it exploits her."[7] In other words, women repeat and exaggerate the roles given to women by patriarchy. It is a little like the technique for relaxation in which one exaggerates the tension in a part of one's body and then releases all the tension. Mimesis is intended to aid women in their attempts to aggravate and de-center the dominant discourse. Using discourse is rooted in Irigaray's critical understanding of what she calls the specular economy—the discursive dynamic (or should I say static) which uses visual metaphors and norms to reduce everything to oneness and sameness. Her project seeks to extricate women from this economy, which defines them as "other" but which actually makes of them only a negative reflection of the Same, and to try to allow women to exist as authentic Other, to "speak (as) woman." Women can choose not to sever their connection with the "other" of the specular economy, but to use it as a political tool of subversion; in this way, women can enter into the philosophical discourse, "the discourse on discourse," to "try to find out what accounts for the power of its systematicity, the force of its cohesion."[8]

As women do this, Irigaray claims, playing the role of "other," of matter, of "femininity," there emerges "some remainder"—something extra which cannot be defined by the character's role, something which resists symbolization and which is truly Other than the Same. This playful repetition "lets loose a 'disruptive excess' that phallocentrism attempts to cover over."[9] The very fact that women can "play" with their designation as "other" suggests that "they are not simply resorbed in its function. They also remain elsewhere."[10] This remnant indicates a reality that is rendered invisible by the

---

[7] Irigaray, *This Sex Which Is Not One*, 220.

[8] Irigaray, "The Power of Discourse and the Subordination of the Feminine," 74.

[9] Ellen T. Armour, "Questioning 'Woman' in Femininst/Womanist Theology," in *Transfigurations: Theology and the French Feminists*, ed. C.W. Maggie Kim, Susan M. St. Ville, and Susan Simonaitis (Minneapolis: Fortress Press, 1993) 163.

[10] Irigaray, "The Power of Discourse and the Subordination of the Feminine," 76.

phallocentric structure of the cognition and discourse. Inasmuch as women are able to resist being inscribed by the dominant discourse—not by feigning masculinity or presuming to jump miraculously outside of its parameters, but by using the strategy of mimesis—there exists the presence of something that is not merely a lack, but which is also not simply the presence of the Same.

This excess of meaning enables the resistance necessary for a feminine syntax to be deciphered, which can undercut and challenge the phallocentrism of the specular economy. Through mimesis, women are enabled to create a space of their own within the phallocratic economy. But this space is not simply a haven for women's escape. Rather, it is the "disruptive excess" that starts in motion the disintegration of the foundations of patriarchy. In this space, armed with the musings of a feminine syntax, the feminine imaginary can "speak/write itself."[11] This "disruptive excess" can "cast phallocentrisim, phallocratism, loose from its moorings in order to return the masculine to its own language, leaving open the possibility of a different language. Which means that the masculine would no longer be 'everything.'"[12] This different possibility is the primordial soup for the development of feminine language. A feminine syntax, imaginary, and symbolic are prerequisites for the possibility of genuine feminine subjectivity. This feminine syntax is not easy to describe or define,

> ...because in that 'syntax' there would no longer be subject or object, 'oneness' would no longer be privileged, there would no longer be proper meanings, proper names, 'proper' attributes...Instead, that 'syntax' would involve nearness, proximity, but in such an extreme form that it would preclude

---

[11] Armour, "Questioning 'Woman' in Femininst/Womanist Theology," 164.
[12] Irigaray, "The Power of Discourse and the Subordination of the Feminine," 80.

any distinction of identities, any establishment of ownership, thus any form of appropriation.[13]

Her goal here is to tap into and create a feminine imaginary, a rich resource of feminine symbols, allusions, metaphors, metonyms, and basically a system of meaning and source of the feminine. This would enable genuine difference to develop and flourish. Following Lacan's psychoanalytical theories, she believes that there is a direct relationship between the structure of language and the structure of subjectivity. This correlation means that in order to enable women's self-determination and self-actualization, she must enable and create a feminine discourse, including grammar and syntax. Remember from the previous chapter that Irigaray suggests a figurative return to the pre-Mirror/pre-Oedipal stage in order to reclaim a feminine experience of woman's own development of self, which would be shaped according to a feminine body with meaning based in feminine metonymy. This process contrasts the phallocentric construction of ego development as articulated by Freud and Lacan.

According to Lacan, the mirror phase is the key to language development. He delivered a lecture in 1949 on the mirror stage "as formative of the function of the *I* as revealed in psychoanalytic experience."[14] The mirror experience is necessary for the formation of the child's sense of being a whole self and marks the turning point for the acquisition of language. Through the image of himself in the mirror, the little boy experiences himself as a singular whole and as distinct from all else in his environment, namely, his mother. This subject/object structure is also the structure of language. In Lacan's accepted schema, this maturation occurs when the little boy identifies himself with the father and distances himself from the mother. He does this according to his conscious awareness of his

---

[13] Luce Irigaray, "Questions," in *This Sex Which Is Not One*, 134.

[14] Jacques Lacan, *Écrits: A Selection*, trans. Alan Sheridan (New York: W.W. Norton and Co., 1977) 1-7.

penis, which she does not have, and subjects to the law of the phallus, which is the master signifier in all language, according to Lacan. In Irigaray's critical Lacanian view, women have entered this significant mirror phase only in terms of their relationship to the phallus. And thus women have learned phallocentrically structured syntax and grammar. Symbolically re-entering the mirror phase, after women have returned to their femininity as experienced in their bodies, may lead to a genuinely feminine syntax and grammar and a feminine symbolic structure. The feminine imaginary is a resource for language development and ego development. Feminine discourse is necessary for the existence of difference in society because the nature of the current phallocentric economy/language is a hierarchical dichotomy of subject/object. Irigaray postulates a correspondence between this dichotomous structure in language and the gender/sex difference dichotomy. Further, she claims that this correspondence is actually a causal relationship, in that the hierarchy of male over female shapes the structure in syntax into a hierarchical dichotomy.

A syntax that grows out of a feminine imaginary and women's experience offers a different way of understanding value and the nature of things. Because the structure of language writes the software for how knowledge and subjectivity is formed, a new and different structure to language offers an alternative to understanding everything, including being a self. Objects and subject can be related in ways that are not opposites, nor even absolutely distinct, but can be next to each other in thought, word, and reality. The subject could "know" the object via conforming itself to that object, so that it is actually taking the object into itself. And the object could impact the subject and impart qualities of itself to the subject. In this way both subject and object could be seen as active and passive. Neither would be exclusively passive nor exclusively active. Further, the way that persons can be related concretely could be viewed differently. A person is not only related to other persons in more intimate and mutually influential ways, but she or he is actually constituted in and by these relationships, both externally and internally.

The imaginary is involved in the child's ego formation in which he identifies with his own image in the mirror. In Lacan's thought, it is "the narcissistic structure of investments which transforms the image of otherness into a representation of the self."[15] It is part of the basic structure of the psyche. The child "imagines" fantasies of himself and the objects of his desire. This entails projecting an ideal onto others and then reclaiming that ideal as oneself. Yet for Lacan, this ideal is always an imagined image and not the real self in itself. The child is always alienated from his true self. This structure sets the stage for the way the child views others and itself. In psychoanalysis the child must split from the mother in order to enter the symbolic, which is the realm of society, language, and distinct subjectivity. In the symbolic the individual submits herself to the law of the Father, which is the rules and regulations and structure of phallocentric grammar. Conforming to the law of the Father breaks the nurturing union of child and mother, which is the imaginary. When the child starts to use the symbolic, it structures the child's subjectivity in a fashion that parallels the syntax of language and thus breaks the fluid connectivity between mother and child. But the child continues to desire union with the mother and this desire is the lack that continues to constitute the adult's ego. In feminist appropriations of Lacan's concept, the imaginary is associated with the pre-Oedipal communion between child and mother. It is the realm of the maternal and thus is often viewed with privilege in feminist circles. It is mostly unconscious and must be sought out through its amorphous presence in the unconscious dimensions of texts and persons. Images and pictorial structures, such as stories, are the best way of finding its expression. For Irigaray, the imaginary can only be accessed in the

---

[15] Elizabeth Grosz, *Sexual Subversions* (Sydney: Allen & Unwin, 1989) xviii.

gaps and margins of the symbolic, such as in dreams and psychoanalysis.

Phallocentrism has excluded the feminine imaginary from conscious expression and has left it in shards and fragments. Women have not been able to utilize the rich resource for creativity and connection of the imaginary. Yet what "if," Irigaray asks:

> the feminine imaginary were to deploy itself, if it could bring itself into play otherwise than as scraps, uncollected debris, would it represent itself, even so, in the form of one universe? Would it even be volume instead of surface? No. Not unless it were understood, yet again, as a privileging of the maternal over the feminine. Of a phallic maternal at that.[16]

Representing the feminine "in the form of one universe" would be closing off woman's self from herself; it is playing his game, and competing against him with his secret rules. It would be merely a reinforcement of the masculine.

But what if woman represents herself in forms that are uniquely feminine? Irigaray answers:

> (Re-)discovering herself, for a woman, thus could only signify the possibility of sacrificing no one of her pleasures to another, of identifying herself with none of them in particular, *of never being simply one*. A sort of expanding universe to which no limits could be fixed and which would not be incoherence nonetheless—nor that polymorphous perversion of the child in which the erogenous zones would lie waiting to be regrouped under the primacy of the phallus.[17]

Here Irigaray hints at a glimpse of what could be true if women could live as authentically feminine and be understood and determined by her own body and her own form, rather than being

---

[16] Luce Irigaray, "This Sex Which is Not One," in *This Sex Which is Not One*, 30.
[17] Ibid., 30-31.

subsumed under the primacy of the phallus. Irigaray notes the plurality possible:

Woman always remains several, but she is kept from dispersion because the other is already within her and is autoerotically familiar to her…She herself enters into a ceaseless exchange of herself with the other without any possibility of identifying either. This puts into question all prevailing economies: their calculations are irremediably stymied by women's pleasure, as it increases indefinitely from its passage in and through the other.[18]

The fourth strategy Irigaray employs is a discursive and literary technique known as metonymy. Metonymy is a figure of speech that consists of using the name of one thing to represent that of another for which it is an attribute or with which it is associated. It is distinguished from a metaphor in that a metaphor is a figure of speech in which a word or phrase which literally denotes one kind of object or idea is used in place of another, to suggest a likeness between the two. A metonymy is actually a part of that which it represents. "*A thousand hands waved goodbye,*" is an example of metonymy. Irigaray uses metonymy most predominantly in her focus on feminine sexuality and female genitalia to represent woman herself. Irigaray favors metonymy over metaphor in her constructive writing because it is more likely to elicit genuine feminine characteristics. Studying actual aspects of an entity to understand the whole is more likely to yield accurate characterizations of that entity.

Irigaray attacks phallocentrism most vehemently and directly on two primary tenets: its deification of maleness and oneness and its association of women with not-oneness. In response to these claims she articulates her famous suggestion that woman is "*This Sex Which is Not One.*" She writes, speaking as woman, "She is neither one nor two. Rigorously speaking, she cannot be identified either as one

---

[18] Irigaray, "This Sex Which is Not One," 31.

person, or as two."[19] In this quintessential formulation of her insights, she brings together three of her techniques in order to locate and imagine what the feminine might be like. First, she holds up what phallocentric discourse has torn down: multiplicity and multiformity. She explores this form/quality from a new non-patriarchal perspective. And she employs her technique of mimesis, of imitating to exaggeration what phallocentric discourse has named as feminine. For instance, Lacan, speaking for Western thought, says that women are the "subject which is not one." (In addition, we have already explored the early foundation of this view in Western theology through Augustine.) Mimetically, Irigaray repeats this "subject which is not one" in "*This Sex Which is Not One*," imitating Lacan's definition of woman. Lacan means that woman does not have a penis and thus does not have direct access to the power of the phallus. Therefore, woman is defined as a *lack* of the male, that which is not one. Irigaray imitates this formula, "not one," but changes the meaning of it. She looks at it from a fresh perspective. "Not one" for Irigaray means *this sex which is many, multiple, more than one, more than oneness*. Not only does this technique yield results in terms of content of the feminine, but also the activity of imitating and repeating on the part of women demonstrates the untruth of Lacan's claim that women are not conscious and intentional subjects on their own. This technique functions a bit like the scene from *Monty Python and the Holy Grail* in which the town dead disposal cart is making its rounds and a man is chanting "Bring out your dead." Another man carries an older man over his shoulder and starts to put him on the cart when the supposed corpse says, "I'm not dead." The collector replies, "He says he's not dead." The young man turns to the body and says to him, "yes you are."[20] The reason this is funny is that the

---

[19] Ibid., 26.

[20] "Plague Village," *Monty Python and the Holy Grail*, DVD, directed by Terry Gilliam and Terry Jones (Culver City CA: Columbia Tristar Home Entertainment, 2001).

supposed dead man has proven that he isn't dead not only by *what* he has said, but also and most convincingly, by the fact that he *has* spoken or *done* anything at all. A woman who imitates and repeats to exaggeration the mask that is put upon her demonstrates that she is more than that mask.

Metonymy is also functioning here in Irigaray's creative take on "not oneness." The metonymy of feminine sexuality as a representative that discloses and suggests feminine characteristics and forms serves her purpose in that using an actual part of women's bodies to theorize about the feminine is more likely to offer an accurate portrayal. Women's sexuality contributes many metaphors/metonyms of the feminine, as Irigaray writes:

> So woman does not have a sex organ? She has at least two of them, but they are not identifiable as ones. Indeed she has many more. Her sexuality, always at least double, goes even further: it is plural…woman has sex organs more or less everywhere. She finds pleasure almost anywhere…The geography of her pleasure is far more diversified, more multiple in its differences, more complex, more subtle, than is commonly imagined in an imaginary rather too narrowly focused on Sameness.[21]

Female sexuality and embodiment suggest that multiplicity and simultaneity are characteristics of the feminine. This plurality of form and complexity can be applied to understanding the feminine in general.

I find her preference for metonymy particularly helpful because it brings attention to the body and strengthens a view of embodied selfhood. Although she is focused on embodiment in general, Irigaray's emphasis here is directly related to her critical response to Lacan and Freud. Recall that her critique of psychoanalysis's theories

---

[21] Irigaray, "This Sex Which is Not One," 28.

concerning ego development for girls and women focuses on the fact that the theories are in terms of penis/phallus. The conceptualizations of female development are simply theories of male development in drag. No consideration is given to women's own bodies. Irigaray argues that little girls' development ought to be understood in terms of her own sexual organs and not male genitalia. This leads to her attention to the insights given from female genitalia and the form of feminine desire. In this way, she is offering a parallel theory of women. Searching within the actual bodies and experiences of women is a clever way to expose a genuine feminine. But we must be careful in making an absolute convergence. Judith Butler suggests that even a woman's body and experience of desire is socially constructed and prescribed by patriarchy, asking, "is 'the body' itself shaped by political forces…?"[22] The body is not a passive entity prior to discourse, but is a figure inscribed with cultural and political signification. Irigaray averts this critique by offering more than one approach in her search for the feminine. In addition to her embodied theorizing, she uses the psychoanalytic technique of highlighting those qualities that have been repressed, as well as the therapeutic strategy of mimesis.

Irigaray also looks to the body because she locates what is uniquely "women-esque" in a most practical and earthy common denominator: women's bodies. We each have our own unique body and our own unique experience of our body. And yet women each share a common anatomy/morphology as female; it is what is most real that women all do share. Women each have a clitoris, a vagina, two pairs of labia. These organs have great potentiality to give pleasure, and often, ecstasy. According to Irigaray, the labia can give constant pleasure, "Woman 'touches herself' all the time…for her genitals are formed of two tips in continuous contact…that caress

---

[22] Judith Butler, *Gender Trouble* (New York: Routledge, 1990) 129.

each other."²³ Irigaray wants to capitalize on this primal experience. And so she begins by grounding her theory in her own and each woman's body, and particularly on women's experience of sexual pleasure. As a psychoanalyst, sexuality and sexual morphology is the context of her discourse.

Irigaray utilizes woman's body for its rich resources and metaphors and metonyms to express concrete genuine feminine realities. For the pairs of labia, Irigaray pens "both at once" as a fundamental feminine metonym to express a genuine reality corresponding to the not-oneness of phallocentrism's projection onto the feminine. The two lips, even the two pairs of lips, represent the feminine. They are simultaneously both singular and double, both open and closed, vertical and horizontal. This metonymy suggests that the feminine is simultaneously both singular and double, open and closed, vertical and horizontal. Irigaray writes:

> Woman is neither open nor closed. She is indefinite, in-finite, form is never complete in her. She is not infinite but neither is she a unit(y), such as letter, number, figure in a series…This incompleteness in her form, her morphology, allows her continually to become something else…No one single thing—no form, act, discourse, subject, masculine, feminine can complete the development of woman's desire.²⁴

Here the fact that feminine selfhood is embodied highlights that it is open, while also maintaining boundaries, and incomplete while in the process of becoming. The feminine brings together elements that appear to be opposite. Further, in the feminine these elements are integrated in a way that does not collapse either side into the other. Irigaray writes:

---

[23] Irigaray, "This Sex Which Is Not One," 24.
[24] Luce Irigaray, *Speculum of the Other Woman*, trans. Gillian C. Gill (Ithaca NY: Cornell University Press, 1985) 229.

the/a woman who doesn't have one sex organ, or a unified sexuality, (and this has usually been interpreted to mean that she has no sex) can not subsume it/herself under one generic or specific term. Body, breasts, pubis, clitoris, labia, vulva, vagina, neck of the uterus, womb...all these foil any attempt at reducing sexual multiplicity to some proper noun, to some proper meaning, to some concept. Woman's sexuality cannot therefore be inscribed as such in any theory.[25]

The characteristics and forms of feminine selfhood that can then be extrapolated from her focus on female sexual organs includes multiplicitiy, "both at once-ness," openness, and contradictoriness and irreducibility. She also removes women's sex and women's subjectivity from the control of phallocentric discourse that might constrict it to a uniform process or a singular expression. She is claiming not only that women's sexual pleasure can be found in multiple areas and experienced in many ways, but that women's entire bodies are the context of their desire and pleasure.

She looks to the form of feminine sexuality and desire as well as to women's actual bodily experience for developing a feminine understanding of women's subjectivity. Feminine desire has been repressed and replaced with whatever men want her to desire. Remember the Freudian formula that woman must renounce her own original desire in order to mature, and then she should desire only to be desired by the male. In contrast to this normative view, Irigaray seeks to elicit genuine feminine *jouissance*. In the French, "*jouissance*" includes the connotation of sexual and sensual pleasure that is lacking in the anglicized "joy." *Jouissance*, Irigaray says, is orgasmic pleasure or delight. But it is also an embodied pleasure. Paula Cooley interprets this notion and its importance in the work of Irigaray as a liberating power. She writes:

---

[25] Ibid., 233.

...for woman consciously to separate herself from man, by rejecting his language and culture, and to explore sexually her own body, alone or in intimacy with other women, is for woman to discover jouissance...Jouissance liberates; it gives rise to woman's identity and language as it simultaneously dismantles patriarchy in its dependence on sexual control over woman to assure patrimony so that power passes from father to son. [It] dismantles patriarchal institutions in that defying sexual repression disrupts control over women as the means of reproduction.[26]

Since feminine *jouissance* is experienced primarily through touching, and not primarily through looking, as is the specular phallocentric economy, the power of *jouissance* raises the subconscious to the surface and thereby releases that which has been repressed.[27] Irigaray seeks to stimulate *jouissance* in women as a means of transcending the language of phallocentrism. Irigaray says women's own desire "upsets the linearity of a project, undermines the goal-object of a desire, diffuses the polarization toward a single pleasure, disconcerts fidelity to a single discourse..."[28] Thus, focusing on the genuine feminine difference is also a strategic move which subverts phallocentrism's emphasis on oneness.

The results of both Irigaray's exploration of these positive expressions of women's bodies and her critical analysis point to multiplicity as a feminine reality. Recalling that the difference between the sexes to originate in psycho-sexual development and through Western society's institutionalization of this dysfunction, particularly expressed in Freud and Lacan's descriptions of Western

---

[26] Paula Cooley, *Religious Imagination and the Body* (New York: Oxford University Press, 1994) 22-23.

[27] Audre Lorde makes a similar claim in "The Uses of the Erotic," in *Sister Outsider: Essays and Speeches* (Berkeley CA: The Crossing Press, 1984).

[28] Irigaray, Luce, "This Sex Which Is Not One," 30.

culture's acceptance of male definitions of women's anatomy and women's experience, Irigaray proclaims that women must reclaim their bodies from the names, words, experiences, and control that men have forced upon women. An example of such discourse-rape is Freud's theory about women's "orgasms." He names the first experience of pleasure for women that occurs solely from stimulation of the clitoris as immature, and preaches that the more "mature" experience is a solely vaginal occurrence. Women are taught that their own bodily experience is immature or wrong. This results in women not trusting their own experiences and makes them especially suspicious of their bodily experience. Irigaray implores women to create their own discourse through experiencing their own bodies and sexuality alone, either in masturbation or in lesbian sexual encounters, without men involved in any way. In this way women can write their own discourse with its own style, its own grammar and structure, and thus they are speaking themselves into becoming real selves.

Almost all Western women have been de-selfed and de-subjected by the Western phallocentric discourse. Thus, the political task at hand is much broader and deeper than we might think at first glance. The task of subverting the discourse that funds patriarchy and defines women as "other" is an important step in the political arena. Commodity capitalism must certainly be challenged, but so must the entire psychological, philosophical, religious, and linguistic framework of Western thought. In order for this kind of subversion to become a reality, the mute—those who have been rendered silent by the One voice of the Same—must begin to speak and break the holy code of silence. Such speech will be difficult, for the only language known is "his." The marginalized voices of women do not make sense to the dominant phallocentric male ear, and feminine grammar will defy all the rules, but feminine discourse will be women's own, *and* it will unsettle, threaten, and decenter phallocentrism.

Once women recognize the urgency of speaking in their own voices and of using their own language, while at the same time continuing their political alignment with one another, the problem becomes the question of *how* such a language can emerge. With what strategies and tools can the dominant discourse be de-centered?

Irigaray is convinced that in order for women to maintain their specificity, a simple turning of the discursive table is not enough. She believes that conventional attempts simply to reclassify women as "subjects" will not work. In Western culture, the category of "subject" is a male-created and male-controlled concept. "Subjectivity" is conceptualized as a oneness, a conformity to the Same, uniform norm. Thus, women can only become "subjects" by becoming like men. Such a change would amount to woman's "renouncing the specificity of her own relationship to the imaginary."[29] She recognizes the incredible complexity of the task at hand and realizes that even the positing of a highly original female metaphysic or epistemology will not change the dualistic grid, which underlies the current thought-world. Strategies like temporary separation from men might be a good idea for those women who are in positions to enjoy such a luxury, and, as Irigaray points out:

>...these are certainly indispensable stages in the escape from their proletarization on the exchange market. *But* if their aim were simply to reverse the order of things, even supposing this to be possible, history would repeat itself in the long run, would revert to sameness: to phallocratism.[30]

Phallocratism is not simply male rule; it is the reign of sameness. Phallocratism is the positing of maleness as the only positive norm of subjectivity. While at the same time it projects the negative characteristics of maleness (perhaps of humanness) onto the feminine, and, further, it also represses that reality which is genuinely feminine.

---

[29] Irigaray, *Speculum of the Other Woman*, 133.
[30] Irigaray, "This Sex Which Is Not One," 33.

Getting rid of the phallocentric/feminine dichotomy demands fundamental changes in every aspect of life, including a different conception of nature and our place in it, and a re-envisioning of our language, our psychology, and, above all, our entire approach to philosophy. Irigaray writes, "Everything has to be (re)invented to avoid the vacuum."[31] It requires challenging the very structure of our thinking—oneness versus difference, sameness versus multiplicity.

Because this task is not simply one "of elaborating a new theory of which woman would be the subject or the object, but of jamming the theoretical machinery itself, of suspending its pre-tension to the production of a truth and of a meaning that are excessively univocal,"[32] Irigaray admits that she has only a vague idea of what such a world would look, sound, feel, or taste like. She also recognizes that the sort of revolutionary changes she is talking about will take time, lots of time, to bring about. She is convinced, however, that the task is still worth doing, even though it may never reach full fruition; "it is," she maintains, "still better to speak in riddles, allusions, hints, [and] parables" than remain stuck in the delimiting language of the phallocratic metaphysic.[33]

Irigaray argues that women need their/our own language in order to assert and develop their/our own selves. Irigaray understands discourse as a grammar that is "man-made," constructed and structured according to men for the function of communication, thinking, and coming to knowledge. This process is akin to Feuerbach's analysis of man's projection onto God. "Man" also projects himself onto language. It is based on man's ways of thinking and expressing, of experiencing and knowing. There is nothing evil in itself about males or male discourse—that is if there were only men in this world. However, phallocentric discourse has become

---

[31] Irigaray, *Speculum of the Other Woman*, 228.
[32] Irigaray, "The Power of Discourse and the Subordination of the Feminine," 78-79.
[33] Irigaray, *Speculum of the Other Woman*, 143.

problematic, beginning with the projection of itself in and onto all else and culminating in the reduction of all otherness to sameness with the male projection, which results in the economy of the Same. The problem lies in the exclusion of women from the creation and development of language (which is oft dubbed as the grand distinction of humanity above other animals). Women have not fully developed into their own selves, because they have tried to fit themselves into these male-centered, hierarchical structures and forms of discourse and values. While the majority of individual men are not responsible for the construction of phallocratism, they are not without blame, for they have inadvertently benefited from this setup and have often perpetrated it knowingly, at the expense of those with less power.

Irigaray's employment of these morphological metaphors and metonymies is not an attempt at naming the "true essence of womanhood." Rather, it is a strategy to contest the dominant illusion of feminine sexuality. What Irigaray has done is to build up the characteristics that have been ignored and denigrated and dismissed. Those attributes that have fallen through the cracks are what patriarchy doesn't want us to know. Her constructive work is not a "new and improved" definition of the essence of woman. Rather, her constructive work builds upon her critique of the phallocentric practice of defining women exclusively according to their relationship to the phallus. She opens that which has been closed to women: women's personal relation to their own organs of sexual pleasure. She makes way for this new "space" in phallocentric discourse by offering it up as suggestions for the emergence of women's own exploration and discovery of the specificity of feminine characteristics, forms, syntax, the imaginary, discourse, and *jouissance*. The feminine is not limited to women, it "cannot signify itself in any proper meaning, proper name, or concept, not even that of woman."[34] The feminine is

---

[34] Irigaray, "Questions," 156.

an ambiguous term that cannot be defined, but only explored and partially discovered by individuals themselves. Irigaray does not seek to construct a theory of women; rather, she shares her thoughts and experiences of the feminine and the feminine imaginary. As she says, "speaking (as) woman is not speaking of woman."[35] Simply by speaking as a woman, she is enacting a feminine language and is contributing to a feminine imaginary.

The phallocentric structure of discourse, words, grammar, experience, articulation, and theology's understanding of God all implies that God must be understood as a "perfect volume, a closed completeness...a matrix coiled back on/in its interiority."[36] "God," for Irigaray, plays a necessary psychological function in the delineation of the boundaries and foundations upon which the self is constituted. Society has proclaimed that the basis of a well-built house is not woman—for woman is associated with fluidity, the shameful flow in Western norms. Irigaray critiques this societal evaluation. "Fluid," she writes, "must remain that secret, sacred, remainder of the one. Blood, but also milk, sperm, lymph, spittle, saliva, tears, humours, gases, waves, airs, fire...light which threaten him with distortion, propagation, evaporation, burning up [consummation], flowing away, in an other difficult to grasp. The 'subject' identifies himself with/in an almost material consistence which is repelled by all fluence."[37] Here Irigaray has identified the phallocentric fear of fluidity and a search for an "almost material consistency," an absolute security or mooring for his subjectivity. Augustine also associates fluidity and flow with the sinful nature of concupiscence, and the holy as the state of continence, the withholding of any flow of any bodily fluids, namely semen. Irigaray's analysis also fits Augustine's fearful quest and almost panicked

---

[35] Ibid., 135.

[36] Luce Irigaray, "Volume Without Contours," in *The Irigaray Reader*, ed. Margaret Whitford, (Malden MA: Blackwell Publishers, Inc., 1991) 63.

[37] Ibid., 64.

appropriation of "God's gift" of continence, the ability to withhold one's fluids. There is a correspondence between Irigaray's analysis of contemporary phallocentric valuing of solids over against the flow of the feminine, on the one hand, and Augustine's theological associations of continence as redemption, while concupiscence, the desire to flow, is the quintessential metaphor for sin, on the other. Again, we see a connection between evil or sin, and women, or feminine form—a connection between women and sin.

There are three primary insights of Irigaray that are particularly fruitful. First is her critique of Western culture and discourse. She analyzes the phallocentric economy of the Same, which I see as a postulate of its exaltation of the one, as a construct that is detrimental to the feminine. Secondly, her technique for discovering the repressed feminine is clever and effective. She looks to what has been repressed to find the feminine. Through the openness and creativity of her technique, she discovers much that has been discarded and lost, especially multiplicity, permeability, and fluidity. The notion that a genuine feminine subject is multiple, permeable, and fluid arises from her critical analysis of the embedded assumptions in the phallocentric discourse. And then this notion is judged against the metonym of the form of feminine sexuality and grounded in women's body experience. This leads to a third area of insight.

She looks to women's concrete *bodily* experience for clues to the recovery of feminine characteristics and forms. This focal point serves as a test for those insights she has derived from her abstract analysis. She argues that the body is the foundation of selfhood. Yet women are not limited by their body in the way that Freud claimed that "anatomy determines destiny." (Nor are men.) In the process of looking for genuine sexual difference, she looks for feminine ways of being subjects. I employ her insights in conceptualizing selfhood as a relational matrix consisting of multiple parts. Building on the firm foundations of bodily actuality and, specifically, on models of feminine sexual organs and sexual pleasure, she constructs feminine subjectivity. This focus yields a paradigmatic metonymy of the feminine, which is the "both at once-ness" of the double labia. The labia are two, but are not reducible into ones. They are paired, pairs of pairs. This metonymy is multiple and has implications of multiplicity for the form of feminine subjectivity. Irigaray locates the certainty of her feminine self in her bodily experience of *jouissance*—the sensuous, sexual pleasure of a woman's body. Irigaray says, "I feel my body, therefore I am." Permeability is another metaphor taken from the structure of women's genitalia. Women are open to the world and take the other inside. This morphology can indicate the importance of external relationships to the constitution of a feminine subjectivity. Fluidity is a third aspect of the female body that Irigaray uses as a metonym for feminine subjectivity. Just as woman's body flows as volume without contours, so too is the feminine self fluid—not static or substance based. It is in process, changing, growing, and developing in its engagements with others. I have highlighted these three of Irigaray's many insights because I will employ them in my new constructive view of theological anthropology in the next chapter.

In summary, Irigaray's critical analysis of the Western tradition, in which she has highlighted the margins and unconsciousness of discourse, reveals the positive presence of multiplicity, simultaneity, and fluidity (among other characteristics and forms). She focuses her search (for that which has been repressed in society) on female bodily experience. She looks to the characteristics and forms of feminine sexual organs and feminine sexual pleasure and process for possible candidates for the lost feminine itself. "What might a genuinely feminine subject be like?" she asks. Let's look at what we know to be feminine, she answers—the female body, the many female sex organs, her sexual joy. Focusing on these areas of women and of the margins of phallocentric discourse, she notes similar qualities and forms. Both techniques of detection reveal multiplicity, simultaneity, and fluidity.

These three themes, including fluidity, simultaneity, and particularly the multiformity of selfhood, are most helpful to the project of writing a constructive view of selfhood that encourages multiplicity and internal relationality. I highlight these qualities of the self and bring them into dialogue with Kierkegaard's insights concerning the notion of the self as a relating relation. These two thinkers brought together in a dialectical way form the foundation of my new theological anthropology. But let's first examine the primary similarities and differences between them.

Comparison and Contrast between Kierkegaard and Irigaray

Irigaray and Kierkegaard have each expressed an alternative to the dominant conceptualization of the self. They differ significantly in terms of influence, method and goals, yet their purposes and conclusions are compatible enough that they can be brought into dialogue with one another. The following section addresses the three major areas of convergence in which I explore the significant differences as well as important points of confluence: (1) purpose and method; (2) critical stance toward the prevailing norm of selfhood; and (3) common conceptualizations of selfhood in which difference, relationality and multiplicity are accepted and authentic selfhood is viewed as holding together difference simultaneously in a single person. While there are many obvious differences between these thinkers, such as divergence in focus, theoretical framework, and purpose, for our purposes here the most interesting differences lie in their conceptualizations of authentic selfhood. I address these differences within the midst of their similarities, arguing that the similarities and differences are best taken together.

1. Method and purpose of critique. Irigaray and Kierkegaard differ in what they hope to effect through their critiques. The purpose of Kierkegaard's authorship is to "edify," to build up the individual's Spirit toward becoming a Christian. Kierkegaard seeks to elucidate the religious sphere, which is a sphere of living that will always be distinct from the norms of culture and discourse. It will always be the sphere accessible only through subjectivity and passion. It is a realm not known through external examination. It is somewhat mystical, not following the logic of universal norms of right and wrong, true and false, real and illusory. The religious follows its own rules, the paradoxical logic of faith. Kierkegaard is not calling for the restructuring of societal norms, for these values are not the religious and will never be. The religious realm is beyond the domain of philosophical discourse. It cannot be integrated into the universal; it is not reducible to societal norms.

Irigaray, on the other hand, seeks to bring the feminine into consciousness. Irigaray's feminine is different from Kierkegaard's religious sphere in that the feminine is not inherently unconscious or opposed to the culture norms. Kierkegaard's religious sphere is opposed to universal cultural norms by definition. Irigaray asserts that current culture and discourse is phallocentric and has repressed the feminine, replacing it with a pseudo-feminine. The current cultural and philosophical norms are unethical for three primary reasons. First, it is problematic because it falsely universalizes itself as "the same." It masquerades as the one *a priori* truth about selfhood, demanding that all selfhood conform to this model of uniformity, uniformly. It is thoroughly phallocentric—its forms and characteristics are based only on male experience and need. Its content is singular, its form is uniform, and its application is absolute. This construct of phallocentrism excludes those who do not fit the norm, rejecting persons and models of selfhood that do not conform to this one phallocentric construct. Irigaray works to build up and expand the conscious expression of culture to include feminine qualities and forms and to rejoice in the genuine difference between male and female.

Kierkegaard argues against the cultural norms because their content has been misapplied to, and identified with, religious truth and salvation. He argues against the common identification of the ultimate with the universal. The cultural norms for selfhood had been associated with human ethical standards and not with Christian criteria. These associations are exemplified by Kant's claims about universal rights and wrongs and Hegel's philosophical claims about the overall progression of history toward harmonious synthesis between the Universal (history) and the Absolute (the Spirit). Kierkegaard generally agrees with Kant about the nature of the universal norms. He disagrees that the Universal and the Absolute are the same, or that the Universal is the way to the Absolute. And for Kierkegaard, the Absolute is the highest goal. The religious sphere is most clearly distinguished from the ethical one in that in the religious sphere one's relationship to the Universal is determined by and through one's relationship to the Absolute. While for the ethical sphere, one's relationship to the Absolute is determined by and through one's relationship to the humanly constructed Universal. Christianity does not bid us to be strictly aesthetic, nor strictly ethical. Rather, the paradigm of faith is Abraham, whose actions do not fit into either of these two distinct dimensions of existence. Abraham's story has elements that are present in both the aesthetic sphere and the ethical sphere, yet he is not limited to this "either/or." Rather, he brings them together in dialectical relation, into a new sphere—a non-empirical sphere that cannot be spoken. This sphere transcends the limits of cultural norms and cultural motifs—the religious sphere is "genuinely different." It is beyond the person's natural ability to reason, know, and articulate.

Cultural norms are not evil in themselves, but they can never be the religious. And religious selfhood is the only genuine selfhood. An individual can look to the universal norms for guidance, and she can look to her own whims and desires. But to become genuinely oneself, one must relate these two ways of living to each other and be in relation to God. The individual self must stand before God as an individual who is solely responsible for her own decisions. The cultural norms will never be adequate to express the religious truth of subjectivity due to their external and universal form. However, please note that the religious realm includes aspects of the self's conformity to the ethical norms of the culture as well as the self's aesthetic rebellion against such conformity as constitutive parts of the religious sphere of existence.

Irigaray, on the other hand, calls into question the universality of what the dominant philosophical discourse claims as universal. The current cultural and discursive norms are unethical due to their exclusivity. The problem is not with a misidentification between cultural norms and religious truths. For Irigaray, phallocentric culture, phallocentric discourse, and phallocentric religion are all correlated in that they all function to uphold male domination. The problem is in the identification between male norms and universal cultural norms. Irigaray wants to change the normative view of the universal so that society and discourse will include the feminine. In fact, she wants to do away with the universal as such. There is such a difference between male and female ways of being that there can be no true universal. She says that she "has no desire to take their speech as they have taken ours, nor to speak 'universal.'"[38] She is not suggesting that the phallocentric universal speech or space be replaced with exclusively feminine speech and space. This would simply lead to another economy of the Same. Instead, she champions an economy of difference.

2. *Critique of normative concepts of Self.* Kierkegaard and Irigaray are both critical of the normative conceptions of the uniformity of selfhood. In response, they both offer a genuinely different model of selfhood. There are similarities in their critical views of cultural expressions of selfhood. Both thinkers evaluate that what passes for selfhood to others on the outside is actually pseudonymous selfhood. Both strive toward enabling those without genuine selfhood to come to it. Kierkegaard believes that persons are in "despair at not willing

---

[38] Luce Irigaray, *Le Corps-a'-corps avec la me're* (Montreal: Pleine Lune, 1981) 64, quoted in Naomi Schor, "This Essentialism Which is Not One," in *Differences*, 1 (Summer 1989): 45.

to be oneself" and in despair at willing to be oneself. Further, they often don't even know that they are in despair. In other words, their despair is unconscious. Kierkegaard seeks to bring that unconscious despair into the person's awareness and "edify" his/her spirit toward "willing to become oneself" before God.

Likewise, Irigaray's critical and constructive project begins with the assertion that genuine sexual difference is repressed, and we are not even aware that it is repressed. Irigaray seeks to "build up" possibilities for genuine sexual difference in selfhood and discourse. In this way both Kierkegaard and Irigaray agree that a problem exists and that most are unconscious of this problem. She sets about to reveal that the feminine has been supplanted with a pseudo-feminine. This pseudo-feminine is not genuine sexual difference. In actuality, it is purely the projections of the dominant discourse's reversed image. In other words, in culture no genuine sexual difference between men and women is acknowledged in our conceptions of male and female. The so-called difference between the sexes is a confabulation of the dominant discourse. The genuine difference has been obfuscated by the repression of the feminine. She seeks to liberate women from this pseudo-selfhood and enable genuine difference to emerge. Kierkegaard's work parallels this aspect of Irigaray's work. He strives to enable the one who is in despair and doesn't know he is in despair to become aware that his pseudo-happiness is exactly the reversal of his true state of being, which is despair.

Kierkegaard's critique of the normative view of the self focuses on the way that religious truth and insights are misunderstood. He brings out the discontinuity between cultural and philosophical values for good existence and the examples of religious living in the Christian tradition. He is particularly disturbed by what he calls the "prodigious illusion of Christendom," in which persons mistakenly believe that they are Christians when, in fact, they are living by the norms of society and not of God.[39] Kierkegaard criticizes the Danish cultural standards of behavior not because these norms are non-inclusive of women and others, but because they have been identified with Christian existence erroneously. He argues against this identification between the external norms of social conformity, found in nineteenth century Danish culture, with religious goodness, holiness, salvation, and selfhood that has led to a pseudo-Christianity, or Christendom. The religious sphere of existence is distinct from the universalization of norms in either culture or reason. Movement toward religious selfhood is a progressively inclusive dialectical movement through the aesthetic sphere and the ethical sphere into a space of becoming in which the elements of existence are held together in a balanced tension, all in the relationship with the Absolute God.

While Kierkegaard offers critiques of the aesthetic sphere and ethical sphere, which together reflect the morals and the norms of the culture and the world, his desired sphere of existence, the religious sphere, takes the other two spheres and their contents up into itself, transcending each. The finiteness of the individual and the world are not lost, not discarded, not demonized, but rather they are transfigured and incorporated into the highest sphere of existence, the religious. This alternative to the cultural social norms not only transcends the norms, but it transfigures them as well by turning them to face each other and enabling a dialectical relationship between the spheres, the elements, and authors. Although Kierkegaard does not have access to the language or principles of psychoanalysis, as does Irigaray, he does search for true subjectivity in that which is under the conscious assertions about religion and about being a self that were prevalent in his "present age." He claims that authentic selfhood is found in the margins and blank spaces of what

---

[39] Søren Kierkegaard, *Attack upon 'Christendom,'* trans. Walter Lowrie (Boston: Beacon Press, 1944).

popular culture names as true and valuable. He even likens his work to revealing a hidden script under the words of the plain text. Genuine subjectivity cannot be expressed externally. He uses a method of indirect communication to highlight where he finds truth.

Irigaray also names the norms of culture as problematic and seeks to subvert the power of the economy of the Same, in which only one way is valued as good and true. Like Kierkegaard, she believes that genuine selfhood lies under the surface of these norms. However, she does not believe that the genuine feminine takes the phallocentric norms of culture into itself. The dominant discourse is problematic due to its exclusive phallocentric content and form. In her utopia the male and the feminine characteristics and forms would relate together consciously in culture.

Irigaray's central analysis of the phallocentric discourse's emphasis upon oneness is helpful to any project of constructing a model of selfhood that is constituted on multiplicity and internal relationality. She has demonstrated that Western discourse's claim of the *a priori* unity of the self/subject is problematic because this conceptualization of the *unity* of the self is a detrimental construct.

Her critique of the Phallocentric discourse and its economy of the Same cracks opens our embedded assumptions about the values ascribed to singularity and begs for our questions and insights concerning the nature of the self.

3. Content and Form of Authentic Selfhood. Irigaray and Kierkegaard also share characteristics and forms in their understanding of authentic selfhood. For Irigaray, genuine subject-hood for women is found in the realm of the feminine, which has been repressed into a sort of collective unconscious. If and when genuine feminine difference emerges from the phallocentrism, phallocentric discourse will not be included as a constitutive aspect of the feminine, for the genuine feminine is invisible in phallocentric thought. For Kierkegaard, however, this third sphere, the religious sphere, encompasses the universal ethical sphere, as well as the aesthetic sphere of social norms. In fact, in some ways the religious realm is the relationship of the universal and the particular, culminating in the absolute.

Next, Irigaray seeks to discover this feminine genuine difference through both her critical analysis of that which phallocentric discourse has obliterated and through the data gathered from women exploring women's own bodies. Kierkegaard seeks to articulate genuine religious selfhood from his reading of the Bible, the Christian tradition, and his religious experience.

Kierkegaard differentiates the religious sphere from the ethical sphere and the aesthetic sphere in several ways. For our purposes we will focus on those aspects that are particularly relevant for my constructive project. First of all, the religious sphere is not a description of what Kierkegaard has observed empirically. It is only known internally and cannot be recognized from the outside. Others cannot know the knight of faith externally. But rather it is an imagined construction, from his religious imagination—his religious experience as a Christian. The religious sphere is his prescription for what is genuine human and Christian existence. The uniqueness of the religious sphere lies not in its content, but in its telos and its form. The telos of the religious sphere is to be related absolutely to the Absolute. The content of the religious sphere is primarily the content of the first two spheres with one major addition: the religious sphere is in relation to the Absolute, God.

Kierkegaard's religious sphere is multiple and relational. It is not uniform, nor is it a duality. Its core is the dialectical movement between the poles of human existence, the finite and the infinite, between the objective and subjective poles of human existence. It is internally relational. Its internal structure is dialectical. This dialectical relation between these inner elements occurs in relation to the Absolute. Through this dialectic of faith, the other spheres, the aesthetic and the ethical, are brought together and held together in tension. Their contradictions and opposing elements are related to each other. These elements are not only relating to each other, their relation is relating to itself as well, all in a web of reflexivity. Thus, the form of subjectivity, the highest form of selfhood, is non-uniform, multiple, and relational.

This "third" sphere can be likened to Irigaray's term, "genuine sexual difference." It is also seen in contradistinction to the accepted cultural norms of selfhood. According to Irigaray's analysis, there are only two accepted ways of living in Western society: phallocentrically and through pseudo-femininity. This so-called feminine is the opposite of the normative in both form and content. The masculine qualities are preferred as mature and positive, while the feminine is the reverse negative image of the male. Irigaray critiques this view as unethical and inadequate to the reality of feminine subject-hood. Like Kierkegaard, Irigaray posits a "third" alternative to the dichotomy of gendered existence, offering suggestions about the qualities and forms of a third alternative. For Irigaray, this third way begins with replacing the feminine that is constructed by phallocentric discourse with a genuine feminine difference. Irigaray further suggests, albeit seldom, that the male model of selfhood is also falsely constructed in this phallocentric discourse. Thus, the masculine would need to be re-examined and transformed as well if the society were to change drastically enough to allow genuine sexual difference. In effect, she is saying that the models for selfhood for males and females are both inadequate and two new models for selfhood are needed. These models should be distinct from one another, yet not limited to stereotypes. This emphasis on gender difference is not present in Kierkegaard's thought on selfhood. Unlike Irigaray, he does not critique patriarchy, he does not consciously recognize a problem with the economy of the Same, and he makes no gender associations between these cultural norms. He sees the society's normative view of selfhood as an inadequate dichotomy that crosses gender.

The metonymy of two lips for the feminine self as posited by Irigaray is an excellent metaphor for Kierkegaard's understanding of human subjectivity. (I say metaphor for Kierkegaard and not metonymy, since it is Irigaray who derives this dynamic from women's labia. Yet if "both-at-once-ness" can be a description of the human body itself, then this could be a metonym.) The human self as a religious self is neither exclusively objective, nor exclusively subjective; he/she is neither totally aesthetic, nor totally ethical, but both at once—neither fully finite, nor fully infinite, but both at once. The dialectic of living is the movement back and forth between these two elements. Human subjectivity is "both-at-once-ness" of existence. It is a dialectical movement of the self's center from one side to the other side, and back again, transformed. This simultaneity is connected with Irigaray's constructive view of genuine selfhood.

Irigaray's "both at once" is similar to Kierkegaard's dialectical relation of the self to itself in structure, form, and content. Recall that Kierkegaard's genuine Christian is the one who is willing to become oneself before God by holding together the oppositional factors of existence. These two factors of existence cannot be completely divided from each other in a real concrete life—a self is not "either" finite "or" infinite, but rather the authentic self in existence is *both* finite *and* infinite. This sounds like a paradox. And Kierkegaard often refers to the paradox of faith.

Irigaray's descriptions of the feminine also sound like a paradox—the feminine does not follow the universal norms of rational non-contradictions, "she is neither one nor two." "She is two that are not reducible into ones." Yet there is some "logic," a logic of the feminine, or as Kierkegaard might call it, the logic of faith found in the paradox of faith. The paradox of faith is not a free for all, with no rules or boundaries or structure. Rather, it breaks the established boundaries and rules of logic and universal rational truth. But truth is real; it is a definable concept, in contrast to other concepts. Irigaray's subversive writing and thinking are similar to Kierkegaard's thought.

Her highlighting the feminine disrupts the boundaries and rules of what patriarchy says is "universal" logic and rational truth. But just as Kierkegaard's thought is not irrational, neither are Irigaray's concepts of the feminine illogical. She is calling for a restructuring of the rational, for what it means to be a subject. Both Kierkegaard's work and Irigaray's work are sometimes labeled as illogical or paradoxical because they are articulating truths that go against the normative modes of thought and value. Their ideas and novel way of speaking subvert the norms of thought and can, thus, evoke charges of illogic.

Both argue that genuine selfhood is not a static being. The problem in both the aesthetic and the ethical spheres, in philosophy in general, is that the not-yet-ness of human existence is ignored. Selfhood, for Kierkegaard is always becoming, for existence is always in process. Irigaray agrees that genuine feminine selfhood is "fluid" and changing, not always the same. She also highlights the fluidity of the feminine as derived from her use of feminine sexuality and bodily experience, as well as from her philosophical claim that the feminine is not definable, for it is changing and changeable.[40]

Many of Irigaray's candidates for the feminine are similar to Kierkegaard's conceptualizations of the religious. This is not surprising, given that both thinkers seek out that which they believe is not emphasized in public universal discourse, but has some power when brought to the surface of individual consciousness. Both have profound insight into what culture ignores and denigrates. Both are seeking to build up an alternate way of being a self. Both see that God/the divine is a necessary power to uphold this selfhood. Both see this selfhood as not following the normative "unity" or oneness of self. Kierkegaard 's multiplicity of selfhood is more limited and follows a tripartite structure, while Irigaray's multiplicity of selfhood

---

[40] She views the self as so changing and changeable that it does not even follow a distinct proscribed direction or progression. This characteristic is different from Kierkegaard's view in which the self is always becoming, but existence is best as it moves progressively, although non-linearly, in relationship with God.

is more open and less controlled. She wants to let all the holds go, to search for candidates of the feminine in what arises once the boundaries and values of phallocentric discourse and culture are cut loose. She uses the morphology and process of female sexuality to guide her suggestions of selfhood.

In the next chapter we will turn these two thinkers to face each other, creating a dialectical conversation that highlights the insights of each in a way that leads to a concept of self as comprised of multivalent factors and relationships between and among these parts. This dialogue between Kierkegaard's dialectic of faith and Irigaray's multiplicity, fluidity and "both-at-once-ness" of the feminine creates a back and forth model for the new theological anthropology I propose in which the self is the multiple parts of the self as they are related to each other simultaneously in a matrix of various centers of connections. We will turn to the elaboration of this constructed theory now.

6

Both at Once Kierkegaard and Irigaray: A Multivalent and Dialectically Relational Self Grounded in Bodily Experience

> "Who am I? How did I come into the world? Why was I not consulted…?"
> —Søren Kierkegaard[1]

In this book I have suggested that the dominant discourse on selfhood in the West is shaped by embedded assumptions of singularity and sameness. These presumptions claim that healthy, holy selves ought to conform to a formal model of internal uniform singularity. Difference, multiplicity and relationality are incompatible with this normative model for selfhood. This assumption and its corollaries have had deleterious affects upon conceptions of the self. The Western conceptualization of the self as a singular entity hinders a relational view of selfhood. Singularity, or oneness, prohibits internal relationality ipso facto because it inhibits multiplicity within a healthy holy self. Multiplicity and difference are necessary conditions for relationality, and relationship requires that there be

---

[1] Søren Kierkegaard, *Repetition: an Essay in Experimental Psychology,* trans. Walter Lowrie (Princeton NJ: Princeton University Press, 1946) 114.

more than one entity. Without irreducible diversity, there would be nothing with which to relate.[2]

This view also has deleterious affects upon society's ability and willingness to accept and relate to diversity outside of itself in the community at large. This book argues that a revised conceptualization of selfhood, which accepts multiplicity, difference, and intra-relationality within each person, would help promote a world in which multiplicity, difference and inter-relationality are also accepted and celebrated.

This exaltation of the One is seen clearly in the legacy of Augustine's theological anthropology and doctrine of sin. Augustine views divisions within the self as part of the paradigm of sin itself. Sin is the actual dividing of the will against itself. Thus, for Augustine and the Augustinian tradition a divided will and a divided self is the mark of sinfulness. The formal structure of sin is division and conflict and multiplicity. A holy self, on the other hand, properly moves toward unity—toward a uniform will. In this way of understanding the process of human existence, multiplicity is squelched. The view of the self that follows from this doctrine of sin demonstrates the problematic structure of the Western bias against multiplicity. Multiplicity is devalued across many dimensions, and this book has argued specifically against the devaluation of multiplicity as it impacts the self. A conceptualization of the self as consisting in a multiplicity of parts that are related to each other is stymied because such a multivalent self is rendered sinful and bad.

There are two problems with Augustine's view. The first concerns the discrepancy between a person's experience of being a self (as divided), on the one hand, and the ideal given as a religious imperative (to be a singular one), on the other. The assumption here is that the human cannot trust her own experience—that one's own

---

[2] This logic is seen in Marjorie Suchocki's *Divinity and Diversity* when she addresses the unity of God, which she says "is created in and through irreducible diversity." *Divinity and Diversity* (Nashville: Abingdon Press, 2003) 66.

experience is wrong or is a consequence of sin and its punishments. Kierkegaard's theological anthropology illustrates both the presence of alternative voices in the tradition and an alternative view of selfhood that accepts the experience of difference and division within the self. Unlike Augustine, Kierkegaard views the paradox, the ambiguity, and tensions of being a person as part of the task that we are called to accomplish. Holding the finite and the infinite together is not a punishment of sin. It is part of complexity of the subjectivity of the religious sphere. The difficulty in holding them in equilibrium is a consequence of sin. Sin is not the division of the self against itself, as Augustine's paradigm claims. Sin is a failure in relationality. Kierkegaard's view of the self as entailing struggle and anxiety counters Augustine's claim. He understands this experience of anxiety as a natural result of the human condition. Kierkegaard describes the state of faith as relating between and among this polarity as part of the essential format of a good and holy self. Irigaray also argues that a genuine self is properly and in its most developed state multiple and "divided." Further, I suggest that the self is a relational relating bundle of relations. If we take these views then, the experience of the self as multiple and divided is a true experience that could be trusted as communicating the form of identity.

The other difficulty with Augustine's conceptualization has been the focus of this book and concerns the exaltation of singularity and sameness. This assumption that this ideal human is, or ought, to be a singular uniform one is about the universality of humanity. It assumes that the ideal human is the same for everyone. This model is patriarchal and phallocentric in that it is formulated out of the experience and desire of only a few homogenous males in power. The experience and needs of others have been discounted, ignored, and repressed. This economy functions and maintains itself on the backs of others, deriving its power from its ability to reduce all others to the Same. I use Luce Irigaray's feminist theory and psychoanalysis of Western discourse to examine this problem with more depth.

Western thought and culture creates what Irigaray calls the economy of the Same. This structure values sameness and is a product of sexism and male exclusivism. The results of her critiques lead to her constructive project, which seeks to encourage multiplicity and genuine difference. She highlights that which has been repressed, ignored and demonized. In this way we can examine the positive and actual reality of selfhood as multiple and relational.

Kierkegaard's theological anthropology also counters the second issue in Augustine's doctrines of theological anthropology and sin. The dominant view of selfhood in which singularity is the original created state of human selfhood is opposed by Kierkegaard's alternative view in which difference, division, relationality, and experience of conflict are understood as given in the human condition. These elements are not evidence of or results from sin.

The self is essentially and inherently relational because it is established by a power outside itself. "Did you make yourself?" the psalmist says. Kierkegaard dwells upon this assertion and argues that it is the foundational truth of human existence. This fact creates a condition in which anxiety ensues and which can easily and inevitably lead to despair, sin, and disrelationship. The self is under the condition of sin. Sin is defined here as a broken relationship—broken between the self with itself and the self with God. A mixed state of part willing ignorance/denial and part unconsciousness accompanies sin.

To counter these assumptions and their corollaries, this book has highlighted alternative perspectives of selfhood given by Kierkegaard and Luce Irigaray. I have focused on both their critiques of this singularity of self and their constructive views of selfhood as relational and multiple, bringing these two thinkers together in a dialectical conceptualization of the self in which multiplicity and difference are accepted both internally and externally.

Kierkegaard and Irigaray may seem like odd dialogue partners.[3] Yet taken together in a dialectical approach, their critical analysis and constructive arguments suggest a model of selfhood that mirrors the very dynamics of selfhood that I am proposing. In other words, the format of this dialogue between Kierkegaard and Irigaray is an example of the actual format of the self itself. Each approach taken by itself alone leans too much to one side or the other. But when brought together in a dialogue (not a synthesis), these two approaches can enable a successful model of selfhood. This structure itself corresponds to Kierkegaard's analysis of the difficult task of becoming oneself in the midst of holding in tension opposed elements that constitute the self. (And in fact I get this model of dialectical relating from Kierkegaard.) The way that I employ these two thinkers represents an example of how to bring together the various parts of the self. It is not meant to be the definitive way, but an example of how one could do this and understand the self as an entity in itself, with difference and plurality within itself. This approach is not typical because I am attempting to imitate the structure of the self that I am constructing in the structure of my articulation.

Kierkegaard and Irigaray differ significantly in terms of influence, method, and goals, yet their purposes and conclusions are compatible enough that they can be brought into dialogue together. The following section is a brief review of the differences and similarities between these thinkers. It then leads into a critical analysis of both the insights and the problems within each thinker and addresses how the dynamic dialectic of the relationship between these two enables them to complement each other.

There are four important areas of comparison and contrast. First, the focal points of their study and their ultimate purposes are

---

[3] Serene Jones is another thinker who has found parallels between Irigaray and an unlikely theologian in her article on Karl Barth and Irigaray entitled "This God Which is Not One," in *Transfigurations: Theology and the French Feminists*, ed. C.W. Maggie Kim, Susan M. St. Ville, and Susan M. Simonaitis (Minneapolis: Fortress Press, 1993).

distinct. Irigaray focuses on women, the feminine and women's bodily experience, seeking to create a world in which sexual difference is accepted, while Kierkegaard hopes to evoke subjectivity and faith in each of his readers regardless of gender.

Second, both of these thinkers are critical of the normative views of the self as a singular entity that prevail in their contemporary philosophical and cultural milieu. Kierkegaard seeks to address the prodigious illusion of Christendom that Christian values are merely the current cultural norms. He differentiates a religious sphere of existence from the universal ethical sphere and the individual aesthetic sphere. Irigaray's critique focuses on the universal claims of phallocentric discourse and its repression of feminine difference.

Third, both Kierkegaard and Irigaray each suggest an alternative view of selfhood that enables multiplicity and relationality. Kierkegaard's multiplicity is found in his three spheres of existence, the polar ontological elements, and his pseudonymous authorship. His emphasis on relationality is clear in his dialectic of faith and subjectivity. Irigaray's view of multiplicity is grounded in her critique of the dominant supposition of oneness and sameness in Western discourse, her psychoanalytical techniques for uncovering the repressed feminine and its characteristics, and her attention to the morphology of female sexuality and women's sexual desire. Irigaray's theory of the realm of feminine subjectivity is comparable to Kierkegaard's concept of the religious sphere of existence. Kierkegaard bases his insights on a Christian structure of existence, while Irigaray employs women's experience of their bodies as feminine for one of the primary resources for her constructive undertaking. Yet Irigaray's metonymy for feminine subjectivity of both-at-once can be applied to Kierkegaard's conception of the authentic self as an oscillating dialectic of polar elements, different spheres, and multiple authors.

I bring these thinkers into dialogue with each other, with special attention to their differences, utilizing several ideas expressed by each as part of my constructive conceptualization of selfhood that respects multiplicity, difference and relationality. Irigaray's emphasis upon an embodied theory of selfhood as open to external and internal difference along with her notion of "both-at-once-ness" provide fruitful models for understanding the self as multiple and externally relational. Kierkegaard's dialectic of faith and the relational form of the religious sphere are helpful in articulating the ways in which the self is internally related to itself. I bring their thoughts together in a multivalent manner that mirrors the format of subjectivity that I seek to expose. In other words, the form of selfhood that I articulate here is a complex network of relating hubs of agency, oscillating between differences and similarities, and between multiplicity and integration. Further, this concept parallels the form of the way that I bring together these two different theorists' insights as elements in my conceptualization of selfhood.

I view the self as primarily a relating entity (rather than a substantial entity) entailing difference and multiplicity within the boundaries of the person as they are usually conceived. As I have argued above, in order for relationality to be truly present, two conditions must be met: multiplicity and difference. There must be more than a singularity within the individual. A relation requires at least two different entities, and true difference requires otherness to be brought into the internality of the self.

Both thinkers are helpful to this conceptualization of selfhood. Irigaray's project seeks to enable genuine difference in the world as well as within the self. She employs feminist and post structural analysis to highlight those qualities and persons who have been repressed/oppressed in the current dominant discourse. Kierkegaard's analysis engages both multiplicity and relationality inside the self. Further, he allows for difference within as well as a particular type of external difference. Difference and multiform are found in three primary ways: in the polar elements (such as finite/infinite) and the grounding in God; in the multiple spheres of existence; and in the polynomity of his pseudonymous authors.

My analysis of Kierkegaard's view of what it means to be a self utilizes three primary parts of his authorship. First, in chapter three I examined his dialectic of faith as put forth in *Sickness Unto Death* and expanded it to provide the format for interpreting the other elements of his theological anthropology. This dialectic is a dynamic and reflexive relationship between polar elements within the self. Secondly, I developed the implications of Kierkegaard's theory of three spheres of existence: aesthetic, ethical, and religious. Applying his dialectic to his theory of spheres enhances both the multiplicity and relationality inherent in the self according to Kierkegaard. I argue that this religious sphere entails a dialectical relating of aspects of the other two spheres. My third focus addressed the variety of voices in his authorship, suggesting that these perspectives represent aspects of Kierkegaard's self. When all the voices are taken together, the relationship of each author to the other authors and to the whole, points to another dimension of multiformity within a single person. I used the dialectic as an organizing framework for understanding the relationship of his various authorial names and personae. I brought these resources together using the dialectic of faith as a central rope running through his work to construct a Kierkegaardian view of the self as a dynamic dialectic.

Kierkegaard offers an alternative view of holy and authentic existence that is characterized by the process of holding together different elements and modes of living within a single person. A self is a synthesis of pairs of polar ontological elements, such as the infinite and finite. This is best understood in two steps. First, the self consists of the relating of these conflicting elements. Further, the relation of these contradictory elements is reflexively related to itself. The self is not precisely the relationship, but rather it consists in the process of self-consciously and reflexively relating to the relation between these poles, such as finite and infinite. Recall his formula:

The self is a relation that relates itself to itself or is the relation's relating itself to itself in the relation; the self is not the relation but is the relation's relating itself to itself.[4]

The self is not merely internally related to itself, it is the very act of relating itself to itself.

It is this dialectic, which is the form of the relationship of these contradictory elements of existence as they are brought into dialogue with each other, that I highlight from Kierkegaard's theological anthropology. This relation of the disparate parts then relates to itself in a dynamic and dialectical way. This reflexive relating constitutes an individual.

Faith, which is the stance of a person in the religious sphere, is defined as the act of dialectical reflexive relationality of these different parts, all transparently grounded on the power that constitutes it. The religious sphere represents his view of authentic subjectivity and is comprised of qualities associated with both the ethical sphere, such as decision-making and continuity through time, as well as those qualities associated with the aesthetic sphere, such as immediacy and capriciousness. Further, the religious sphere entails a conscious relating of these qualities and spheres without evacuating either completely.

Kierkegaard's pseudonymous authorship employs a variety of names with a diversity of styles and viewpoints and also hints at his attempt to give objectification to all the perspectives in his thinking. He says that he uses different voices to engage different people wherever they are, but I wonder if he is not also engaging different parts of the same people in their multiple viewpoints and questions about existence and truth.

The dialectic in Kierkegaard's authorship is a complex web that forms both the structure of the content of his thought, as seen in the

---

[4] Søren Kierkegaard, *The Sickness Unto Death*, trans. and ed. Howard V. Hong and Edna H. Hong (Princeton NJ: Princeton University Press, 1980) 13.

relationship of the existential elements, and also the form of his polemical method, demonstrated in the mode of his pseudonymous authorship. His authors are related to each other by name and by argument. He creates a web of interrelated authors/characters who dialogue among themselves. His method is also dialectical in that he desires to engage his reader in a conversation.

Kierkegaard's understanding of selfhood and subjectivity is profoundly relational. The self consists in the dynamics of relation. This relationality is further compounded by the fact that this relating spirit is essentially related to the power that established it—God. This external relationship (relationship with something other than the self) is not a mere fact of an external or objective relationship, for it is the necessary depth dimension for the self to be able to relate to itself. And it is this relation that is the self in itself. In other words, for Kierkegaard, the human being is a created entity that requires the continual and mutually active presence of its creator. I say *mutually active* to indicate that God is an active participant in the continuing constitution of the self and the self must be intentionally and actively relating itself to this foundation of its being.[5] (By using the term "mutuality," I do not mean to suggest an equality of contribution.) Further, this self is a dialectical spirit that seeks to balance three sets of polar elements while also relating this balancing relation reflexively to itself. The total package then is relational—internally within itself, and externally with God. As we shall see below in the section on critique, the external relationality, while primary, however, is limited to God and does not include the relationships with other persons outside of the self.

---

[5] This aspect is a bit like Schleiermacher's concept of "Feelings of Absolute Dependence" in *The Christian Faith* and Tillich's conceptualization of God as the Ground of Being developed in *The Courage to Be* and in his *Systematic Theology*.

Critique of Kierkegaard

Kierkegaard's theological anthropology provides helpful implications for the development of a new model of selfhood. His theory of three spheres of existence and the notion of the religious sphere as including the relation of the other spheres of existence, indicate multiple modes of being that are internal to the self. His insightful articulation of the dialectic of faith as the internal relating of parts offers a complex and coherent way of addressing the internal tension between different parts. If the finite and the infinite can be held together within one person, then parts/modes that are not as different can be held together as well. The advantages to Kierkegaard's conclusions include his openness to multiplicity on a variety of levels and most particularly his profound understanding of relationships between the various parts within the self. I will return to his dialectic after a review of Irigaray's insights and suggest that Kierkegaard's relationality offers a way to understand the relationality of the different aspects and multiple hubs within the self in a way that does not lead to dispersion.

Yet there are also several difficulties with his conceptualization. His structure of three definite spheres and two factors facilitates the internal relationality of the dialectic view of multiplicity, yet it is limited. There are three spheres. It is not open to other possible spheres or models. There are complexities within each sphere and between the spheres. But the basic structure of three spheres and two factors of existence are not negotiable. This characteristic is both limiting and delimiting. Kierkegaard does not have the space for including radically new notions or experiences. However, observing and naming the relating of two or three defined elements clearly is much easier and obvious than the relating of an indefinite number and type of elements. This clarity and containment is helpful, but by itself this view still stands as inadequate to our current project.

The relationality is limited to the limited character of these ontological polarities; the type of relation is conscious balancing or juggling of these polarities. The limitation, which is also an advantage in some instances, is the clarity and limited quality of the polar relationship of the internal dialectic. These parts of the self are in tension and opposition to each other. They must be balanced like a seesaw. They are related exclusively in a linear opposition to each other. As we shall see in greater detail below, Irigaray's analysis yields a more open and varied complex of aspects, forms, and types of relationships within the self.

Another significant concern is the lack of explicit embodiment in Kierkegaard's conception of selfhood. The body is not a foundation of selfhood. He follows Augustine's de-emphasis on the body as witnessed by his exclusion of the body from the *Imago Dei*. Kierkegaard's multiplicity stems from his religious experience of healing the conflict, contradiction, and ambiguity in existence, not from his embodied experience. His emphasis on subjectivity leads us away from the immediate and physical experience of the body.

Lastly, his emphasis upon the internality of the solitary individual is problematic in two significant ways. In Kierkegaard's dialectic of subjectivity the essential external relationship is limited to God. The only essential relationship the self has with an entity outside of itself is that with God. The neighbor is important as an object of one's duty to love and share God's love, but the neighbor is not an essential element in the constitution of the self. There is not a mechanism in which the context, the other, the neighbor can enter and become a part of the self. The direction of energy flows outward from the self through God to the neighbor, but the neighbor does not necessarily flow back to the self. Difference is internalized/absorbed only from God. The love for the other, the neighbor is a necessary aspect of being a Christian for Kierkegaard, but it is not an essential aspect of becoming oneself. The relationality that constitutes a Kierkegaardian self is limited to either reflexive relationship with oneself or the relationship to God.

In spite of his profound insights into the relationality of the self within itself, Kierkegaard's view is inadequate to my conceptualization because he seems to forget and discard the profound essential effect of external relationships upon the self. I argue that the self is relational both internally and externally. The internal relationality of the self is a network of relations and centers of connection that enables external relations with difference and others outside the self. Relationships with others are a part of the self. A self is not exclusively inward. I argue that even inner subjectivity is not solitary—one brings one's relations to and with others into the very core and constitution of oneself. Further, one's inner awareness of one's genuine self has effects externally as well. Faith is not simply a matter of one's private relation to God, but involves one's public and communal relations with others. The inner and outer are connected. The internal relationality enabled by the balanced relation of opposite factors of existence of Kierkegaard's religious sphere I believe ought to further enable deeper and more inclusive external relationships with others outside of the self. Like the internal dialectic of the factors of existence, the spheres, and the pseudonyms, there could be an external dialectic relationship between the self and others. I argue that the structure of the self as a relational matrix in itself yields a model that is more open to external relationships. This view of the self allows the effects from outside the self, such as other persons and the environment, to become more easily absorbed and included in one's own self. A structure that is a related, relational, and relating complex web of hubs is more adequate to include and address external difference and influences than is a model of the self as a self-contained substance.

Kierkegaard's way of understanding the self provides several helpful pieces to the puzzle of selfhood in the twenty-first century. But his view is limited in several ways. These limitations are met to some degree in Irigaray's constructive project. Yet Irigaray's suggestions are also not completely adequate to the task either.

Kierkegaard's clarity and distinctness offer the containment that is sometimes helpful in organizing and making boundaries for the self. His view can be a corrective to the unbridledness of Irigaray's open fluidity of genuine selfhood. Irigaray answers the limitedness in Kierkegaard's relationality by her view that genuine feminine subjectivity is open to difference from outside as well as greater multiplicity within the self.

Kierkegaard's religious sphere is more defined than Irigaray's open suggestions of the feminine. He is more clear and explicit in his articulations about the nature and forms of the highest expression of human existence. Irigaray's work is intentionally experimental and constructive. This openness makes Irigaray's feminine realm less defined and less structured, less conscripted and less constricted. She is open to exploring all that has been repressed. Arguing against the notion of paradigms, she does not put forth one paradigm of authentic selfhood, as does Kierkegaard. The only structure and content provided is loose, so that project can remain open to new possibilities of the feminine. Her analysis of metonyms of the female body and feminine sexuality yield possible candidates and she cross checks them with those characteristics and forms that are repressed in phallocentric discourse.

Irigaray's work thus has the advantage over Kierkegaard's thought in being more apt to reveal the novel ways of being a self. It is more likely to elicit creative ways of being a self that are more adequate for persons who are oppressed in the current culture. Her suggestions of multiplicity and multiformity of the feminine self are more open to diversity and difference within and between persons. Further, she speaks for those who have been rendered voiceless historically. Her work highlights the contributions of those who have been oppressed. In any reconstruction of a Christian theological anthropology, we need to pay close attention to the experience of those who have been systematically ignored and prohibited from contributing to the norms of discourse and interpretation. Irigaray's analysis provides just such a gateway to bringing the images of the oppressed into our focus.

Kierkegaard's work, while helpful in his assertion that selfhood is not a uniform synthesis, is more limited in his creative expression of selfhood. Selfhood consists of these three spheres of existence and variations on this tripartite structure. All personal characteristics have to fit into one of these three. And even though the content of selfhood is quite varied, both within and across an individual's experience, given the dialectic, processive character of Kierkegaard's view of subjectivity, Kierkegaard's structure of becoming oneself is fairly fixed and universal. There are three spheres each with their own type of qualities. Further, the self is a synthesis of two opposite factors: finite and infinite. Within an individual, these three spheres and factors are related in a similar manner. Even though not everyone is at the same place in the structure, all persons must progress through the same structure toward religious selfhood, and each individual must balance these conflicting elements together.

I am not suggesting that we pick and choose amongst the insights of these profound thinkers to create a synthesis. I am suggesting that we take the insights of these thinkers and put them into dialogue with each other so that their insights can relate to each other in a way akin to Kierkegaard's dialectic of faith. Yet the dialectic here is more expanded in that it not only moves back and forth, side to side, but also all around. In other words, sometimes the self is closely united with itself, other times it is dissociated into various parts. Sometimes these parts are related in oppositional ways like Kierkegaard's polar ontological elements, other times these parts are related in analogous, supplemental, or even skewed ways.

The key here is *form* as well as the content. I have proposed a conceptualization of selfhood that focuses on the general form of selfhood as both relational and multiple. I am not suggesting a mere synthesis of two thinkers that complement each other. Rather, I am positing a relational dialectic in which the focus oscillates between the insights and viewpoints of Kierkegaard and Irigaray.

Irigaray

While Kierkegaard's work is distinct from Irigaray's in several ways, there are many points of resonance. Whereas Irigaray's view is grounded in the Psychoanalytic schema concerned with ego development and is influenced by Lacan's theory of language as the foundation of the structure of subjectivity, Kierkegaard's conceptualizations grow forth from roots in the philosophy of the Enlightenment and his view of the structure of existence as formed by relationship to God. Irigaray's primary insights for this project include her critique of phallocentric discourse and the economy of the Same, her creative methods for discerning genuine feminine identity, and her constructive conclusions about the nature of a genuine feminine.

First, Irigaray not only provides a thorough critique of the unilateral uniformity which she calls "the economy of the Same," but also provides the tools to facilitate further critical analysis of this devaluation of multiplicity. This bias against multiplicity and difference is problematic because it represses significant, powerful, and real aspects of society, culture, individuals, and discourse. Further, she demonstrates an association between that which is repressed and the feminine, on the one hand, and an association between that which represses it and the dominant male discourse, on the other. In other words, the dominant phallocentric discourse represses the feminine in society, culture, thought, and expression, as well as individuals. There is a correlation between this repression and its exclusivity as demonstrated in the economy of the Same and the demand for uniformity of self. The repression of sexual difference is the basis of the repression of all difference, which leads to the economy of the Same in which conformity with the single and singular model of selfhood is venerated and expected.

Her critique of the hegemony of the one is insightful and leads toward her construction of a more adequate and creative model of subjectivity. She demonstrates that the so-called oppositeness between the sexes is actually a monism of maleness and its reverse. This construction of pseudo-gender as sexual difference is detrimental to women and to society. Irigaray claims that this so-called female is not really a genuine difference, but is merely the underside or the projection of those qualities that are rejected by the dominant discourse. Instead, she proclaims that the feminine is not simply "not-male," but the feminine is something qualitatively different than male or not-male.[6]

Next, Irigaray believes that the genuine feminine is accessible to our current experience in several ways. She applies psychoanalytical techniques to her analysis of phallocentric discourse in three particularly significant approaches. One crucial technique is her work in upholding and highlighting those characteristics that culture and discourse repress and ignore. A less well-known technique is mimesis, in which women exaggerate the proscribed ways of being feminine to reveal a remnant transcending the parameters proscribed by patriarchy. This is a technique that is often used in humor and satire, such as drag. A third resource for discovering the genuine feminine is women's bodies themselves. Irigaray looks to women's sexuality, physical pleasures, and embodied experiences as resources for uncovering and enabling genuine feminine differences. The morphology of women's bodies, both the whole body and the specific locale of sexuality, provide metonyms[7] and metaphors for understanding feminine reality, imaginary, symbolic, and discourse. These various techniques yield fruitful results and work together for

---

[6] The male and views of maleness are also truncated in this dichotomous view.

[7] A metonym is a figure of speech in which the name of one thing is used "for that of another of which it is an attribute or with which it is associated (as 'crown' in 'lands belonging to the crown')." See *Merriam-Webster Dictionary,* s.v. "metonymy."

both Irigaray's project, in her theorizing about qualities and forms of a genuine feminine, and my own work here.

In using metonyms of the morphology of women's bodies and sexuality, Irigaray posits four particularly significant characteristics for the feminine: multiplicity, simultaneity, openness, and fluidity. First, unlike the focus of Freud, Lacan, and other psychoanalytic theory on male morphology/experience, women's sex is not reducible to one single organ, but rather is multiple and multiform. Women's sexuality, Irigaray says, is plural, diversified, and multiple.

One of the primary feminine metonyms Irigaray uses is "both at once." The pairs of labia are two, doubled together and doubly paired. Yet they cannot be separated from each other. The two lips and the two pairs of lips represent the multiplicity and simultaneity of a genuine feminine subject-ivity. They are simultaneously both singular and double, both open and closed, vertical and horizontal. Feminine subjectivity is not one, nor is it two, it is both at once—it is neither one, nor two, it is *both* one *and* two. Recall Irigaray's assertion that woman is "neither one nor two. Rigorously speaking, she cannot be identified either as one person, or as two."[8]

Another metonym yields another significant quality of the feminine—openness. Women's body and sexuality is both partially open and partially closed, and "woman is neither open nor closed. She is indefinite...."[9] Woman takes the other into herself and incorporates otherness as part of her self, and yet she also has closed boundaries. This receptivity to the environment suggests that external relationships are constitutive parts of the genuine feminine self.

The fourth quality I will highlight here, fluidity, suggests that the feminine is moving, flowing into difference and change. It is not a

---

[8] Luce Irigaray, "This Sex Which is Not One," in *This Sex Which is Not One* (Ithaca NY: Cornell University Press, 1985) 26.

[9] Luce Irigaray, *Speculum of the Other Woman* (Ithaca NY: Cornell University Press, 1985) 229.

static entity and cannot be contained by patriarchal logic or definition. Here her claim that subjectivity is a process, not an end, is reminiscent of Kierkegaard's claim that being is the process of willing to become oneself.

Irigaray's insights concerning simultaneity and multiplicity can be further developed into ways of talking about the self as characterized by having multiple centers and connections that cannot be separated from each other, nor collapsed into each other. These hubs and relationships are not merely one, nor merely a conglomeration of many-ness, but are *both* one *and* many at the same time, like Irigaray's feminine. The self, I suggest, is like Irigaray's feminine in that the form is not a singular self-contained identity but is a multiform network that is capable of holding together differences without disintegrating. In fact, the multiplicity enhances the richness of the self. The multiform network, which I suggest is the self, is open to internal difference and complexity as well as otherness from outside the self.

Another way her methodology works together is in her psychoanalytic approach as she seeks to create a feminine syntax by getting women to symbolically return to an earlier stage of development, the pre-Mirror stage, and to transverse it anew (born again) as genuine feminine subjects. She hopes that this would accomplish two things. First, it would enable women to develop a structure of language that is not based on the law of the phallus (which operates as a dichotomy of subject versus object that mimics the process of the male child's identification with the father through differentiation from the mother), but rather on the positive connections with the maternal. Secondly, this foundation also offers an excellent and genuine space for women to connect and reconnect with themselves and other women, especially leading to reconnections between mother and daughter as adults as well as for a future in which female children can transit the early developmental stage in a genuine feminine way in actuality. A new linguistic and cognitive structure leads to a different way of expressing the feminine, which in turn leads to alternative ways of understanding subjectivity itself. Irigaray uncovers that which has been covered over and ignored by the dominant discourse for her project, such as multiplicity, openness, simultaneity within a single person, fluidity, relationality, proximity. These are clues and possibilities for the genuine feminine. For my project, this critical analysis of embedded assumptions of oneness and sameness and the results of her constructive work open the possibilities for thinking and expressing the self in alternative ways.

Critique of Irigaray

Irigaray's critical work and her constructive projects have proven invaluable to my project, but I also have critiques of her thought. Many of the earlier American and British readers of Irigaray have critiqued her thought as essentialist.[10] This is due in part to her desire to highlight and find a genuine feminine and her assertion that the fact of sexual difference is a universal experience.[11] The exact meaning of this critique is confused as Naomi Schor points out in her article "This Essentialism Which is Not One: Coming to Grips with Irigaray." There are many definitions and connotations to this term, some of which perhaps deserve the blanket rejection given by most feminists, while other employments of the idea are strategic and necessary. In general, the term simply means that things have essences, that one thing is different from another, fundamentally. At one level, the claim that there are genuine differences between things is in a line with claims that many feminists have made concerning a

---

[10] See Andrea Nye, *Feminist Theology and the Philosophies of Man* (London: Croom Helm, 1988) and Toril Moi, *Sexual/Textual Politics: Feminist Literary Theory* (London: Routledge, 1988).

[11].See Luce Irigaray, "Equal or Different," in *The Irigaray Reader*, ed. Margaret Whitford (Malden MA: Blackwell Publishing, Inc., 1991).

genuine and irreducible difference between the sexes/genders. The essentialism that is problematic claims that women are defined essentially by their anatomy and its so-called destiny. Implied in this claim is a "denial of the very real lived differences—sexual, racial, national, cultural, economic, generational—that divide women from each other."[12] Yet Irigaray does not argue for either of these claims. But rather argues that women are different from men and from what has been named as the feminine by phallocentric discourse. Further, she claims that women and the feminine are not definable per se. Recent interpreters have further addressed this charge with success. Ellen Armour, among others, reframes her assertion of feminine characteristics as a political strategy.[13] Further, Amy Hollywood points out that one of the issues is that the first works of Irigaray translated into English did not address real women, but emphasized the feminine abstractly as a "philosophical construct."[14] I will not rehash the many capable and thorough responses to this issue.[15]

My primary concerns with Irigaray fall into three categories: her psychoanalytic framework; her exclusive focus on women and the feminine; and her inattention to the internal integrity of the self. Her Lacanian/psychoanalytic framework seizes upon sexuality, conceiving of the development of the self and maturation exclusively in terms of

---

[12] Noami Schor, "This Essentialism Which is Not One: Coming to Grips with Irigaray," in *Engaging With Irigaray*, ed. Carolyn Burke, Naomi Schor, and Margaret Whitford (New York: Columbia University Press, 1994). 62.

[13] Ellen T. Armour, *Subverting the Race/Gender Divide: Deconstruction, Feminist Theory, and the Problem of Difference* (Chicago: University of Chicago Press, 1999).

[14] Amy Hollywood, *Sensible Ecstasy: Mysticism, Sexual Difference, and the Demands of History* (Chicago: University of Chicago Press, 2002) 189.

[15] See Diana Fuss, *Essentially Speaking: Feminism, Nature and Difference* (New York: Routledge, 1989); Margaret Whitford, "Reading Irigaray in the Nineties," and Alison Stone, "From Political to Realist Essentialism," in *Feminist Theory*, 5/1 (2004): 5-23; Elizabeth Weed, "The Question of Style," and Noami Schor, "This Essentialism Which is Not One: Coming to Grips with Irigaray," in *Engaging With Irigaray*.

sexual feelings, the repression of these impulses, and the overcoming of the unfulfilled sexual desires. The sexual organs and the sexual process of women is almost her exclusive focal point for her discovery of the feminine through the body. I agree that the multiplicity of woman's genitalia and its quality of both-at-once-ness make excellent metonyms/metaphors for speaking and writing, thinking and knowing about the multiplicity of subjectivity, and I also find this focus helpful because it brings our attention to the body and shows that the body is the grounding cord of subjectivity. However, I see that the body itself as a whole also makes an excellent metonym and metaphor for the multiplicity of subjectivity. Embodiment is the most authentic foundation for human selfhood. This is the case for both male subjects and female subjects. Her work takes me here, to embodiment; but once I am here, I can remain here through an emphasis on the body as a whole.

The exclusivity of her emphasis on sexuality is also limiting. It limits the applicability of her constructive suggestions about the multiplicity of selfhood to women. And even further, it limits it to women who are able to make a positive connection with their sexuality. For instance, many women have been sexually abused, and such focus on sexual organs may be painful. These women would be at a disadvantage (again) in Irigaray's experiment. There are also women who are not sexual for other reasons, such as the celibate, or the elderly, and others. Further, Irigaray's constructive work, like her critical analysis, remains in a Freudian framework, which asserts the primary significance of sexual experience in early childhood and Freud's focus on the male sexual member. However, I wonder if the feminine is actually so focused on sexuality, feminine sexuality, or phallic sexuality. Perhaps women's ways of becoming selves, of constituting their subjectivity, has less to do with sexuality itself than does male/phallocentric development. Perhaps women are more affected by their body as a whole and sensual pleasure in general. Or as Carol Gilligan suggests, maybe women are constituted by the early childhood relational dynamics with their mothers.[16] Perhaps women do not exclusively emphasize sexual pleasure or desire. Irigaray's focus on the embodied sexuality of women can be transformed to an employment of embodiment in general, as the basis of selfhood. I propose that this new view of the self should employ the multiplicity of the body as a whole for the fundamental constituting modes of selfhood. The self is an embodied self. The human body is multifaceted and yet, for the most part, the different parts work together as a unity. The self is not disembodied. I believe that Irigaray's metonym, "both-at-once-ness," is in continuity with extending the elements that constitute the self beyond their Irigaraian original placement in female sexuality to the body as a whole. The body itself is not reducible to oneness. I like the cleverness and aptness of her metaphor of two lips. And I believe that she would not disapprove of my expansion.

Further, I wonder if the bodily experience of pain is also actually an important factor in the forming of subjectivity. Sexual experience is not the only type of experience in the body, neither is it always pleasurable. Unfortunately many women have experienced violation and suffering in sexual encounters, and all persons experience the body as source of pain and discomfort at times. Surely these types of experiences are significant, if not more powerful in forming one's sense of self. One might even suggest that it is the experience of pain that opens a person to empathy with others. I may not understand your particular context, but I can relate to pain and suffering. Irigaray's schema does not address these issues explicitly or in any appropriate depth. Pain could be taken into account in the very structure of selfhood as part of the ambiguity, difference and distance necessary for the self to develop its multiple aspects and the complex form of multiplicity. The value given to absolute singularity of self

---

[16] See Carol Gilligan, *In a Different Voice: Psychological Theory and Women's Development* (Cambridge MA: Harvard University Press, 1982) and *The Birth of Pleasure* (New York: Alfred Knopf, 2002).

inhibits healthy recognition of the significance of pain and discomfort. A conceptualization of self as multiple and inclusive of difference offers a greater openness to the ambiguity of life. Embodied experiences not only lend themselves to metonyms, synecdoches, or other ways of thinking about the whole self, but also to a grounded theory of selfhood.

My second issue is not so much a critique of her work as it is a recognition that her aim and my aim diverge at the point of application of multiplicity and relationality to selfhood for all humanity. While the project of this book is consanguine with Irigaray's own, it is also different, in that it articulates liberating concepts of human selfhood in general. Irigaray's focus is to liberate the feminine from its repressed and oppressed position. The focus of this is to propose models of human selfhood that are free from society's normative over-emphasis on singularity and synthetic uniformity. I understand Irigaray's focus on the feminine and her silence on the male. But for the purposes of this project and beyond, it is not strategic to limit multiplicity of selfhood to the feminine.

While I do not seek to construct a conceptualization of the feminine self to be understood in contrast to the singular masculine self, Irigaray's analysis of phallocentrism is a helpful critique of the normative description of selfhood as a uniform singularity and the absolute valuation of this ideal. It is problematic not only due to its male bias, but it is also inadequate to articulate human selfhood in general. I seek to offer a conceptualization of human selfhood, male and female, to be understood in contrast to this phallocratic norm of the self.

Irigaray finds phallocentrism problematic because of its sexism. A corollary to this is that it represses all difference and multiplicity. I argue against the normative philosophical assumptions that exalt the One and sameness because difference and multiplicity are repressed. In my schema it is the sexism that is the corollary. Patriarchy represses difference, all differences. The characteristics of multiplicity and fluidity are repressed in whomever they appear—a male or a female. Of course I agree that women are oppressed and that the feminine is repressed in Western discourse and Western culture. The norms and values of selfhood are determined and patterned after male paradigms. Men have constructed the society's values and concepts of the self, of good and bad, and of truth that fit their experience of life and their desires and needs. *And* women have suffered from this set-up. Women are mistreated, given less than male value, have less representation. Certain male persons who want certain things in their women construct femininity. But there are others who are repressed too. Irigaray often proceeds as if she assumes that all that is repressed is the feminine, and all the feminine is repressed. This is a mistaken assumption. All that is repressed could be possible candidates for the lost feminine, since we don't know what is feminine. However, in fishing for the feminine in the sea of the unconscious, she might hook other entities and forms that are lurking in the depths of the unconscious.[17] It may also release other undesirable vestiges, such as violence, unacceptable desires, and other phylogenetically primitive qualities. Here I wonder if Irigaray is inadvertently identifying the feminine and the unconscious, the id, and possibly evil. This identification has problematic implications for feminism in general.

Another concern I have with her analysis is that she reduces the Western tradition to a singularity itself, a solo if you will, proclaiming one view with a single voice. Now I agree that there are embedded assumptions in traditional Western discourse that exalt sameness and consistency and exaggerate the value of singularity and the One. These assumptions are not only prevalent and pervasive, but also benefit those in power. However, they are not absolute. The

---

[17] Like Joseph Newirth in his *Between Emotion and Cognition* (New York: Other Press, 2003) I disagree with the common assumption in American psychology that the unconscious harbors only destructive energies or problematic memories, but I do believe that people often do carry with them destructive and problematic elements unconsciously.

tradition is not monolithic. Although the distinctiveness of alternative perspectives are sometimes downplayed or misinterpreted, there have been other voices in the choir of Western discourse. Søren Kierkegaard's theological anthropology is only one example of this richness. This assertion is important not only strategically, but also because it is true. Irigaray's reductionist claim about the homogeneity of Western discourse can paint feminists into a corner. It makes it difficult to speak and write and even think as persons who disagree with the normative theories and to articulate a critical perspective. Western history is much more rich and complex than this.

My fourth concern focuses on the unbridled multiplicity and openness to difference. It is related to my suspicion addressed above that everything in the unconscious is not associated with the feminine. But even more specifically, Irigaray's constructive suggestions for the feminine are too wide open. A self, an individual subject, needs some way of limiting the multiplicity and maintaining at least some contained boundaries. I suggest that Kierkegaard's concept of the relationality of the dialectic can provide a structure for how to relate the difference within the feminine self that is even sometimes conflicting with the other in a positive way. His dialectical relatedness could also provide a structure for addressing the ambiguous openness and fluidity without contours. In other words, I like Irigaray's no holds barred approach but I think it needs to be reigned in sometimes. I suggest that this dialectic relationality be a way of enabling the self to be one way at one time and another way at another time. It can oscillate from a being characterized as centered, to being dispersed, to being focused on the relating of the relations, and perhaps to other forms of selfhood as well. The self is a dialectic that is *both/and* not either/or. Using Kierkegaard's model allows this model to focus on the relationality and not the disparate parts or conflicting voices all the time, but to shift one's attention from one to the other. In this way the self is a relating of many relations. The self is related, relational, and relating. *Related* signifies the external relationships with other persons and environmental factors that are constitutive of the self. *Relational* is the form of the self. It is a relational network. This is the format of the structure of the self. *Relating* signifies the process of movement of connections and relations within the self and between the parts of the self, as well as with external entities.

A New Philosophical Anthropology of Multiplicity

I bring together Kierkegaard's relational dialectic and Irigaray's multiple and embodied feminine for my purposes of suggesting selfhood as a network of multiple relations and oscillations between relationship and connection. I appropriate Kierkegaard's idea of reflexive relationality between these disparate parts as a means of holding together the contrasting elements in Irigaray's feminine subject. These notions of simultaneity and relationality of different elements within the self are helpful in my construction of selfhood.

Building upon these ideas, I suggest that the self is multiple: multifaceted, multivalent, multidimensional, relational, and dynamic. These qualities and forms of subjectivity are not limited to the substance thinking that dominates common discourse about selfhood. They are systemically connected with each other, build upon each other, and are interdependent. One quality calls to mind the other. They are not linear in their relationship to each other—not literally or literarily. It is difficult to distinguish them even to analyze or discuss each individually. This is the case, because these realities, like Irigaray's feminine imaginary and symbolic, are not based on a logic of linear expression/truth nor on the economy of the Same. Rather, a three or four or more dimensional format for expressing ideas would be more suitable for this alternative way of thinking about the self. Kierkegaard's distaste for linear logic as the norm for human subjectivity is apparent here as well.

The self is a matrix of interrelated self-states that are also open to more and to other relationships. There are sub-selves, which are centers of connection, memory, and tendencies, and secondly, connectors, which are conduits of relation. This conglomeration of stuff is a network with many points of concentration as well as wires that flow both forth and back in all directions.

Positive relation requires three conditions: difference, multiplicity and openness. There must be more than one entity or part of entity for relationship to occur. Without difference and separation between two or more entities or parts of entities, there can be no interaction. A single entity cannot exhibit genuine relationality. Further, openness to the other, to that which is outside of the self, is essential. This openness could be a mind open to change from external influences, or a physical/metaphysical permeability to that which is outside oneself, or somewhere in between. The ability for an entity to be affected by otherness, whether within the self or outside the self, is a necessary condition for the possibility of relation.

My image of the self is a little like an old-fashioned tinker toy erector set in which a round piece, or sub-self, can have several sticks (indicating connections to other sub-selves) emanating/emerging from it toward other pieces. The dowels can be of different colors or qualities, and different lengths and going in different directions. The pieces themselves also come in different sizes and different colors. And some are shaped like spheres, while others are like wheels, while still others are shaped cylindrically. Connections happen horizontally and vertically, in skewed ways, through direct connections and proximate connections. This metaphor is helpful in expressing the multiplicity of the self, but it is still inadequate in several ways. First, these dowels need to be understood as intangible, fluid, and energized relating. Further, the degree of fluidity and energy, as well as the thickness and mutability, are wide-ranging and changing. The self is dynamic, and yet even that dynamism is variable. Some parts are more enduring than others. Some are so fleeting that they are only present for a moment, some without full conscious awareness. Another difference between a tinker toy model and my concept of selfhood is that the relationships between the pieces emerge from the piece and from the energy fields between the parts. The primary aspects of the self are not limited to the centers or hubs of connection, but include the dowels that conduct and enable those connections. Selfhood then is like a matrix of entities pulling toward each other and pushing away from collapse into each other. It is like what Wittgenstein once said of Shakespeare: "He shows you a city with no main road." The self has no main road, but many avenues and boulevards going in various directions, a little like Boston and San Francisco.

This model is much more fruitful and appropriate to imaging selfhood as internally related to itself as a network of connections, connectors, and connectedness for conceptualizing a self as relational with others as well. The image here is like a solar system, with multiple planets, moons, comets, and other cosmic entities orbiting at different speeds and angles and even different planes. The self is the whole network together. To stretch the metaphor we might imagine that one subject share an orbiting object or two with another subject as a metaphor for understanding the intimate nature of relationships. We share parts and are constituted by each other.

In his recent work on theological anthropology, F. LeRon Shults talks of a shift toward emphasizing relationality in philosophy and psychology and in ways of thinking about human reality. He believes that this "turn to relationality" means that "we must now engage in reforming theological anthropology" to doctrine that focuses on relationships between persons and views the self as relational.[18] Yet in order to move our understanding toward relational thinking about the self in terms of the importance of relationships with others in constituting the subject, we need also to rethink the way we understand the internal consistency of the self as relational. What I

---

[18] F. LeRon Shults, *Reforming Theological Anthropology* (Grand Rapids MI: Wm. B. Eerdmans, 2003) 2.

am offering here does just that. It looks at the self as internally related—as related to itself, as relational both in terms of its introspection, its past, present, and future openness to relations. In fact, it could be argued that the relating between the parts are the most significant aspects of the self and not the apparent fixed coherence that we observe when we glance in the mirror.

Shults traces the history of the role of relationship in philosophical understanding of human selfhood. He writes of a distinction between internal and external relations in which internal relations are essential to one's self, while external relations are nonessential. Essential means that it is necessary to one's self and will never change. The examples given are telling. An example of internal relation is that I am younger than my uncle, while an example of an external relation is that I am east of the Mississippi River. The former cannot change and reflects the fact that there is a relation between my uncle and myself, but it does not say anything about the nature of that relation. Further, it makes no reference to whether or not this relation is conscious or had any impact upon my life. The latter example is clearly an external relation and an irrelevant one. This designation as external and nonessential indicates that this fact of the relation of the river to me makes no difference to my life. These distinctions are clear, but they are not so helpful. It seems to me that they are both designations of external, negative relations. Kierkegaard's distinction between positive and negative relations is more clarifying and helpful. Instead of focusing on the nature of the relation as essential or nonessential, he talks of negative and positive relations. An example of a negative relation is a mere objective observation about the relation between two lines on the chalkboard. Everyone in the room can see that the yellow line is longer than the white one. This relation is something observed by those outside of the lines and is not a fact noted by the lines themselves. A positive relation, however, is one in which both aspects of the relation are affected by each other. They are intentionally related to each other, and this relating creates a third entity. This relation, or activity of relating, indicates that both parts (parties to the relation) are affected by the other, and by the relation itself. Let's return to Shults's example of what he terms an internal relation. I am younger than my uncle. This relation may be necessary in that it cannot be escaped nor changed; however, it is itself not essentially constitutive to my subjectivity. It may not affect me at all or have little significance to my sense of self or to the qualities that make up my personhood.

Kierkegaard's distinction between positive and negative relations is more meaningful with regards to subjectivity. The activity of reflexively relating different elements implies mutual and significant influence. This view lends itself to the argument for multiplicity within the self. Being able to be changed by difference outside oneself as well as difference within the self is the key to a relational subject.

This relating is the core of the self—the nitty gritty or the integrity of the subject. It is relational at its core. Being relational internally enables external relationality in several ways. First, it is more consistent to view the self as relational inside and outside. If philosophy has truly taken a "turn to relationality" in which the self is understood as a self-in-community, then it follows that the self-itself is understood as an internal community, dynamic and relational within itself. Kierkegaard's insights help us delve into this notion more deeply.

Secondly, when the self is understood as a relational entity in itself, otherness (as opposed to the sameness in a singular self) is already a part of the self. This means that external otherness can be incorporated into the self more easily and naturally. A multiple self is already in a relational format. There is no impermeable boundary that must be trespassed or violated for an external object to influence the self. There is already a mechanism for integrating otherness and a criterion for how to integrate.

Further, accepting oneself as multivalent and complex enables one to identify and empathize with a variety of others. This increases the quality of one's relationships as well as the quality of the community. Instead of valuing another person or religion or culture based upon the similarity to one's own, this approach seeks to value the differences between individuals, religions, culture, etcetera, by starting with valuing the difference within oneself. The issue is about the value ascribed to difference and multiplicity. If we can learn to accept and value difference because it is different within ourselves, it will be easier and more natural to accept and celebrate differences outside of ourselves. The fact of multiplicity won't scare us so much.

I have utilized the insights of Irigaray and Kierkegaard explicated above to give flesh and depth to these ideas and images. Irigaray's work will help us with uncovering the multiplicity within and with accepting and listening to the embodiedness of selfhood. Kierkegaard's insights help us with understanding the multiplicity and the way the parts are always dynamically relating to each other.

My constructive conceptualization of selfhood is similar to process theology in many ways. This is a work that would fall into the category of relational thinking. This is a book about relationality within the self. The details of the differences between this view and that from a process thought perspective will have to wait until the next project. Suffice it to say that this author is deeply influenced by process thought in its various manifestations. I have remained oddly silent on process in this work because I want to formulate a relational view of the self that is not dependent upon process metaphysics in order to be better able to dialogue with process feminist thought in my next project. However, I will mention a few differences and similarities at this point. There are clear similarities in my emphasis on external and internal relationality. I use the terms a little differently. But the common sensibility that values relationality is clear. Our focus is the same, but our understanding of the details is different. This model I put forth here is a metaphor for the self and not necessarily a metaphysical claim. In this model I argue that the self is compromised of multiple parts that are truly different from each other all relating to each other simultaneously. The distinction between process and my thought rests upon the simultaneity of the multiplicity.

The other similarity is that process is open to difference and multiplicity. Process seeks to enable difference and multiplicity, but not at the same time. In the end it gives priority to harmony and unity. "The many become one, and are increased by one."[19] My constructive thought posits a complex web of relation within the self with different parts present simultaneously.

Further, I use the terms internal relation and external relation slightly differently. Process theology argues that each entity is constituted by its relationships to past entities. The past impacts the present—provides the fodder for the becoming moment. Internal relation for process theology signifies this process of becoming in which the past, perished entity is grasped by the becoming occasion and becomes an internal part of the present entity. This is the meaning of internal relation. The present occasion takes the past entity into itself and uses the past entity as the concrete stuff of becoming in the moment. This is part of what Whitehead meant when he said, "life is robbery."[20] The past that becomes an internal part of the present is no longer present, no longer has subjectivity. My model argues that the self is a multiplicity in and of itself, without relations to other entities. This claim is hypothetical because the self is never actually without relations to others. That said, however, the view I espouse argues that internal relations exist within the self between aspects of the self. We could call these aspects sub-selves. The self is the relating of these sub-selves with and to each other. This network of interwoven connections and hubs of connection then is the core of the self—a unity of many parts coming together. The integrity is maintained by three important functions:

---

[19] Alfred North Whitehead, *Process and Reality: Corrected Edition,* ed. David Ray Griffin and Donald W. Sherburne (New York: Free Press, 1978) 21.
[20] Ibid., 160.

the boundaries of the body, its memories and intimacy with itself, and the periodic oscillations of the self's attention to the whole. This is not to give priority to unity and is not to assert that there is difference only secondarily.

The self as a network of relating, relational, and related multiple sub-selves/sub-states yields a more clear and consistent model for understanding the self as relational to others in the universe. If the self is itself a network of relating, then relations with entities outside of the self can more easily be understood as becoming a part of the network.

This book has provided the groundwork for re-visioning theological anthropology in the current postmodern world. It has explicated the problem of Western discourse's emphasis upon oneness for the conception of selfhood. It has demonstrated how the Christian norms of selfhood, exhibited in Augustine's doctrine of sin as the internal division of the self, have inhibited a conception of the self as multiple and internally related to itself. Further, it has provided a thorough and insightful critique of the phallocentric discourse, especially in regards to the detrimental effects upon women. Thus, it is imperative that the characteristics and forms of the feminine be stressed in a new vision of theological anthropology. This book has examined two views of selfhood that challenge this monarchy of the self. Kierkegaard writes from a Christian religious perspective and frames his vision in terms of subjectivity in relation to God. Subjectivity as the dialectic of faith is the ontological reality of human existence. With Kierkegaard's emphasis on subjectivity, he misses the fundamental importance of the body for selfhood. Luce Irigaray picks up this dropped ball and explores the multiplicity of selfhood as found through the embodiment of the feminine. She highlights the experiences and truths of those who have been excluded in the phallocentric proclivity toward singularity and oneness. Taking these two thinkers and their insights together has provided a model of selfhood that is both multiple and integrated, different and related, embodied and transcending, internally and externally related. It is a dialectical, multivalent matrix of relating relations, interconnected, yet not reducible to a uniform substance.

I have proposed a genuinely different view of selfhood in which genuine difference is accepted and celebrated. This model enables and encourages a self-matrix that is inherently related to itself internally. These internal relations are logically prior to the effects and projections of external relationships, although in actual living the essential relationships that constitute the self are both internal and external. These different parts of the self, along with the ambiguities, are held together within the self. This model is applicable to both male selves and female selves. Not only is the variegated multiplicity within the self embraced, but the diversity outside of the self can also more readily be embraced.

This groundwork speaks of difference, then, in two ways: difference between the self and other; and difference between the parts within the self. One part of the self is genuinely different from another part of the self, which is different from another part, and so on. Thus, difference becomes a part of the self. Once difference can be accepted internally as a self that is multivalent in character, then difference can be accepted and valued outside in society. Different parts of the self and different parts of society relate to each other. Thus, an entity, whether a self or a community, is a multivalent matrix of internally related hubs, connections, and centers. This book has raised many questions and offered only a few answers, but its fundamental contribution is to provide the ground for a new Christian articulation of theological anthropology. This new anthropology needs to acknowledge and encourage the characteristics and forms of selfhood that have been put forth in this work. Selfhood is grounded in embodiment; it is comprised of multiple parts; these parts are internally related to each other. The self is a relational matrix-reflexively relational both prior to the effects of external relations, and in the relations with others. Difference is embraced, both internally and externally, both personally and socially.

Another implication of the reconstructed anthropology has to do with the understanding of sin. The paradigm of internal division with the soul and the will, which is the Augustinian basis of sin, is incompatible with this new construction of selfhood. In fact, the emphasis upon singularity and uniformity in the self and in the community facilitates sinfulness. A formula to describe sin is better articulated as not willing to become oneself before God. In the context of the multiplicity and relationality of selfhood, this formulation of sin entails not accepting oneself in all one's multiplicity. Further, sin is being afraid of the difference and ambiguity within the self. It is repressing the possibility of internal relations. It is oppressing the differences within oneself and outside of oneself. The formula of sin as not willing to become oneself before God is adequate for many sins, but it does not cover the more violent and extremely abusive acts. These acts, so prevalent in our increasingly violent society are more adequately referred to as "demonic." Another category of sin needs to be explored.

Moreover, there are implications for Christian spirituality from this re-visioning of selfhood. Spirituality is not conforming one's multiplicity and complexity into a uniform singularity. Rather, spirituality is encouraging the development of more of one's differences. It is practicing the spiritual discipline of holding together in tension more and more ambiguity and difference in one's self and interrelating these differences. Meditation is listening to the voices within, giving the embodied parts ear and participation in the action and decisions of the whole self. The effects of such "contemplation" are to bring the energy of difference and acceptance into conscious time and space. The more ambiguity and difference a person can hold together, the bigger the person, the more complex she is, and the more love she can and does have for herself and others.

And finally, the traditional view of the divine-human relation is called into question with this new formulation of human selfhood, of sin, and of spirituality. God is already given the model of selfhood that is multiple, or at least Trinitarian; and further, God is inherently internally related to God's self. This view of human selfhood facilitates the divine-human relationship.

There is much work ahead if indeed a theological anthropology of multiplicity replaces the current theological anthropology of the One. This juxtaposition of Kierkegaard and Irigaray provides the rationale and the signposts for the continuing task.

Bibliography

Armour, Ellen T. "Questioning 'Woman' in Feminist/Womanist Theology." In *Transfigurations: Theology and the French Feminists.* Edited by C. W. Maggie Kim, Susan M. St. Ville, and Susan Simonaitis. Minneapolis: Fortress Press, 1993.

—————. *Subverting the Race Gender Divide: Deconstruction, Feminist Theology, and the Problem of Difference.* Chicago: The University of Chicago Press, 1999.

Armstrong, Arthur H., ed. *Cambridge History of Later Greek and Early Medieval Philosophy.* London: Cambridge University Press, 1967.

Augustine. "Against Julian." Translated by Richard Stothert. Volume 5 of *The Nicene and Post Nicene Fathers of the Christian Church.* Edited by Philip Scheff. Grand Rapids MI: Wm. B. Eerdmans Publishing Company, 1956.

—————. *City of God.* Translated by Marcus Dods. New York: The Modern Library, 1950.

—————. "Concerning Two Souls, Against the Manicheans." Translated by Richard Stothert. Volume 4 of *The Nicene and Post Nicene Fathers of the Christian Church.* Edited by Philip Scheff. Grand Rapids MI: Wm. B. Eerdmans Publishing Company, 1956.

—————. *Confessions.* Trans. R. S. Pine-Coffin. London: Penguin Books, 1961.

—————. "The Literal Meaning of Genesis." Translated by John Hammond Taylor. Vol. 2 of *Ancient Christian Writers.* New York: The Newman Press, 1982.

—————. "Of True Religion." In *Augustine: Earlier Writings.* Translated by John H. S. Burleigh. Philadelphia: Westminster Press, 1953.

—————. "On Continence." Translated by C. L. Cornish. Volume 3 of *The Nicene and Post-Nicene Fathers of the Christian Church.* Edited by Philip Scheff. Grand Rapids MI: Wm. B. Eerdmans Publishing Company, 1956.

—————. *On the Trinity.* Translated by Stephen MacKenna. New York: Cambridge University Press, 2002.

Borch-Jacobsen, Mikkel. *The Emotional Tie.* Translated by Michael Brick and others. Stanford CA: Stanford University Press, 1993.

Bretall, Robert, ed. *A Kierkegaard Anthology.* New York: The Modern Library, 1970.

Burkey, Carolyn, Naomi Schor, and Margaret Whitford, eds. *Engaging with Irigaray: Feminist Philosophy and Modern European Thought.* New York: Columbia University Press, 1994.

Burns, James Patout. "Grace: the Augustinian Foundation." In *Christian Spirituality, Origins to the Twelfth Century*. Volume 16 of *Encyclopedia of World Spirituality*. Edited by Bernard McGinn and John Meyerdorff. New York: Crossroad, 1985.

Butler, Judith. *Gender Trouble*. New York: Routledge, 1990.

Connell, George. *To Be One Thing: Personal Unity in Kierkegaard's Thought*. Macon GA: Mercer University Press, 1985.

Cooley, Paula. *Religious Imagination and the Body*. New York: Oxford University Press, 1994.

Derrida, Jacques. *Of Grammatology*. Translated by Gayatri Chakravorty Spivak. Baltimore: The Johns Hopkins University Press, 1974.

Dupré, Louis. *Kierkegaard as Theologian, the Dialectic of Christian Existence*. New York: Sheed and Ward, 1963.

Eilberg-Schwartz, Howard. *God's Phallus*. Boston: Beacon Press, 1994.

Evans, C. Stephen. *Kierkegaard's Fragments and Postscript: The Religious Philosophy of Johannes Climacus*. Atlantic Highlands NJ: Humanities Press, 1983.

Fredriksen, Paula. "Beyond the Body/Soul Dichotomy: Augustine's Answer to Mani, Plotinus, and Julian." In *Paul and the Legacies of Paul*. Edited by William S. Babcock. Dallas: Southern Methodist University Press, 1990.

Freud, Sigmund. "Anatomical Distinction Between the Sexes." In vol. 8 of *The Standard Edition of the Complete Psychological Works of Sigmund Freud*. Translated and edited by James Strachey. London: Hogarth Press, 1957.

——————. "Mourning and Melancholia." In volume 14 of *The Standard Edition of the Complete Psychological Works of Sigmund Freud*. Translated and edited by James Strachey. London: Hogarth Press, 1957.

——————. "On Narcissism: An Introduction." In volume 14 of *The Standard Edition of the Complete Psychological Works of Sigmund Freud*. Translated and edited by James Strachey. London: Hogarth Press, 1957.

Fuss, Diana. *Essentially Speaking: Feminism, Nature and Difference*. New York: Routledge, 1989.

Gilligan, Carol. *In a Different voice: Psychological theory and women's development*. Cambridge MA: Harvard University Press, 1982.

——————. *The Birth of Pleasure*. New York: Knopf, 2002.

Grosz, Elizabeth. *Jacques Lacan: A Feminist Introduction*. New York: Routledge, 1990.

——————. *Sexual Subversions*. Syndey: Allen and Unwin, 1989.

Hanby, Michael. *Augustine and Modernity*. New York: Routledge, 2003.

Hearts of Darkness: A Filmmaker's Apocalypse. Directed by Fax Bahr and George Hickenlooper. Hollywood CA: Paramount Pictures, 1991.

Hollywood, Amy. *Sensible Ecstasy: Mysticism, Sexual Difference, and the Demands of History*. Chicago: University of Chicago Press, 2002.
Hundert, E.J. "Augustine and the Sources of the Divided Self." *Political Theory* 20/1 (Feb 1992): 87-89.
Irigaray, Luce. "Equal or Different?" In *The Irigaray Reader*. Edited by Margaret Whitford. Malden MA: Blackwell Publishers, Inc., 1991.
───────. *The Ethics of Sexual Difference*. Ithaca NY: Cornell University Press, 1993.
───────. *Le Corps-a'-corps avec la me're*. Montreal: Pleine Lune, 1981.
───────. *Parler n'est jamais neuter*. Translated by Margaret Whitford. Paris: Minuit, 1985.
───────. "The Poverty of Psychoanalysis." In *The Irigaray Reader*. Edited by Margaret Whitford. Malden MA: Blackwell Publishers, Inc., 1991.
───────. *Sexes and Genealogies*. Translated by Gillian C. Gill. New York: Columbia University Press, 1993.
───────. "Sexual Difference." In *The Ethics of Sexual Difference*. Ithaca NY: Cornell University Press, 1993.
───────. *Speculum of the Other Woman*. Translated by Gillian C. Gill. Ithaca NY: Cornell University Press, 1985.
───────. *This Sex Which is Not One*. Ithaca NY: Cornell University Press, 1985.
───────. "Volume Without Contours." In *The Irigaray Reader*. Edited by Margaret Whitford. Malden MA: Blackwell Publishers, Inc., 1991.
───────. "Women's Exile." In *Ideology and Consciousness* 1 (1977): 62-76.
Jones, Serene. "This God Which is Not One." In *Transfigurations: Theology and the French Feminists*. Edited by C.W. Maggie Kim, Susan M. St. Ville, and Susan M. Simonaitis. Minneapolis: Fortress Press, 1993.
Kierkegaard, Søren. *Attack Upon 'Christendom'*. Translated by Walter Lowrie. Boston: Beacon Press, 1971.
───────. *Concluding Unscientific Postscript*. Translated and edited by Howard V. Hong and Edna H. Hong. Princeton NJ: Princeton University Press, 1974.
───────. *Concluding Unscientific Postscript*. Translated and edited by Walter Lowrie. Princeton NJ: Princeton University Press, 1941.
───────. *Either/Or*. Translated and edited by Howard V. Hong and Edna H. Hong. Princeton NJ: Princeton University Press, 1987.
───────. *Either/Or*. (abridged) Edited by Stephen L. Ross, translated by George L. Stengren. New York: Harper and Row, 1986.
───────. *Fear and Trembling*. Translated and edited by Howard V. Hong and Edna H. Hong. Princeton NJ: Princeton University Press, 1970.

―――――. *Journals and Papers.* Translated and edited by Howard V. Hong and Edna H. Hong. Bloomington IN: Indiana University Press, 1967.
―――――. *Repetition: an Essay in Experimental Psychology.* Translated by Walter Lowrie. Princeton NJ: Princeton University Press, 1946.
―――――. *The Point of View of My Work as an Author.* New York: Harper Torchbooks, 1962.
―――――. *The Sickness Unto Death.* Translated and edited by Howard V. Hong and Edna H. Hong. Princeton NJ: Princeton University Press, 1980.
―――――. *The Sickness Unto Death.* Translated by Walter Lowrie. Princeton NJ: Princeton University Press, 1970.
―――――. *Upbuilding Discourses in Various Spirits.* Translated and edited by Howard V. Hong and Edna H. Hong. Princeton NJ: Princeton University Press, 1993.
Krentz, Arthur. "Kierkegaard's Dialectical Image of Human Existence in the *Concluding Unscientific Postscript* to the *Philosophical Fragments.*" *Philosophy Today* Summer (1997).
Lacan, Jacques. *Écritis, A Selection.* London: Tavistock, 1977.
―――――. *Écritis, A Selection.* Translated by Alan Sheridan. New York: W. W. Norton and Co., 1977.
―――――. *The Seminar XX, Encore: On Feminine Sexuality, the Limits of Love and Knowledge.* Edited by Jacques-Alain Miller, translated by Bruce Fink. New York: W.W. Norton and Co., 1998.
Levin, Jerome David. *Theories of the Self.* Philadelphia: Hemisphere Publishing Corporation, 1992.
Lorde, Audre. "The Uses of the Erotic." In *Sister Outsider: Essays and Speeches.* Berkeley CA: The Crossing Press, 1984.
Lowrie, Walter. *A Short Life of Kierkegaard.* Princeton NJ: Princeton University Press, 1970.
Miles, Margaret. *Delight and Desire.* New York: Crossroads, 1992.
Moi, Toril. *Sexual/Texual Politics: Feminist Literary Theory.* London: Routledge, 1988.
Muller, Robert. *Dictionary of Latin and Greek Theological Terms.* Grand Rapids MI: Baker Book House, 1985.
Newirth, Joseph. *Beyond Emotion and Cognition.* New York: Other Press, 2005.
Nye, Andrea. *Feminist Theology and the Philosophies of Man.* London: Croom Helm, 1988.
O'Connell, Robert. *The Origin of the Soul in St. Augustine's Later Works.* New York: Fordham University Press, 1987.

Pattison, George. Speech, Kierkegaard Society Dinner at the annual American Academy of Religion meeting, Philadelphia PA, 1994.

Phillips, D. Z. "Authorship and Authenticity: Kierkegaard and Wittgenstein." *Midwest Studies in Philosophy*, 17 (1992): 177-193.

—————. "Critical Notice." *Philosophical Investigations* 9/1 (January 1986): 66-77.

—————. "Purity of Heart." Lecture, Claremont Graduate University. Claremont CA, February 8, 1994.

"Plague Village." *Monty Python and the Holy Grail.* DVD, directed by Terry Gilliam and Terry Jones. Culver City CA: Columbia Tristar Home Entertainment, 2001.

Plotinus. *The Enneads*. Translated by Stephen MacKenna. New York: Pantheon Books Inc., 1957.

Sands, Kathleen. *Escape From Paradise*. Minneapolis: Fortress Press, 1994.

Schacht, Richard. *Hegel and After*. Pittsburgh: University of Pittsburgh Press, 1975.

Schneider, Laurel. *Re-imaging the Divine*. Cleveland OH: Pilgrim Press, 2000.

Schor, Naomi. "This Essentialism Which is Not One." *Differences* 11/2 (Summer 1989): 76-105.

Schor, Noami. "This Essentialism Which is Not One: Coming to Grips with Irigaray." In *Engaging With Irigaray*. Edited by Carolyn Burke, Naomi Schor, and Margaret Whitford. New York: Columbia University Press, 1994.

Shults, F. LeRon. *Reforming Theological Anthropology*. Grand Rapids MI: Wm. B. Eerdmans Publishing Compnay, 2003.

Suchocki, Marjorie. "The Correlation between God and Evil." Ph.D. dissertation, School of Religion, Claremont Graduate School, 1974.

Suchocki, Marjorie. *Divinity and Diversity*. Nashville: Abingdon Press, 2003.

Taylor, Mark C. *Imagologies: Media Philosophy*. New York: Routledge, 1994.

—————. *Kierkegaard's Pseudonymous Authorship*. Princeton NJ: Princeton University Press, 1975.

Thompson, Josiah. *The Lonely Labyrinth: Kierkegaard's Pseudonymous Works*. Carbondale IL: Southern Illinois Press, 1967.

Tillich, Paul. *Dynamics of Faith*. New York: Perennial Classics, 2001.

—————. *Nineteenth and Twentieth Century Protestant Theology*. New York: Harper and Row Publishers, 1967.

Torjesen, Karen Jo. "The Body." Unpublished paper, Claremont Graduate University, 1993.

Walker, Jeremy. *To Will One Thing*. Montreal: McGill-Queens University Press, 1972.

West, Cornel. *Prophesy Deliverance!* Philadelphia: Westminster Press, 1982.

Weston, Michael. *Kierkegaard and Modern Continental Philosophy*. New York: Routledge, 1994.
Westphal, Merold. *Becoming a Self.* West Lafayette IN: Purdue University Press, 1996.
———. "The Teleological Suspension of Religiousness B." In *Foundations of Kierkegaard's Vision of Community*. Edited by George Connell and C. Stephen Evans. Atlantic Highlands NJ: Humanities Press, 1991.
Whitehead, Alfred North. *Process and Reality: Corrected Edition*. Edited by David Ray Griffin and Donald W. Sherburne. New York: Free Press, 1979.
Whitford, Margaret. *Philosophy in the Feminine*. New York City: Routledge, 1991.

Index

Aristotle, 185
Armour, Ellen, 175, 187, 188, 239
Augustine, 6, 19-56, 171, 194, 204, 205, 220-222, 230
Borch-Jakobsen, Mikkel, 155
Bretall, Robert, 133
Butler, Judith, 196
Connell, George, 71, 73, 74, 75, 76, 77, 80, 81, 92, 102, 111-115
Deconstruction (post-structuralism), 6, 225
Derrida, Jacques, 139
Dialectic, 6, 9, 11, 15, 17, 82-93, 223, 253
Dupre, Luis, 64, 86, 91, 102, 128, 131, 137
Dubois, W.E.B., 18
Eilberg-Schwartz, Howard, 156
Evans, C. Stephen, 103, 104
Feuerbach, L.V., 168, 202
Fuss, Diana, 239
Gilligan, Carol, 240
God, 11, 14, 19-20, 37, 42, 52, 228, 230, 252, 255
Grant, Jacquelyn, 18
Grosz, Elizabeth, 138, 139, 156, 191
Hegel, 9-10, 79, 83, 125, 209
Hollywood, Amy, 186, 239
Impoverishment of diversity, 175
Indirect communication, 95,127
Irigaray, Luce, 3, 6, 8, 12-15, 17, 56, 135; Disruptive excess, 187, 188
Freud, Sigmund, 12, 13, 139, 146, 147, 149, 151, 152, 153, 155-168, 178, 180, 195, 200, 205, 236; Ho(m)mosexuality, 178; Jouissance, 182, 198, 199, 203, 206
Lacan, Jacques, 12, 13, 138, 139,144, 151, 154-168, 178, 180, 189, 190, 191, 194, 195, 234, 236

Lost (repressed) Feminine/difference, 135, 139, 140, 143, 144, 145, 157, 164, 172, 179, 180, 181, 184, 199, 211, 232, 234, 242
Metonymy, 193, 194, 195, 203, 205, 216, 224, 232, 235, 236, 240, 241
Mimesis, 177, 185, 186, 194, 196, 235
Multiplicity/multiformity, 138, 140, 172, 174, 176, 182, 185, 194, 195, 198, 206, 212, 224, 229, 232, 235, 236, 242, 244, 252
Oedipal phase/complex, 148, 158, 162, 163, 167
Phallocentrism/phallocratism, 12, 138, 139, 143, 144, 150, 153, 162, 166, 168, 169, 173, 176, 177, 181, 184, 185, 188, 190, 191, 192, 193, 200, 201, 202, 203, 205, 206, 208, 210, 212, 214, 215, 224, 235, 240, 242, 252; Position of mastery, 144
Irigaray's texts:
—*Ethics of Sexual Difference*, The, 142, 183, 186
—*Ideology and Consciousness*, 165,
—*Speculum of the Other Woman*, The, 146, 149, 150, 153, 154, 183, 197, 201, 202, 236,
This Sex Which is Not One, 143, 154, 157, 162, 170, 171, 179, 186, 189, 192, 193,
194, 197, 201, 236; *Sexes and Geneologies*, 167
Jones, Serene, 213
Kierkegaard, 3, 6, 8-10, 14, 17, 56, 57-93, 174, 207
Spheres of Existence, 8, 9, 10, 11, 14, 57-93, 95, 131, 207, 208, 209, 212, 214, 215, 216, 221, 224, 227, 229, 233

Dialectic, 8, 9, 10, 11, 14, 56, 58, 59, 71, 87, 90, 91-92, 124, 125, 126, 128, 136, 212, 214, 226, 227, 228, 232, 244
Faith, 9, 14, 67, 76, 91, 128, 136, 214, 216, 226, 232
Despair, 64,65, 91, 134, 211
Pseudonymous authorship, 57, 94-135, 136, 227, 228
Kierkegaard's texts:
Attack Upon Christendom, 212
Concluding Unscientific Postscript, 65, 66, 68, 79, 81, 83, 85, 86, 96, 104, 107, 114, 132
Either/Or, 10, 60, 61, 62, 63, 64, 65, 66, 74, 76, 90, 97, 98, 120
Fear and Trembling, 67, 68, 69, 88, 96, 99, 100, 121
Journals and Papers, 107
My Point of View of My Work as an Author, 69, 97, 101, 105, 107, 119, 122, 131, 133
Philosophical Fragments, 96
Purity of Heart is to Will One Thing, 77, 78
Repetition, 96, 219
Sickness Unto Death, The, 11, 57, 58, 72, 74, 77, 80, 83, 84, 85, 88, 89, 91, 93, 94, 96, 113, 125, 132, 134, 136, 226
Stages on Life's Way, 96
Three Edifying Discourses, 97
Training in Christianity, 96
Two Edifying discourses, 97
Upbuilding Discourses in Various Spirits, 127
Love, 230, 254
Multiplicity, 2, 4, 5, 6, 7, 15, 16-18, 39, 48, 57, 59, 67, 77, 95, 99, 115, 207, 218, 220, 221, 222, 224, 225, 232, 237, 238, 244, 246, 250, 251
Marx, Karl, 169
Multiple Personality Disorder (Dissociative Identity Disorder), 17

Multivalent Integration, 92, 197, 218, 220, 225, 237, 245, 249, 253
Newirth, Joseph, 243
Nye, Andrea, 238
Pain, 241
Pattison, George, 131
Phillips, D. Z., 69, 81, 101, 103-110, 117, 126
Plotinus, 26-29
Process theology/thought, 6, 250-252
Relation, 6, 10, 11, 14, 226-229, 231-233, 244-245, 247-249, 252, 254
Ross, Stephen, 90
Sands, Kathleen, 5
Schacht, Richard, 67
Schleiermacher, F., 228
Schor, Naomi, 210, 238, 239,
Schneider, Laurel, 6
Schults, F. LeRon, 247
Self, multiple, 2-8, 10, 12-15, 16, 17, 138, 218, 232, 242, 245, 246, 249, 252-253
Self, singular, 2-8, 15, 19-22, 50, 219, 224, 234
Subjectivity, 6, 8, 10, 12, 14, 51, 58, 68, 80, 85-87, 112, 123, 125, 130, 185, 190, 191, 198, 210, 215, 221, 224, 225, 228, 230, 231, 235, 240, 252
Suchocki, Marjorie, 28-29, 220
Taylor, Mark, C, 61, 70-72, 89, 92, 102, 116, 117, 118
Thompson, Josiah, 70
Tillich, Paul, 89, 123, 131, 228
Walker, Jeremy, 73
West, Cornel, 4
Westphal, Merold, 67, 121, 122
Whitford, Margaret, 140, 239
Whitehead, Alfred North, 251